THINKING ABOUT
PROTECTION PRAC

Case studies for critical
and discussion

Jadwiga Leigh and Jane Laing

P

First published in Great Britain in 2018 by

Policy Press
University of Bristol
1-9 Old Park Hill
Bristol
BS2 8BB
UK
t: +44 (0)117 954 5940
pp-info@bristol.ac.uk
www.policypress.co.uk

North America office:
Policy Press
c/o The University of Chicago Press
1427 East 60th Street
Chicago, IL 60637, USA
t: +1 773 702 7700
f: +1 773-702-9756
sales@press.uchicago.edu
www.press.uchicago.edu

© Policy Press 2018

British Library Cataloguing in Publication Data
A catalogue record for this book is available from the British Library

Library of Congress Cataloging-in-Publication Data
A catalog record for this book has been requested

ISBN 978-1-4473-3280-0 paperback
ISBN 978-1-4473-3279-4 hardcover
ISBN 978-1-4473-3282-4 ePub
ISBN 978-1-4473-3283-1 Mobi
ISBN 978-1-4473-3281-7 ePdf

The right of Jadwiga Leigh and Jane Laing to be identified as authors of this work has been asserted by them in accordance with the Copyright, Designs and Patents Act 1988.

All rights reserved: no part of this publication may be reproduced, stored in a retrieval system, or transmitted in any form or by any means, electronic, mechanical, photocopying, recording, or otherwise without the prior permission of Policy Press.

The statements and opinions contained within this publication are solely those of the authors and not of the University of Bristol or Policy Press. The University of Bristol and Policy Press disclaim responsibility for any injury to persons or property resulting from any material published in this publication.

Policy Press works to counter discrimination on grounds of gender, race, disability, age and sexuality.

Cover design by Andrew Corbett
Front cover image: www.alamy.com
Printed and bound in Great Britain by Clays Ltd, St Ives plc
Policy Press uses environmentally responsible print partners

Contents

Acknowledgements

Jadwiga: For social work.

Jane: For Mum who always knew I could; Lynn who showed me how and Josh who will always be the why and for Jane Burton who always asked when?

For Lynda Hughes, Jackie Southam and in memory of Carole Bale.

Glossary of terms

Affect, emotion and object relations: affect is the experience of feeling or emotion. Emotion is an affective state characterised by intense mental activity and a high degree of pleasure or displeasure. An affect is different to an emotion because it is something that is produced by the body, or the mind, when an interaction has occurred with another body or mind. This interaction subsequently increases or diminishes the body's power of activity. Object relations theory is a psychoanalytic theory that emphasises the dynamics of interpersonal relations (see Chapter 4).

Attachment theory: states that a strong emotional and physical attachment, or bond, to at least one primary caregiver is critical to personal development. John Bowlby first coined the term as a result of his studies involving the developmental psychology of children from various backgrounds. Research also indicates that attachments are developed over time and affect the emotional state and behaviour of adults as well as children (see Chapter 6).

Dramaturgy: developed by Erving Goffman, the dramaturgical approach makes us realise how when we act, we worry about our 'audience' and how they will judge our performance to see if we will slip up and show how we really act 'behind the scenes' (see Chapter 2).

Internal working model: the child's attachment relationship with their primary caregiver leads to the development of an internal working model. This is a cognitive framework comprising mental representations for understanding the world, self and others. A person's interaction with others is guided by memories and expectations from their internal model that influence and help evaluate their contact with others (see Chapter 8).

Management theory: addresses how managers and supervisors relate to their organisations and its objectives. It also seeks to explore how the implementation of effective methods can accomplish ideal goals as well as how employees can be motivated to perform to the highest standard (see Chapter 3).

Managing risk: In child protection social work, managing risk is an integral part of practice and often involves completing, or considering, risk. Risk assessments involve understanding the likelihood of beneficial and harmful outcomes occurring within a particular timescale. Despite pressure on social workers to adopt defensive risk management, considering and acting on all forms of risk, it is widely recognised that it is impossible to eliminate risk (see Chapter 5).

Motivational Interviewing: refers to a counselling approach developed in part by clinical psychologists William R. Miller and Stephen Rollnick. The main goals are to engage clients, elicit change talk (where the client articulates their own rationale for behaviour change) and evoke motivation to make positive changes for the client (see Chapter 7).

Performativity: the terms 'performativity' and 'performance' derive from the verb 'to perform'. They define how an action is executed. In this context, it refers to what the audience experiences as well as the actors involved in the action directly (see Chapter 2).

Person–centred approach (to care): an approach that developed from the work of the psychologist Dr Carl Rogers (1902–1987). It is a way of thinking and doing things that sees the people using health and social services as equal partners in planning, developing and monitoring care to make sure it meets their needs (see Chapter 1).

Professionalisation: a social process by which an occupation transforms itself into a profession so that it can attain the highest form of integrity and competence. Professionalisation tends to result once the professional has established acceptable qualifications, and is deemed to be able to practice and oversee the conduct of members of the profession (see Chapter 2).

Single– and double–loop learning: according to Chris Argyris (psychologist) and Donald Schön (philosopher), single– and double–loop learning is required so that the organisation and its employees will improve their understanding of the cause of problems and the effective way of solving them. Single-loop learning involves the detection and correction of error. This normally occurs when something goes wrong and people look for another strategy. However, double-loop learning is an alternative response and involves people questioning and subjecting the governing variables to critical scrutiny. This form of learning may then lead to a shift in the way in which future strategies and consequences are framed (see Chapter 3).

Symbolic interactionism: a sociological perspective that developed from the American philosophy of pragmatism and particularly from the work of George Herbert Mead. It is the view of social behaviour that emphasises linguistic or gestural communication and its subjective understanding, especially the role of language in the formation of a social being (see Chapter 1).

Systems theory: premised on the idea that an effective system is based on the individual needs, rewards, expectations and attributes of the people living in the system. The theory is designed on the structures, and sub-systems, that surround a service user, for example, the family, organisations and institutions to which that service user belongs. The theory also recognises that any change in one part of the system tends to have repercussions for the other parts (see Chapter 1).

Theory of mind and space: theory of mind (often abbreviated to ToM) is the ability to attribute mental states – beliefs, intents, desires, pretending, knowledge, etc – to oneself and others and to understand that others have beliefs, desires, intentions and perspectives that are different from one's own (see Chapter 7).

Introduction

This book has emerged as a result of our own frustration – reading books where case studies have been used as a means of providing practice examples for social workers. We'd often find that after reading snippets of the case, and thinking about what we were meant to do, we were left with no real understanding of what we may actually do if we encountered a similar situation. Therefore, rather than providing us with the direction we were looking for, we were left with more questions. Instead of feeling better informed and more confident, we felt confused and unsure. So we decided that when we taught our students how to reflect and to explore 'the outside world of practice' in the confined space of the classroom, one way to do this would be to take them on a journey that we had once travelled.

Rather than ask students to read a brief case study and answer some questions about it, we decided to act out the scenario with them. By drawing from our own practice experiences we found that students engaged more willingly; they were lured into the case study because they played a significant part in it. By pausing at different stages and openly discussing the uncomfortable situations that they had encountered, they began to relate to that which we had experienced. In turn, when they then went out into practice, they felt more comfortable when faced with situations that they had not previously been prepared for. They drew from the theoretical perspectives we had introduced them to and were encouraged to find research data that supported their decision-making processes. They became, in effect, creative social scientists.

This persuaded us that if we could succeed in enabling students to weave in theory and research into their practice, while reflecting at the same time, we could also encourage qualified social workers and managers to do the same, using the same technique. We have run a few workshops using this method with practitioners, and found that these have been effective in providing social workers with the opportunities to pause, reflect on what has happened, feel reassured that they are not alone, and then be provided with possible solutions that they could implement to affect positive change.

Child protection work involves working with families and other services to safeguard children and young people. It is challenging work that requires making critical decisions in complex situations amidst organisational, political and emotional pressures. Reflection is an essential activity that should take place across all areas of social work, and so the aim of this book is to use detailed case examples to explore typical situations that any child protection social worker may be likely to face in practice. By doing it this way we hope to provide the reader with an atmospheric sensation while reading it, one that will hopefully leave them feeling as if they were also part of the situation. By weaving in theory and research into the study to support or critique our reflections, the reader will also be provided with an idea of how unpredictable events can emerge in practice.

They may also come across ideas that they may (or may not) want to implement in their practice if they find they are faced with a similar predicament in their work.

There are already several books in circulation that explain how students and practitioners can reflect, and there are also those that use small case studies to do so. Our intention is not to replicate these approaches. Instead, we want to frame situations by using detailed case examples of real–life situations that we have faced inside and outside of the office. All the following chapters will take readers on a particular journey of a situation we have experienced 'in practice'. By beginning at the beginning, we will start by exploring the nature of the situation, the theoretical perspectives that we drew from, what we were thinking as it was happening and what we thought after the event, before ending with a conclusion of what happened and what we have learned from that experience.

The material we have drawn from has been taken from field notes and our own reflective diaries. However, it is important to note that we recognise protecting the privacy of others within the text is crucial. We have subsequently altered several identifying characteristics such as, for example, certain circumstances surrounding incidents, locations, places and personal characteristics that include gender, age and name.

Although this book is technically a 'how to do it' book, it will also explore the 'how not to do' aspects of practice. Each chapter will be dedicated to exploring one case study in great detail. This collection of chapters aims to provide readers with a range of different experiences that may be useful for students, social workers and managers.

Reflection 'in' and 'on' action

Donald Alan Schön (1930–97) originally trained as a philosopher, but his concern with the development of reflective practice and learning systems has been of great importance to education and practice in the fields of health and social care. The term reflection 'in' action developed from Schön's reading of philosophers Michael Polanyi (1967) and Gilbert Ryle (1949) as he started to recognise how many practitioners revealed their knowledge during an action. Drawing from Polanyi (1967, p 4), who argued that 'we know more than we can tell', Schön (1992) recognised that skilled practice can reveal a kind of knowing that doesn't stem from a previous intellectual know-how. Therefore, although practitioners sometimes reflect before action, much of their unplanned behaviour will stem from a knowledge that is ordinarily tacit or implicit in their patterns of action (Schön, 1983). In other words, Schön recognised that practitioners found it difficult to explain how they felt for the things that they were doing or dealing with, but they nonetheless dealt with the situations they encountered by drawing from an internal knowledge base.

Schön (1983) felt that often people encountered situations that they felt unprepared for because they would draw from previous learned knowledge that was perhaps inappropriate for the new event. Schön's ideas therefore drew our attention towards an embodied kind of reflection, one that was associated with the development of professional knowledge. He felt that if practitioners were to avoid using preconceived ideas about what should be done in a particular situation, they would need to develop an understanding of frame reflection.

Schön used the term 'frame reflection' to demonstrate that different individuals, disciplines and policy-makers bring different frames, or perspectives, to the same events. Thus, depending on the role, people will see a situation in their own way. In addition, Schön recognised that different disciplines frequently held conflicting views of the same situation, and that, in many cases, they were unlikely to resolve their disagreement because they tended to pay attention to a different set of facts. This is an important point to consider given that professional boundaries are eroding in the contemporary social work setting (White, 2006).

However, some writers have challenged the notion of reflection altogether, and argued that there is no such thing (Ixer, 1999, 2011). Ixer's (2016) issues stem from the social work education whole-heartedly accepting the concept without a stable empirical evidence base underpinning its approach to the performance of practice tasks. Furthermore, Ixer is concerned that the process of reflection and critical reflection is hidden, and often only becomes necessary to externalise and bring to the public arena when required for measuring performance in assessment purposes.

However, although Schön (1983, 1987) recognised that the contexts of practice are messy, complex and laden with value conflicts, he felt that if professionals were to reach an agreement, they would need to understand the perspective of the other. Only by doing this would they then discover and appreciate the different tacit cognitive strategies involved, and use this understanding to comprehend the other's framing of the situation. Thus, their ability to come to a practical agreement is contingent on their ability to frame reflection.

If reflection 'in' action occurs while the actor is in the midst of doing or being involved in an activity, then reflection 'on' action is concerned with thinking critically after the activity has taken place. The purpose of reflecting after the event is important because it gives the practitioner an opportunity to review, analyse and evaluate the situation. This process can enable the individual to move from the stage of unconscious knowing in action to a juncture that encourages the reflector to describe their tacit knowledge. This stage of reflection rarely, however, involves just looking back on experiences and exploring the reasoning behind the actions that were taken. Instead, it brings into action ways of responding to the problematic situations that were faced by framing the practical knowledge with conceptual theory. This stage therefore helps the reflector identify and analyse how the practical knowledge used in a particular situation was influenced by language and dominant discourses. Practice in welfare settings takes place, after all, in the context of powerful organisational and professional cultures (White, 2006).

Professional development therefore only begins once a person reflects 'on' action because this is the time when they are able to (re)examine a situation or encounter through a critical lens. By exploring what happened, why it happened in the way that it did, and taking into perspective the views and feelings of others, the reflector can, with the support of the wider literature, engage in critical reflection. Schön (1987) argued that people were more likely to develop their understanding of the situation and create solutions for future practice if they applied a research-based theory technique to their reflections 'on' action.

At some point in social work, there may come a time when practitioners observe their colleagues, with plenty of experience, get 'stuck' in certain situations. They appear unable 'to navigate the swamps' within which they are trapped, and the predicament they find themselves in only seems to get messier and messier (Kinsella, 2010, p 566). This can occur when the social worker doesn't have the time or space to reflect on their own practice or take the time to see a situation from a different perspective. Schön (1987, 1992) has argued that it is the ability of the practitioner to engage in reflection 'in' and 'on' action that will make the difference in terms of how future tricky encounters are addressed.

However, White (2006) warns the practitioner to tread carefully when drawing from fashionable or powerful ideas to analyse moral reasoning as it can interrupt the reflector's capacity to engage critically with their endeavour. Social workers may feel 'free and purposeful agents', but they are not in conditions of their own making (White, 2006, p 23). Therefore, when practitioners act in a certain way, or make a case for a specific action, they may be unaware that they are invoking a particular idea because it is a popular one promoted by their organisation, but not necessarily the most desirable or appropriate one for that situation.

It is often argued that there are gaps between theoretical/research knowledge and practice knowledge in social work. Indeed, Schön (1987, 1992) often contended that professionals faced a crisis of knowledge. However, in recent years there has been a significant drive towards bridging the theory/practice gap in social work practice. This activity has been referred to as knowledge translation or the ability to demonstrate how evidence is used in practice (see BASW, no date). By reflecting 'in' and 'on' action, and by drawing from the relevant theories to enable a critical form of analysis, we hope to use this book to demonstrate how social workers can generate knowledge for their own practice.

In the following chapters we have drawn from Donald Schön's concepts in each case study. The case studies we have included tell a story that is personal and indicative of the journeys we have taken when we were in practice. By re-telling these stories in this context, we hope to encourage the reader to pause during the 'in' action reflections, and to consider what is happening in each of our narratives. This technique has been designed to persuade the reader to think about what she or he may have done if they had been faced with the same situation.

Although it is hard to recognise when one is reflecting 'in' action, and Ixer (2016, p 814) has even stated that 'reflection in action is an impossible skill', we use it in this context to show the social worker in action in a given situation. As mentioned earlier, we have drawn from research field notes and practice diaries, so have written these case studies up from notes that were made after the events took place. While we agree that it is impossible to know which of these thoughts are therefore a direct result of reflection or outputs of tacit knowledge and intuition, we do recognise that it is our moral characters that have guided our thinking, decision-making and action, and therefore perhaps our own reflection too. We found that this method does have its benefits in taking the reader on the journey with us, but obviously, a journey that is only told from our perspective.

To try and demonstrate how different views matter in practice, each chapter draws from different theoretical perspectives in an attempt to explore the way in which a particular situation unfolded. We hope that this approach will provide the reader with a better understanding of what was happening and the reasons why it perhaps happened in the way that it did. It is important to remember that everyone is an individual, and social workers approach practice in many different ways. Therefore, there is not one ideal way to resolve the predicaments that we encountered.

We hope that each chapter can provide material that might be useful for practice educators or work-based supervisors to use with students or for managers to use with social workers in supervision or in team meetings. There are many different styles for writing reflective accounts and doing reflective thinking. We have shaped each chapter differently to reveal this variable landscape. We recognise that although reflective writing is a product of reflective thinking, it is difficult to identify how the student or practitioner is learning. Some supervisors fear that reflective exercises merely reflect what the supervisor wants to see, not what the practitioner actually feels. It is hard for supervisors to assess whether they are encountering reflection, analysis or critical thinking. Indeed, Ixer (2016) has argued that many writers have failed to explain reflection or consider its links to virtue ethics and values.

Taking Ixer's (2016) argument into consideration, when the case studies conclude, we use reflection 'on' action to try and highlight our own ethics and value base by discussing what happened after the activity had taken place. Although as social workers we attempted to practice ethically in accordance with defined social work values (see BASW, 2012), when translated into practice this can mean different things for individual practitioners. This section therefore provides the reader with an opportunity to think about what we (and others) did, and with the use of the wider literature, to explore what happened in more detail. The chapters conclude with a summary examining what could have happened if a different approach had been adopted and how this may have resulted in different outcomes.

References

BASW (British Association of Social Workers) (2012) *The code of ethics for social work: Statement of principles* (http://cdn.basw.co.uk/upload/basw_112315-7.pdf).

BASW (no date) 'Professional Capabilities Framework' (www.basw.co.uk/pcf/PCF06ASYELevelCapabilities.pdf).

Ixer, G. (1999) 'There is no such things as reflection', *British Journal of Social Work*, vol 29, pp 513–27.

Ixer, G. (2011) 'There's no such thing as reflection – 10 years on', *The Journal of Practice Teaching in Health and Social Work*, vol 10, no 1, pp 75–93.

Ixer, G. (2016) 'The concept of reflection: Is it skill based or values?', *Social Work Education*, vol 35, no 7, pp 809–24, doi:10.1080/02615479.2016.1193136.

Kinsella, E.A. (2010) 'The art of reflective practice in health and social care: Reflections on the legacy of Donald Schön', *Journal of Reflective Practice*, vol 11, no 4, pp 565–75.

Polanyi, M. (1967) *The tacit dimension*, London: Routledge.

Ryle, G. (1949) *The concept of mind*, London: Hutchinson.Schön, D.A. (1983) *The reflective practitioner: How professionals think in action*, New York: Basic Books.

Schön, D.A. (1987) *Educating the reflective practitioner*, San Francisco, CA: Jossey-Bass.

Schön, D.A. (1992) 'The theory of inquiry: Dewey's legacy to education', *Curriculum Inquiry*, vol 22, no 2, pp 119–39.

White, S. (2006) 'Unsettling reflections: The reflexive practitioner as "trickster" in interprofessional work', in S. White, J. Fook and F. Garnder (eds) *Critical reflection in health and social care*, Maidenhead: Open University Press, pp 21–40.

1

Applying a person-centred approach

Introduction

This chapter explores a case where the family had been known to Children's Services for a long time. The mother was a single parent to two boys. She suffered with depression, and several agencies were expressing concerns about the welfare of her children because the boys were arriving at school late, appeared unkempt, and were always getting into trouble inside and outside school. In addition, the Family Support Service had developed an unwritten policy that stated that they would not work with any parent who was 'depressed' and not receiving medication for their depression.

The story begins by explaining why the author opened the referral and how a case that appeared to be 'child in need' quickly progressed to 'child protection'. It follows the trials and errors made by the author who became the allocated caseworker. The author, who, while responding to the fears of other professionals and trying to deal with not being supported by the Family Support Service, soon started to act as a parent to the mother of the family. Therefore, although the author did begin working *with* the family, her narrative soon changed to that of someone who 'knows best' as she struggled to balance the fears of other professionals with the needs of the family.

Drawing from a *symbolic interactionist perspective*, the author uses this framework to explore the different views of the family and the professionals involved in the case. She also draws from a *person-centred approach* in the case study to demonstrate how this model could have alleviated some of the problems that she faced, before concluding with a *systems theory approach* to explain how a 'bad' situation turned 'good'. Throughout this chapter, the author draws from current research to explain why an emancipatory style of working is far more beneficial in producing change than that of a dictatorial approach.

Symbolic interactionism

Symbolic interactionism is a sociological perspective that developed around the middle of the 20th century and derived from the American philosophy of pragmatism, and particularly from the work of George Herbert Mead (1863–1931). Symbolic interactionism is basically therefore a distinctive approach to the study of human life and human conduct (Blumer, 1969). This viewpoint sees people as being active agents in shaping their world, rather than as entities that are acted on by society (Herman and Reynolds, 1994). Reality is thus seen as being a social activity as it is developed in interaction with others. Joel Charon (2010) has argued that there are five central ideas behind this approach:

- The human being must be understood as a *social person*. It is the constant search for social interaction that leads us to do what we do. Instead of focusing on the individual and his or her personality, or on how the society or a social situation causes human behaviour, symbolic interactionism focuses on the activities that take place between actors. What we do depends on our interaction with others earlier in our lifetimes, and it depends on our interaction right now
- The human being must be understood as a *thinking being*. Human action is not only interaction among individuals, but also interaction within the individual. It is not our ideas or attitudes or values that are as important as the constant, active, ongoing process of thinking.
- Humans do not sense their environment directly; instead, humans *define the situation they are in*. An environment may exist, but it is our definition of it that is important. Definition doesn't simply randomly happen; instead, it results from ongoing social interaction and thinking.
- The cause of human action is the result of *what is occurring in our present situation*. Cause unfolds in the present social interaction, present thinking and present definition. It is not society's encounters with us in our past that causes action, nor is it our own past experience. It is, instead, social interaction, thinking and a definition of the situation that takes place in the present. Our past enters into our actions primarily because we think about it and apply it to the definition of the present situation.
- Human beings are described as *active beings in relation to their environment*. Words such as 'conditioning', 'responding', 'controlled', 'imprisoned' and 'formed' are not used to describe the human being in symbolic interaction. In contrast to other social-scientific perspectives, humans are not thought of as being passive in relation to their surroundings, but actively involved in what they do.

Person-centred theory

If symbolic interactionism is a perspective that recognises individuals are active-thinking agents who draw from the past to interpret interactions that happen in the present, a person–centred approach can help social workers apply this theoretical framework to practice. Person–centred theory (also known as humanistic theory) accepts people as they are despite the chaos and complex issues they are situated in. It is believed that if social workers consistently and actively demonstrate this acceptance through their behaviour, they can create the conditions necessary for people to become the people they have always had the capacity to become.

The person–centred approach developed from the work of the psychologist Dr Carl Rogers (1902–87). This approach to practice moved away from the idea that the therapist was the expert and towards a theory that trusted the intrinsic tendency of human beings to find realisation of their personal potential. An important part of this approach is that in a particular environment, the fulfilment of personal potential includes the need to be with other human beings and the desire to know and be known by other people. It also involves being open to experience, being trusting and trustworthy, being curious about the world, and being creative and compassionate.

The psychological environment described by Rogers was one where a person felt free from threat, both physically and psychologically. This environment could be achieved when being in a relationship with a person who was deeply understanding (empathic), accepting (having unconditional positive regard) and genuine (congruent) (see www.bapca.org.uk). Over the years many social workers have associated themselves philosophically with the person–centred approach. The reason for this association is because it is based on the concept that social issues are at the root of people's difficulties. However, if social workers work with people as self–determining actors in their own lives, then social and personal change can be brought about (Sanders, 2005; Proctor et al, 2006).

Systems theory

Systems theory has developed from several perspectives and directions such as cybernetics (Wiener, 1948), general systems theory (von Bertalanffy, 1968), structural–functionalist systems theory (Parsons, 1951), functionalist–structural systems theory (Luhmann, 1990) and social ecological theory (Germain, 1978). All of these perspectives have influenced social work practice over the years in various ways. Systems theories view human behaviour as being a product of complex systems. This theory is designed on the structures that surround a service user, for example, the family, organisations and institutions to which that service user belongs (Payne, 2007). It also encourages the development of a social order, and shows how other individuals within the community can be included to help a service user resolve a problem.

Systems theory has helped developed social workers' understanding of human behaviour in the social environment by encouraging practitioners to focus on understanding where the person is in relation to cross–cultural elements. It is based on the idea that an effective system recognises the individual needs, rewards, expectations and attributes of the people living in the system. Therefore, if a problem is to be resolved, those who are directly connected to the person at the centre of the dilemma will be involved in helping them overcome their difficulties. Social workers can support change to take place by identifying how different people can connect, interact and work together to reach the desirable outcomes.

All three of these theories, symbolic interactionism, a person-centred approach and systems theory, are drawn from in this case study.

Case study

Context

This chapter discusses the interactions that took place with the Taylor family. Trina Taylor was 30 years old at the time, and the mother of Peter aged 12 and Sam aged 9. Peter and Sam had different fathers and different surnames. They lived alone with Trina and neither had contact with, or knew the whereabouts of, their fathers. This case was one of the first families I was allocated as a newly qualified social worker. I had only been in practice for a few weeks when I picked it up. It was considered a 'child in need' case, and was opened after the following referral was received.

Referral details

T/C (telephone call) from the community mental health nurse. He had just been to the house to check on Trina. He couldn't gain access again, but he knew Trina was in because he saw the curtains move upstairs. He was worried because the garden was full of bin bags, and he found one of Trina's sons, Sam (9), smoking around the corner with some older kids. When he asked him what he was doing, Sam told him that he had been caught setting fire to a neighbour's shed and that when Trina had found out, she had gone mad and thrown him out of the house. He didn't have anywhere to sleep that night.

When I checked the system I noticed that there had been a number of referrals made to our service about this family, and they had been made by a wide range of different people such as the postman who was concerned because the mail he posted daily was mounting inside the front door; the headmistress from the primary school because she was concerned that Sam always appeared unkempt; neighbours who were complaining about the boys' anti-social behaviour; the community health nurse (the most recent referrer); and even a referral from housing expressing concerns about the condition of the home. I also noticed that this case had been open and closed many times over the years, starting from when Sam had been a baby.

I had only been in post a few weeks when I received this case. I was keen and eager to get going. I wanted to apply all my learning from university and start 'doing' social work. This was a case I thought I could get my teeth into, and I was told by my manager that it was a typical 'child in need' case. From what I had read in the previous referrals it had sounded to me as if there were several other concerns, but when I raised this with my team manager, she calmly reassured me that our first approach to the case needed to be a supportive one. Despite hearing this advice, I was still convinced that there was more going on and I felt it was my mission to find out what was happening. However, engaging with Trina was not going to be easy. I had tried calling her numerous times but she didn't answer her phone and didn't call me back. I knew that my main priority was to find out quickly if Sam had a place to stay that evening, and so I decided to visit the house.

The Taylor family lived in a terraced council house, and I could see on arrival that the community mental health nurse had been correct, the front garden was full of bin bags. As I walked up the path I could see that it stood out from the others – it looked the most dilapidated on the street. When I knocked on the door there was no answer. I called through the letterbox but no one replied and I couldn't hear any movement inside either. I could, however, smell a strong odour. It was pungent and seemed to be a mixture of damp and urine. I left a note for Trina with my phone number on it and went back to the car. I sat and waited, watching the house and looking for movement. There was none.

Reflection points

1. What could I have done before I'd gone around to Trina's house?
   Contact other professionals to find out if they had concerns or had involvement with Trina.
2. What do you think might be the best way to make contact with Trina?
   A letter or an email explaining that a referral had been received and a meeting to talk it over would have been one way of informing Trina of my involvement.
3. Do you think that the lack of engagement from Trina is concerning?
   It does appear as if Trina is avoiding contact, but it may be that Trina's number has changed.

After about 30 minutes I noticed a boy walking down the path that ran between the two lines of terraced houses that faced each other. He had a school uniform on, and it looked like it was from the same school that Peter was supposed to attend. I watched what he did and when he turned towards the Taylor's house I jumped out of the car and walked quickly behind him. It was not until he entered the house that he noticed I was behind him. I walked in with him and introduced myself. He didn't look surprised to see me, and without talking walked into the house. Once inside the sitting room he called to his mother.

Nicolas (2015) suggests that home visits should build a picture of what life is like for the child, and that this may differ from the social worker's initial thoughts before the visit. While it is always important to consider the family's strengths, it is also helpful to be realistic about risks and concerns.

I was thinking about what life may be like for Peter and Sam in the Taylor home when I noticed Trina coming down the stairs in her nightie. When she walked into the room and saw me, it was immediately apparent that she was not impressed with my tactical entrance. But rather than express her annoyance by shouting at me or telling me to get out, she sat down on the couch and said nothing. I took this as a cue that I could stay, so I sat down next to Trina and proceeded to tell her about the referral and the concerns that I had from reading the previous contacts that were on the system.

As I talked I noticed that I could not read Trina's thoughts or feelings. At this point in time I was not thinking about symbolic interactionism (Charon, 2010) or a person–centred approach (Rogers, 1957). I was just conscious that the atmosphere was tense and difficult.

Payne (2007) argues that knowledge and theory is integral to all social work practice because it is embodied in the worker. Therefore, the worker as a 'wise person' draws from their knowledge to inform their social work practice and so produces an improvised embodied performance.

I am not sure whether I was feeling particularly wise at that moment, but what I did know was that Trina didn't react to what I was saying, either physically or emotionally. She didn't disagree with what I was saying, but she didn't contribute anything to the conversation either. It was almost as if she didn't care. When I asked her questions about what was happening, she replied by shrugging her shoulders. I realised I was finding it difficult to gauge what Trina felt at all. The only comment that Trina made was that she had not thrown Sam out and that he had already been back for his tea.

Reflection points
1. How would you have interpreted Trina's behaviour?
2. What technique might you have employed to encourage the conversation to develop?
   A SAVI (System for Analysing Verbal Information) tool may have been useful here, especially active listening and turn taking when talking (see Koprowska, 2008, p 77). It is important to remain patient and avoid repetition, otherwise this will lead to frustration for both parties.

During this awkward interaction Peter left the house, and I noticed that when he did, he didn't tell his mother where he was going. And she didn't ask. I sought permission from Trina to speak to Peter and Sam at school the next day, and Trina agreed that I could. However, when I asked if Trina could show me around the house, she said it wasn't appropriate, and it was only at this point that I noticed a slight change in her presentation. She shifted uncomfortably in her seat and reached for a cigarette. I was tempted to push the matter further, but as Nicolas (2015) suggests, making a home visit should always be respectful, and it is important to strike a fine balance between being authoritative and arrogant. Also, drawing from a person–centred approach, I didn't want to appear threatening towards Trina; I wanted to build a relationship that had the right ingredients to produce the therapeutic conditions of empathy, unconditional positive regard and genuineness (see Wilson et al, 2009). I considered this theoretical argument as I left Trina's house that evening. I felt proud that I had used my detective skills to stealthily gain entrance to the house, but at the same time, I felt foolish for not having used my relationship–building skills effectively to engage with either Trina or Peter.

The next day when I spoke to my manager she told me that I should perhaps consider involving a family support worker, one who had worked with Trina before and who had a relationship with her. I agreed, but before I called the Family Support Service, I made an appointment to see the boys at school. Peter's teachers didn't have much to say about him. They said he was easy to overlook. He didn't contribute in class, but he did attend. He wasn't any trouble, but he didn't have any friends to get in trouble with. When I asked them to describe him, they couldn't. I realised that Peter was absent even when he was present. He did a good job of slipping into the background, and it was because of this that no one had noticed Peter at all.

When I talked to Peter alone, it felt like I was talking to Trina. He didn't respond to any of my questions, and didn't elaborate on any of the answers he gave me when he did. I did learn, however, that he felt there were "no problems at home". He told me that all was fine and I needed to leave them alone. I explained my role and what I hoped to achieve with them all if they engaged with me and with others. Peter nodded as if to consent, but I wasn't entirely sure if that meant he was going to work with me or just accept that I was going to be around for a while.

Reflection points

1. How would you have read Peter's behaviour?
2. What do you think about how Peter's teachers described him?
   Being easy to overlook doesn't always mean that a child is problem-free, but that they able to conceal their problems from view.
3. What could I have done to have built a better relationship with Peter?
   Used language and interaction more effectively; encouraged reciprocity; waited for your utterances to be processed; remembered power imbalance; asked Peter to tell you to slow down; used simple language; been specific – one question at a time; asked broad and narrow questions; considered the location of the meeting (see Koprowska, 2008, p 104).

Although I didn't employ any method other than talking to Peter, research carried out by Dillenburger et al (2008) has suggested that using art with children is one way in which communication with children can be improved. Art can be applied in a variety of settings and with a large number of different client groups. It has been used for aesthetic, educational and clinical reasons. In this situation, drawing from a symbolic interactionist perspective (Charon, 2010), and remembering that the past often influences the way someone behaves in the present, I could have asked Peter to have drawn a typical evening at home. Using different characters, and drawing from a person-centred perspective, I could have gently asked him who was present in his life and what was happening. The idea behind this form of practice is that the art encourages the young person to relax, so that they may reveal more about a situation they find difficult to describe. This process of pairing can help both the social worker and young person to overcome anxiety, the assumption being that relaxation reciprocally inhibits the anxiety response, leading to 'a weakening of the association between stimuli and anxiety' (O'Sullivan and Dryden, 1990, p 253).

My reception at Sam's school was entirely different. It was Sam's headmistress, Janet, who greeted me and was eager to tell me all about Sam and Trina. She told me that Sam had been walking to and from school by himself, which, although it was not too far, still concerned her because he had started mixing with children who were a lot older than he was. This had, she believed, been getting him into trouble, both inside and outside of school. Inside school, Sam found it "difficult to concentrate" and was a "nuisance in class". He was also prone to swearing, and Janet found this upset the other children. Despite focusing on the negative aspects of Sam's behaviour, it was also evident that Janet was fond of him. She told me that because he had been so disruptive in class he spent a lot of time in her office. At first Janet found this unpleasant because he was a distraction, but the longer they spent together, the more Janet realised that he was "a nice kid".

Janet described how she had tried to engage Trina in turning the situation around, but how she had found it difficult because there was "no one home". By this she meant that although Trina was present, she was absent. Janet felt that Trina was more wrapped up in her own problems and, as a result, had neglected her children's needs. She told me several times in the conversation that Trina needed "a good talking to". I felt that there was a subtext to this inference that indicated that the person who should give the good talking to Trina should be me.

When I met with Sam it was clear that he was a completely different character to Peter. He had lots to say and wanted to say it all at once. He was keen to tell me about his adventures and was almost boasting when he informed me of setting fire to his neighbour's shed. It was evident that he did not spend much time at home, however, and that his mother didn't know where he was because she didn't ask. He felt this was because she didn't like him much, and he admitted that he wasn't sure if he liked her. He said he only went home to get food when he was hungry; the rest of the time he liked to play out with his friends.

Reflection points

1. What kind of information do you think has been gathered from the children at this point?
   The two children are different, have different relationships with their mother

and the schools that they attend. The youngest, Sam, appears to have been neglected, both physically and emotionally.

2. What could have been my next step?
   Talked to community crime prevention services to find out what kind of support Sam or Trina were being offered.
3. Is this still a typical 'child in need' case?
   Different agencies have different thresholds, but at this point, Trina and the children appear to be in need of support, even if they are not saying that explicitly, and therefore the focus should be on building relationships with the family.

The meetings with both schools, although different, were collectively informative, and I felt I was beginning to gain a bigger and clearer picture of the Taylor family's issues. In my view, they appeared to all be stemming from Trina, her poor parenting and her lack of willingness to engage with professional services. Drawing from what I considered to be a symbolic interactionist perspective, where the person is seen to be an active being in relation to their environment (see Charon, 2010), I came to the conclusion that Trina was primarily responsible for the problems she was facing. As I had also learned that these issues had been ongoing for years, and that during that time a number of different agencies had been involved and tried to help Trina make changes, I was even more convinced that Trina was the cause of the problems.

However, I did acknowledge that the one agency that had remained distant was my agency, and this lack of intervention and constant re-referral back to schools, health and support services had left our partner agencies unsure of how to best progress with the situation. Learning this information left me feeling annoyed with my own manager for always passing it back, but I was also annoyed with Trina. Why did she not accept help when she was given it? Why was she making life so difficult for herself? And why was she not bothered about her children? Whatever the answers were to these questions, I knew that I was not going to let this case drift any longer, and I made a promise to myself that I would get to the bottom of the issues once and for all.

Yet, to do so I needed to find someone who had worked with Trina before and who had had a good relationship with her. I contacted our Family Support Service and spoke to the team manager, Harriet, the gatekeeper who would decide if my request for support held any merit and if she would be willing to allocate me the right person for the case. After explaining the dilemma to Harriet, I quickly learned that the Family Support Service had developed a policy of their own recently, one that had been created because of a reduction in resources and workers. Harriet told me that she would not be able to provide me with a service because, from what I had said, it sounded like Trina was depressed, and she had agreed with her workers that they would not work with parents who didn't access support for their depression. This, Harriet thought, was the first step that parents needed to make if they were to engage effectively with a support worker.

I put down the phone to Harriet feeling shocked and disappointed. It took me a while to figure out why exactly, but it wasn't long before I realised that this approach that Harriet had devised was not only oppressive, but also contradicted the purpose of 'support work'. The primary role of the support worker is to provide support and enable independence, whether or not someone has depression. Manthorpe (2008, p 8) has defined support work as:

> A person who is employed on an individual basis to foster independence and provide assistance for a service user in areas of ordinary life such as communication, employment, social participation and who may take on secondary tasks in respect of advocacy, personal care and learning.

Because I had been unaware of this new rule and was unprepared for the outcome I would encounter by sharing Trina's behavioural position with Harriet, I had rather naively presented Trina as 'depressed' to seek support when I didn't actually know for sure if Trina had been medically diagnosed as such.

I called my team manager, Sue, and told her of my blunder. She sympathised and then said, "Well, you know what you should do? Pass it back to school. It sounds like it's their issue, not ours." This lack of ownership and what I perceived as unwillingness to progress with the case annoyed me, and without thinking I retaliated, "Actually it's not their problem, it's ours." I then proceeded to argue that refusing to offer a service to someone who may or may not be depressed was discriminatory and constituted oppressive practice (see Thompson, 2006). I didn't feel it was right that the Family Support Service could say that they would only work with Trina once she had agreed to take and had been on anti-depressants for a period of a month. I also felt that what my manager should be doing, rather than making the easy call of sending it back to the school, was to pick up the phone and call Harriet, and tell her that this approach was not only inappropriate but also highly unacceptable. Sue didn't say a word, but when I finally stopped talking she just said, "I think you need to come into the office straight away."

The drive to the office was a blur. I felt anxious all the way there, believing that I had over-stepped the mark and that this meeting I had been called to was not going to be a pleasant one. But I also felt deep down that I was right – all this theory I had learned at university had to have been for a reason, and what better reason than now, I thought. Determined to stand my ground, I strode into the office prepared for a heated discussion. But Sue was more reasonable than I had anticipated, and appeared to have sympathy for my argument. After a good debate, therefore, Sue agreed to call Harriet and "have a word". It wasn't long after that I received a call from a family support worker called Debbie. Although she couldn't carry out direct work with Trina, she could meet with me to tell me what she knew about the family.

Reflection points

1. What do you think about the Family Support Service decision to not work with parents who suffer with depression?
2. Do you think there may have been a reason why such a decision had been made?

   The service had to deal with financial constraints and therefore developed criteria that allowed support workers to work with families who would benefit from short periods of intervention. This would free support workers from being embroiled with cases that were likely to require a lot of involvement.

I wasn't overly pleased with the outcome from the Family Support Service, but I did feel proud that I had stayed true to my beliefs. Although I had only been qualified for a few weeks, I felt I was applying my knowledge and developing skills quickly. This led me to feeling more confident, in control and eager to progress with the case. I wanted to resolve the issues for the Taylor family and achieve a great outcome for them all, and I was of the mindset that if no one else could help me, then I would have to do it by myself.

I decided to call around to see Trina and find out how things were going. When I knocked on the door I wasn't surprised that I didn't get an answer, but when I called through the letterbox cheerfully, "Trina, it's me. I know you're in there and I'm not going away till you answer the door", I was pleased to hear movement and see Trina, once again in her nightie, walking down the stairs towards me. My methods are clearly working, I thought to myself.

I asked Trina how she was feeling, and she once again shrugged her shoulders and said nothing. I proceeded to tell her about my day and the meetings I'd had. Although my news may have been exciting for me, it didn't appear to have the same effect for Trina. The lack of engagement and interaction from her was starting to annoy me and made me feel unappreciated – how could she not see all the effort I was putting into this case for her? If I had been in her shoes I would have been grateful that someone was finally willing to help, I thought to myself.

I started to wonder if Trina really was depressed or actually just rude. I almost felt relieved when Sam walked in the door as he did seem pleased to see me. And then suddenly, while sitting there, a thought occurred to me, and without pausing to consider Rogers' (1957) person-centred practice, or the advice of Nicolas (2015), I asked Sam if he could give me a tour of the house, starting with his bedroom. He agreed, and before Trina could intervene, both Sam and I walked up the stairs.

It soon became clear why Trina was reluctant to show me upstairs. Sam's bedroom was completely bare – there were no curtains, no bed, no carpet, no wardrobe, nothing. There were, however, bin bags on the floor that were full. Sam didn't seem to notice my shock and took me to his window to show me the view from his room – I looked into the back garden and noticed it, too, was full of bin bags. My head was spinning as I was trying to work out what to say, and all that came out was, "Where do you sleep?" Sam put the bin bags in his room together and pointed to them, "On there", he said. He showed me that inside the bin bags were his clothes, not rubbish, as I had presumed. He got out a coat and told me that he used it as a cover, and when it was cold, he put two on.

When I saw his brother's room I wasn't surprised to see that it was exactly the same as Sam's, but when I saw his mother's room, I was really concerned. Trina's room did have a bed, a duvet, bedding, pillows, curtains and a bit of a carpet. Sam didn't comment on the fact that his mother had somewhere comfortable to sleep, and so neither did I. When I went into the bathroom it instantly made sense why I had smelt a strong smell of urine and damp. There was mould all over the walls and the toilet was broken – it wouldn't flush. Sam told me that they had to fill a bucket to get rid of their waste, and because he couldn't be bothered to do this, he would just pee in the bath.

Reflection points

1. What do you think these findings suggest in terms of using a person-centred approach?
   I had, perhaps, become so focused on building a relationship with Trina that I was overlooking the children and the home environment.
2. Do you think this approach was the right one to adopt in this circumstance?
   I could have asked Trina if she would show me around the home and been more open in my approach.

When I came down the stairs I looked at Trina and she looked mortified; it was the first time she had expressed any emotion, and even though I was pleased to see she could feel emotion, I couldn't respond because I was in shock and didn't quite know what to say. I followed Sam into the kitchen. I almost sighed with relief when I saw a cooker and a fridge, but then Sam showed me that neither worked, they were just there for show. I looked in the cupboards and they were almost bare – all that was there were two pot noodles and a packet of crisps.

Trina came into the kitchen and said, "I can explain". I wasn't properly listening, however; instead, I was thinking that trying to consider Trina's feeling with positive unconditional regard was not a functional method at all (see Rogers, 1961); I was more motivated in looking for someone to blame. I replied rather tersely, "I think you better had". She proceeded to tell me that a few months previously she had started to get into bad debt, she couldn't afford to pay her rent, and so borrowed from loan sharks, but this had made the situation worse as she couldn't afford to pay them either.

The loan sharks came around and took pieces of her furniture as payment, which is why the boys had lost their beds, their furniture and why the items in the kitchen weren't working. "But that doesn't explain why they have no quilts or bedding, Trina, and why you have a bed and bedding!" I snapped loudly. I could feel myself getting annoyed as I was convinced Trina was lying to me. She couldn't answer me. This irritated me even more, and before I knew it I was quoting extracts from all the 'good parenting' handbooks I had ever read, building up evidence that would support my theory that Trina was an emotionally absent and neglectful parent. I only stopped ranting on when I noticed Trina sit down and start to cry. She said, "You are right, I am shit." To which I replied sternly, "I think we need an emergency meeting with everyone tomorrow, and I hope you can make it this time."

I left the house feeling self-righteous and pleased with my delivery. I was a good social worker because I had told Trina what I thought of her and given her the "good talking to" that Janet said was well overdue. But as soon as I got to my car and sat down, I felt terrible. I started thinking back over everything I had said, over Trina's reaction, my lack of empathy, my poor listening skills, the fact that I had not even thought about where the children were or how they would have felt if they had heard what I'd said to Trina. I had been so focused on 'finding out the truth' behind Trina's behaviour that I hadn't even thought properly about the way I was doing it. Rather than thinking about why the home conditions were as they were, perhaps considering the symbolic interactionist notion that something had occurred in the past to affect the present environment (see Charon, 2010), I had stormed ahead, driven by my own agenda to make her feel bad for being a poor parent. I drove home and kept hearing Trina's voice saying, "You are right, I am shit."

The next morning, I met with my team manager. I told Sue everything that had happened yesterday, keeping my eyes glued to her face, waiting to see if her expression would reflect her disappointment in me. It didn't. She told me that she was pleased to have me on the team because although I had acted like a bull in a china shop, I had quickly realised that this wasn't the right way to be a social worker. The wise person approach that Payne (2007) argues embodies most social workers in practice had not been the performance I had acted out in my encounter with Trina. Sue made me feel slightly better by warning me not to be so hard on myself.

Sue and I talked at length about what I could do to rectify the situation and how I needed to spend some time planning what should happen next. We agreed that I would organise a meeting with both schools, health and support services for as soon as possible. Once I had a time and date I would go around to Trina's and apologise. I was just about to leave our meeting when the phone rang. Sue answered it; it was Janet, Headmistress at Sam's school.

Janet told Sue that Sam had arrived with the police that morning. They had dropped him off and told Janet that they had arrested Trina. They couldn't give Janet any further details at that time, but they promised they would be in touch shortly. When the police left, Sam told Janet that they had arrived around 6am and seized Trina's laptop. They had also searched the house and he had heard them asking his mother if he and Peter had been aware of the websites she had been looking at. Sam then said to Janet, "It's probably the dirty sites she looks at with her boyfriends that they've done her for." Janet ended the call stating that she wanted it noting that she was recommending the children be removed from their home with immediate effect and placed in care.

Sue told Janet that she would ask me to organise an emergency meeting for Trina and all professionals to come together to discuss recent events and concerns, and to decide on the best way to proceed. When Sue put down the phone we went through what the next steps should be. It looked like this news was going to trigger a Section 47 (Children Act 1989), which is when a local authority has reasonable cause to suspect that a child in their area is suffering, or is likely to suffer, significant harm; enquiries are then made that enable them to decide whether they should take any action to safeguard or promote the child's welfare. We also agreed that this new piece of information had shed new light on the situation and potentially explained why Trina had been behaving in the way she had. But we also agreed that there was so much that was still not known that without clarifying further could affect the next decisions that were made. We decided that the first step should involve calling the police and finding out what it was they had arrested Trina for. Only once this information was obtained would I then be able to decide whether the children were at risk of harm or not.

The police were pleased to inform me that there was no material of concern on Trina's laptop, but that they were concerned about one of her boyfriends. It emerged that Trina was a worker for an online escort agency, and their concerns related to one of the men she had been working for who had visited her house on several occasions. While this news was not as bad as I had originally anticipated, in that Trina had not been arrested for downloading child abuse images, it did highlight fresh concerns that I had not previously considered. I hadn't even thought about asking whether there was anyone involved in Trina's life other than trying to find out whether Peter and Sam's fathers were around. I had now learned that there was not just one other man in Trina's life but potentially several, and that one of these men posed a risk to children. He may also have had contact with Peter and Sam. I agreed with the police that I would pick Trina up in an hour from the police station and take her home.

Before I went to collect Trina, I called the other professionals involved in the case and arranged an emergency meeting for everyone to attend at Sam's school for the next afternoon. I then drove to the police station, all the while thinking about what I was going to say to Trina about my last visit and the recent revelations. When I met Trina in the foyer of the police station I could see that she looked nervous. This confirmed that my approach had been inappropriate. I had some work to do to make it up to her.

When we were in the car together alone, the first thing I said was "Sorry", to which Trina replied, "You have nothing to be sorry for." I explained that I did, and I went on to explain why. I said that it had been inappropriate and unprofessional of me to have searched her house in the way I had, and how I had effectively told her off and made her cry without once stopping to listen to her or think about whether the children could hear me. My apology appeared to surprise Trina as she looked choked and tearful, but after she regained composure she started to talk. And once she started talking she couldn't stop.

Trina told me that at the age of 10 she had been placed into foster care because of concerns relating to neglect. When she was 11, she had moved into a residential home, and as soon as she told me the name of that residential home I instantly recognised it. It had been one that had closed down recently due to allegations of historic physical and sexual abuse by staff. I asked Trina if she had experienced abuse while in the home, and she nodded. She had tried to run away, she told me, on a number of occasions, but when found was always taken back to the same place despite pleading to go elsewhere. She was seen by her social worker as a trouble maker and by the police as a nuisance.

When she had left care, she had fallen into a relationship with Peter's father, a man who was 15 years older and who she thought would look after her. She realised that this was not going to be the case as soon as she fell pregnant. He didn't want to have a baby, she said, and he left. She met Sam's father, Alfie, while she was pregnant, and was happy that he was willing to have a relationship with her despite not being the father of the baby she was carrying. However, once Peter was born, Alfie started drinking heavily and was on occasion violent towards her. Trina told me that she was more scared of being alone with a new baby than putting up with "the odd beating", so she stayed. She thought that Alfie was jealous of Peter as he wasn't his father. Trina thought that if Alfie had his own baby he would change and that is why they had Sam. It was when Sam was only a few weeks old that Alfie hit Trina at the top of the stairs. She fell down the steps and nearly died.

Trina didn't have to leave the house, however; Alfie did. She said that he was shocked at what he had done to her and that when she returned from hospital he packed his bags and she never saw him again. Trina was upset that Alfie had gone, but was also relieved that he had made that decision for her. She decided at that point that she would be better off alone and that she should never have a boyfriend again. She decided she would try to bring up Peter and Sam by herself. She was, she said, aware that in trying to do it alone she had been a "shit mother" and that she had made many mistakes. However, she said she had tried to show the boys that she loved them even though they annoyed her daily. I asked Trina if she did love the boys, showing them love was not the same as loving them. "I don't know what love is" Trina said. It was at this point that I realised it was me who didn't know what to say. Trina had stunned me into silence.

Trina then told me about the online escort agency that she said was not about escorting anyone anywhere, it was more like being a sex-worker. She had taken up the job because she had fallen into bad debt and had been given an eviction notice from housing because she had gone into arrears with her rent. She said her overdraft was unauthorised, so whatever benefits did get paid into her account were being swallowed instantly by her bank. She had borrowed money from loan sharks but couldn't repay them, and so they had taken possession of her white goods, furniture, the TV and Peter's Xbox. The one thing that they were not aware she owned was her laptop. Trina decided that she needed to earn money, and the easiest way for her to do this without paying tax was to move into prostitution.

I learned more about Trina on that car journey that I had from the family's case notes, files or from the conversations I had tried to have with her at home. I realised that I had been so intent on pursuing my own line of enquiry that I had not thought to spend quality time implementing a person–centred approach to building a relationship with Trina, or properly considered the five central elements of symbolic interactionism.

Reflection 'on' action

My eagerness as a newly qualified social worker combined with learning 'the truth' dominated over simple aspects of social work practice such as trying to connect with the children and their parent. Although this did happen eventually, it could also easily not have. Listening to people's life stories, placing them at the centre of the process, is crucial. As Murphy et al (2013) note, although social workers are likely to be familiar with the term 'person–centred', they are not likely to be specifically trained as therapists in the person–centred approach, to have an in–depth knowledge of the theory or have an appreciation of applying the subtle nuances of this theory in practice. Thus, social workers who claim to be operating in a person–centred way within a relationship–based approach are, in effect, using the relationship instrumentally as a utilitarian function (Murphy et al, 2013). For example, I used the idea of building a relationship with Trina to facilitate engagement and find out what she was thinking so that I could try to develop a rapport with her so she might be more likely to comply with my future suggestions for change.

In addition, although I considered symbolic interactionism (see Charon, 2010) as being a key theoretical perspective when attempting to interact with Trina, Sam and Peter, my adoption of this concept was only loosely applied to the people I was interacting with. I used the idea that they were active agents and responsible for the situation they were in without properly considering how the Taylors defined the situation they were in in the way that they did. Perhaps if I had moved outside of my 'own view of the environment' and taken on their perspective, I could have developed a better understanding of their situation (Charon, 2010, p 104).

However, because I was focused on my view of the situation I needed to consider what had influenced this view. Symbolic interactionism draws from the notion that although we are active thinking beings, we develop ways of knowing and saying when in interaction with others (see Charon, 2010). It is important to acknowledge that I was influenced largely by Janet's views. She was a strong and confident person in a position of authority. I felt she did know what was best for Sam, and I also felt guilty that our services had let the case drift. I realised that these two factors had spurred me to take on the case and make sure it led to a successful outcome. The problem was, I didn't know what was best for the family. It was only when I started to reflect on my behaviour (see Schön, 1987) that I started to also realise that Janet often came across as overbearing. But once I reflected on why this was, it soon became clear that it was because she did have Sam's best interests at heart.

After the strategy meeting with the police, Janet decided that we should have a meeting with the professionals and the family to see what we should do next. At that meeting, everyone present agreed that a lot more support was needed for the whole family. Trina didn't say very much, but when she did speak, it was to explain that she couldn't cope with the way things were and that she needed help. She wanted help with her children, her life, her depression and her debts. She said she would no longer be working as an online escort and wanted to find a "proper job", but she also added that she didn't know where to begin.

Peter and Sam came in for the second half of the meeting and expressed their views. Peter wanted to stay living with his mother but Sam wanted to go somewhere else for a while. It was agreed that the case would progress to child protection but that, in the meantime, with the help of the support worker, community health and both schools, we would begin to tackle the issues that were affecting the family. Trina also agreed that we could contact her aunt, who she had not been in touch with for a while but who she knew would be willing to look after Sam for a while if needed.

Systems can organise and, if allowed, can produce their own structures and other components. These 'autopoietic systems' can decide, not with respect to a person but to the communication, whether help or no help should be granted (Luhmann, 1990). Luhmann called social systems autopoietics because they produced themselves through communication (Luhmann, 1990). But for communication to be effective, a synthesis of three selections was required: about what (information), how (ways of utterances) and which reaction (understanding and misunderstanding). Throughout my involvement I had been focused on Trina, the children and the absent fathers, but I hadn't explained what was expected of Trina, or offered her a way of solving the problem. It hadn't occurred to me that Trina would be able to draw from her own autopoietic system and decide who she wanted support from and in what way. This misunderstanding had prevented Trina from drawing from her own system that was already in place, but lying dormant.

Summary

The dilemma that many practitioners in social work face is knowing which theoretical perspective to draw from and apply to a particular situation to achieve the best results. It is evident that in this case, the two I concentrated on to begin with were not always applied well and may not have been the most useful in this situation. Critically reflecting on the approaches chosen is important in social work practice as it helps practitioners consider the model and its efficacy.

The person–centred approach has faced criticism over the years for its lack of evidence base, its inability to address political context and overall positive human assumptions (Harms, 2015). The criticism that there is little evidence to show the efficacy of this approach is a criticism that can also be applied to the other two perspectives used in this chapter. Nonetheless, it is an approach that is still popular in practice today, and is often used in trauma work with service users (see Murphy et al, 2013).

Symbolic interactionism is another theory that has faced criticism relating to Mead's emphasis on the power of the actor to create reality, in other words, a situation is real if the actors define it as so. Yet it has been argued that this assertion ignores the extent to which people live in a world that is not of their own making. Erving Goffman (1983) contended that this concept, although true, ignored the physical reality of certain situations. For example, if Janet and her children agreed that she was an excellent mother, this would have been a reality for them. Yet it wouldn't acknowledge the fact that children's services and the school had concerns.

However, although symbolic interactionists do have their critics, they argue that they do recognise the validity of constraint, but also emphasise the importance of shared meanings. It therefore remains an exploratory and enduring theory. Although it is most commonly used in research in multiple contexts, it is constantly being developed and extended, and can easily be applied to the context of social work practice. It also provides the foundation for many other theories used in this book.

Systems theory has also been criticised for the lack of explanatory power that it holds. Although this approach can provide an understanding of wider family and community structure, there is little research evidence that supports the influences these supports have on the system (Harms, 2015). Luhmann's systems theory has also been criticised for focusing on existing systems and institutional order, produced and maintained by a communication that has been reduced to codes. Although this perspective invites a consideration of individuals, it doesn't include autonomous and self-realising individuals in this invitation. Its autopoietic character therefore implies that change can only occur from the inside, which suggests that changes on the outside will be rendered meaningless (Kihlstrom, 2011).

As different theoretical perspectives have both strengths and weaknesses, it is important for practitioners to ensure that they consider these elements when utilising them in practice. By reflecting 'in' action and 'on' action, however, the practitioner is given many opportunities to consider how and why a particular encounter evolved in the way that it did. It is essential to remember that there is no standard way for approaching different situations, and as each social worker is an individual, it is highly likely that there will be distinctive responses to practice encounters because of the different characters involved. The benefit of drawing from a range of theoretical perspectives, however, throughout a case study, is that it enables practitioners to develop their knowledge and explore the way a situation evolved in more detail.

Further reading

Charon, J. (2010) *Symbolic interactionism: An introduction, an interpretation, an integration*, London: Prentice Hall

  This book is a great introduction to the theoretical perspective of symbolic interactionism. It attempts to grapple with some of the following: Who are we? What are our qualities? Why do we do what we do? How is it possible to live together in society? Why do some succeed? And why do some get into trouble?

Rogers, C.R. (1961) *On becoming a person*, Boston, MA: Houghton Mifflin

  On becoming a person is not a single piece of writing but a collection of pieces Rogers wrote over a decade. The book is the accumulation of wisdom of a career in psychotherapy; while not an easy read, once you 'get' the ideas it can be a very inspiring read. The result is an original and revolutionary way of dealing with a person's issues that overturned the traditional psychologist–patient model, and developed broader implications for successful human interaction.

Harms, L. (2015) *Understanding trauma and resilience*, Basingstoke: Palgrave Macmillan

  Understanding trauma and resilience addresses the multifaceted nature of trauma by bringing together the many theoretical perspectives that explain how people cope with traumatic life experiences. Ranging between attachment, person-centred and anti-oppressive approaches, each chapter takes a contemporary approach, and provides students and practitioners with an in-depth analysis of the histories, core assumptions and critiques of each perspective. Rich in theory and practice, case examples and case scenarios run throughout to demonstrate the integration of each approach in to real-life practice, and to illustrate the different responses to trauma.

Koprowska, J. (2008) *Communication and interpersonal skills in social work* (2nd edn), Exeter: Learning Matters Ltd

  Good communication skills are at the heart of effective social work practice. This book enables students to develop a flexible and responsive approach to communicating with the most vulnerable people in society, paying particular attention to young people, adults and families. The emphasis of this book is not on any particular 'right way' to communicate, but more the ability of the student to be pro-active and aware in different situations.

References

Blumer, H. (1969) *Symbolic interactionism: Perspective and method*, Berkeley, CA: University of California Press.

Charon, J. (2010) *Symbolic interactionism: An introduction, an interpretation, an integration*, London: Prentice Hall.

Dillenburger, K., Fargas, M. and Akhonzada, R. (2008) 'Evidence based practice: An exploration of the effectiveness of voluntary sector services for victims of community violence', *British Journal of Social Work*, vol 38, no 8, pp 1630–47.

Germain, C. (1978) 'General-systems theory and ego psychology: An ecological perspective', *Social Service Review*, vol 52, no 4, pp 534–50.

Goffman, E. (1983) 'The interaction order', *American Sociological Review*, vol 48, pp 1–17.

Harms, L. (2015) *Understanding trauma and resilience*, Basingstoke: Palgrave Macmillan.

Herman, N.J. and Reynolds, L.T. (eds) (1994) *Symbolic interaction*, New York: General Hall, Inc.

Kihlstrom, A. (2011) 'Luhmann's system theory in social work: Criticism and reflections', *Journal of Social Work*, vol 12, issue 3, pp 287–99.

Koprowska, J. (2008) *Communication and interpersonal skills in social work* (2nd edn), Exeter: Learning Matters Ltd.

Luhmann, N. (1990) *Essays on self-reference*, New York: Columbia University Press.

Manthorpe, J. (2008) *Support workers: Their role and tasks. A scoping review*, Social Care Work Force Unit (www.kcl.ac.uk/sspp/policy-institute/scwru/pubs/2008/manthorpeandmartineau2008support.pdf).

Murphy, D., Duggan, M. and Joseph, S. (2013) 'Relationship-based social work and its compatibility with the person–centred approach: Principled versus instrumental perspectives', *British Journal of Social Work*, vol 43, pp 703–19.

Nicolas, J. (2015) 'Why do home visits matter in child protection?', *Community Care*, 2 September (www.communitycare.co.uk/2015/09/02/home-visits-matter-child-protection/).

O'Sullivan, K.R. and Dryden, W. (1990) 'A survey of clinical psychologists in the South East Thames Health Region: Activities, role and theoretical orientation', *Clinical Psychology Forum*, October, pp 21–6.

Parsons, T. (1951) *The social system. The Free Press of Glencoe*, London: Collier Macmillan Limited.

Payne, M. (2007) 'Performing as a "wise person" in social work practice', *Practice*, vol 19, no 2.

Proctor, G., Cooper, M., Sanders, P. and Malcolm, B. (2006) *Politicising the person-centred approach: An agenda for social change*, Ross-on-Wye: PCCS Books.

Rogers, C.R. (1957) 'The necessary and sufficient conditions of therapeutic personality change', *Journal of Consulting Psychology*, vol 21, pp 95–103.

Rogers, C.R. (1961) *On becoming a person*, Boston, MA: Houghton Mifflin, pp 21–42.

Sanders, P. (2005) 'Principled and strategic opposition to the medicalisation of distress and all of its apparatus', in S. Joseph and R. Worsley (eds) *Person-centred psycho-pathology: A positive psychology of mental health*, Ross-on-Wye: PCCS Books, pp 21–42.

Schön, D.A. (1987) *Educating the reflective practitioner*, San Francisco, CA: Jossey-Bass.

Thompson, N. (2006) *Anti-discriminatory practice*, London: Palgrave Macmillan.

von Bertalanffy, L. (1968) *General system theory*, New York: George Bratziller.

Wiener, N. (1948) *Cybernetics*, Cambridge, MA: MIT Press.

Wilson, K., Ruch, G., Lymbery, M. and Cooper, A. (2009) *Social work: An introduction to contemporary practice*, London: Longman.

2

Managing different professional perspectives

Introduction

This chapter explores a situation in which a student approached one of the authors for advice and support. This was the author's first student in her new role of senior practitioner. The author had agreed to be mentored by her own manager, the work-based supervisor for the student. As the author was new to the authority and the manager had also just been promoted, this chapter begins by exploring the transitions both professionals had to make, and the complications that arose as a result of positioning, credibility and identity. However, what made the situation even more complex was the way in which they each related to the student.

The student had been assigned a case that both the author and her mentor struggled to agree on. It involved a family who had been known to the service for a long time. Both parents suffered with mental health issues and regularly misused alcohol. They had been provided with many opportunities to turn the situation around, and the work-based supervisor, after initially being optimistic about the case, felt that it was time to progress and refer the family to conference. The student, however, did not agree. She felt that the family had been known to Children's Social Care (CSC) for so long because they had not been provided with the right kind of support, and were therefore not aware of how they were failing to meet expectations. The author agreed with the student that the family was in need of a different service that would be more appropriately tailored to meeting their needs. However, issues arose when they tried to share these new ideas with the work-based supervisor who appeared upset that the pair disagreed with his decision-making.

This chapter refers to theoretical perspectives on positioning, credibility and identity construction. It explores how difficult and awkward situations can arise when two professionals disagree on the way practice should be conducted. It also draws from recent research exploring the nature of mental health issues and alcohol abuse with parents who then subsequently neglect their children.

Positioning, credibility and identity

Exploring the context in which the field of child protection social work is currently situated is important if we are to then consider what being a professional means to its members. Freidson (1986, p 230) once described 'professionalism' as the impact a profession has on its members. He recognised that the professional's attitude and their commitment to their career became that of their own identity because professionals were their areas of practice; they represented their profession through who they were and what they did.

Exploring how the self is constructed is particularly important in this context if we are to consider where social workers are situated. There are some who argue that the field of child protection is currently located in a culture entrenched in blame and as a result, commentators and critics are right to worry over social work's apparent loss of identity (Ferguson, 2011). This is mainly because when a child dies, an atmosphere of blame and criticism emerges as tabloids extort the facts and sensationalise the coverage through 'provocative and accusing headlines' (Reder et al, 1993, p 1). Such emotive subjects can lead to a form of reportage that will inevitably influence all who read it and subsequently affect public opinion (Franklin, 1989).

The cultural narrative surrounding the field of child protection has therefore had to emerge amidst multifarious moral issues due to much of its beleaguered history being marked by insecurity and anxiety. Social workers have, in turn, had to construct and re-construct their understanding of being a professional within this current, active, socio-political climate. This is evident from the literature that examines the role organisations play and the impact culture can have on the self and credible performances.

One scholar who dedicated his attention to exploring the behaviour of people in organisations was Erving Goffman (1922–82), a Canadian–American sociologist. In his seminal study, *The presentation of self* (1959), Goffman's attention was drawn particularly towards the performances that individuals 'put on' in social situations that were supported in 'the context of a given status hierarchy' (Lemert and Branaman, 1997, p xlvi). As a micro-sociologist Goffman was inherently interested in how the self, as a social product, depended on validation awarded and withheld in accordance with the norms of a stratified society (Manning, 1992). Indeed, Philip Manning (2008, p 284) once suggested that credibility was 'the quality of being believable' and that this quality was 'integral to both trust and deception'. Drawing on Goffman's work, Manning further argued that the 'production of credibility' was a way in which people made their actions convincing to other people (2008, p 284).

The organisational ethnographic work of White (1997) and Pithouse (1998) is relevant here because they revealed that social work is a profession that is firmly situated in, and subject to the power of, hierarchical bureaucracies. Maintaining a formidable reputation is not only the concern of managers; it is an activity that is prevalent and will affect all throughout the organisation, from the frontline social worker to the area director and on to elected councillors. Constructing credible performances to impress others is therefore an organisational issue and one that emerges from cultural routines, linguistic practices and storytelling sessions that all take place within a social work department (White, 1997).

Yet external organisational influences also bestow social work teams with pressing and contradictory issues to consider, especially as conflict, unpredictability and blame is now more pronounced than ever before (Pithouse, 1998). This substantial change in organisational temperament has led some to believe that the identity of social work has been 'threatened' and 'spoiled' (1998, p 2). In recent years the customary political game of criticising social workers and the 'unduly vindictive and sensational attention' from the media has subsequently led to the emergence of certain defensive organisational practices that have, in turn, prompted many to develop the 'watch your back' narrative (White, 1997). Managers are often of the belief that if cases are inspected effectively, poor practice can be identified and subsequently eliminated. This approach has, in turn, prompted the development of a 'them and us' mentality to arise between managers and social workers, leading to social workers feeling discredited and undervalued (Gibbs, 2009, p 295).

Attempting to prove to others that you are a 'credible practitioner' is an activity of social work that can take place in many different forms. It is not just an activity that takes place intra–agency, but also one that dominates interactions with others outside of the agency. Credibility is an activity that many try to achieve in social work, but the way it is acquired varies depending on the interface taking place. What is widely recognised, however, is that wider culture affects the organisation within which these interactions take place, because being counted as a 'credible practitioner' is an aspect of social work practice that is often overshadowed by the fear of making mistakes or feeling inadequate.

Cultural norms therefore play an important role when individuals seek approval and acceptance because it determines whether practitioners should be rewarded with social status or receive punishment (Leigh, 2013). Although the concept of feeling not 'good enough' is an inevitable human experience, it is the kind of experience that is not always tolerated by society, social work organisations or even social workers themselves (Gibson, 2014, 2015). While it is recognised that the challenges many social workers confront are often characterised by fear, shame, anxiety and distress, further analysis of these studies indicate that professional credibility also plays a substantial role in practice. Making a good impression in the minds of others therefore enables social workers to feel valued and accepted as professionals (Greenwald and Harder, 1998).

By drawing from a Goffmanesque perspective that focuses in particular on the dramaturgical aspect of organisational social work activity and the regions where this takes place, I explore the interplay between practitioners, managers and their inside and outside audience in more detail. Goffman (1959) developed the theory of impression management while carrying out anthropological fieldwork in the Shetland Isles. He found that communication between individuals took the form of the linguistic (verbal) and non–linguistic (body language). These gestures were employed between individuals when in interaction with others. By observing the local crofter culture closely, Goffman discovered that individuals who over-communicated gestures were trying to reinforce their desired self, while those who under–communicated gestures were detracting from their desired self (Lewin and Reeves, 2011). Impressions of the self were therefore managed actively by individuals during their social interactions, a process that Goffman termed 'impression management', and in order to be seen as credible, they relied on the intimate cooperation of more than one participant.

The presentations that individuals performed were undertaken in two distinct areas: the front region and the back region (Goffman, 1959). In the front region, Goffman observed performances as more formal and restrained in nature, whereas in the back region, performances were more relaxed and informal, and thus allowed the individual to step out of their front region character. However, Goffman also felt that individuals used the back stage to prepare for front stage performances. Each region therefore has different rules of behaviour – the back region is where the show is prepared and rehearsed; the front region is where the performance is presented to another audience (Joseph, 1990).

Case study

Context

This event occurred shortly after I had joined the organisation as a senior practitioner. This position was a promotion and in a new environment I was keen to make sure that the team I was supposed to be supporting felt comfortable and confident in my practice, so that they felt they were receiving the right advice when they asked for it. The safeguarding team that I joined was the Duty Referral and Assessment Team, and the position I took up was the former role of the newly promoted manager, Andrew. Therefore, both Andrew and I were in new roles on the same team working closely with one another.

I knew that part of my role would involve being a work-based supervisor for a student social worker. This was an activity I was looking forward to and which I hoped would not only help me consolidate my learning but also be of benefit to the student for their future practice. As this was a new role for me, Andrew and I agreed that he would be my mentor and we would both act as supervisors for the student; I would therefore shadow Andrew. This meant that the student would be learning from me and Andrew, and I would be learning from Andrew and the student.

Before I started with the organisation, Andrew had already met with the student, Lexi, and together they had agreed on what her needs were and how the placement would be able to meet these needs. As this was Lexi's first placement, Andrew had agreed that he would only pass over 'child in need' cases for Lexi to work on, and then perhaps towards the end of her placement she would be able to co-work a few child protection cases with me. This case study relates to one of the cases that Andrew passed over to Lexi, the Smith family.

The Smith family had been known to CSC for some time, and concerns related to mental health issues and alcohol misuse. Rachel and Gareth Smith were the parents of two children, Jane and John, both of whom attended primary school. The most recent referral made to the CSC had been made by school over concerns relating to Jane and John's appearance. They often presented in dirty school uniform, appeared to have poor hygiene, and were regularly falling asleep in class.

Day 1

I woke up in the morning feeling quite relaxed and confident about the day ahead. I'd had a good summer, and this was technically my first day back at work. I had only been with the organisation for two months, so I was still 'bedding in', but I had enjoyed my new role so far. Today was also the first day that I would properly meet my first new student, Lexi. Because she was my first student she was going to be primarily supervised by my newly appointed manager, Andrew. I kept wondering how this would go because I didn't know Andrew very well and I didn't know Lexi well either. I wanted us, as a 'team', to get on brilliantly, without egos and arrogance, and I suppose deep down I wanted them to like me too.

We decided that we would meet at the office and then go to a 'child in need' meeting together. This was a case that Andrew thought Lexi should pick up from him, and we agreed that this would be a good place for us to make introductions to the family. We collected Lexi and together we walked to a bench outside the office to sit down and talk through the plans for the day. It gave me a chance to say a proper 'hello' to Lexi. She looked nervous but she looked nice. I thought that I was going to like her. As I sat between the two of them I tried to work out what the next few months would be like together – would we have ups and downs? Would we all get on? Or would we dislike each other intensely by the end? I also wondered what they were thinking about me.

Andrew started to tell us about the last meeting he went to for this case, the Smith family – how well it had gone and how impressed he was with what they had achieved. He thought he had struck a good working relationship with Rachel, the mother, and Gareth, the father. He told us how their issues were related to drink and mental health issues, but that a quick parenting programme should 'do the trick' and it should be a straightforward case to work with. He then told us who we should expect to meet in the meeting, and he joked that even though he had invited all involved, we should only probably expect to have about one or two present. However, we found the meeting was full. Both Rachel and Gareth were present, as well as all the relevant professionals. There were three spaces left for us.

Andrew started talking to them all, and in between informing them about the needs of the Smith family and how these may be met, he made jokes and kept it all light hearted. He was the confident professional I thought, and I appreciated the way he related to both the family and the professionals in the meeting. When he finished talking he passed the conversation on to me and I aimed to match his performance by filling in the gaps in the same calm and collected manner. I explained who I was and what my role would be in terms of supporting Lexi and shadowing this case. I was aware of those watching me, but felt pleased when I saw them nod and smile. Lexi told them about who she was and what she thought her role would be. She talked about the experience she had had so far, and how she was impressed with the authority and the way we practised. They all seemed to like this approach and I saw much more nodding and smiling. I was impressed with Lexi's introduction, and I felt comfortable with the new situation. I thought that the family felt comfortable with our presence, and we left feeling content about what the future would hold.

Reflection points

Think about how you have felt in a new work situation.

1. How did it affect your performance?
2. What kind of views did you hold of the people you were working with?
3. Have you ever considered how you may have come across to them?

Day 2

The next visit we made was to the Smith family home. The atmosphere was warm and pleasant when we arrived, but the conversation took a turn when they started to ask us about whether they would have to be involved with CSC. Gareth talked about consent and how he had heard that a 'child in need' plan didn't mean you had to be involved with a social worker if you didn't want to. He had heard that his participation was voluntary. Rachel agreed and asked, "Do we have a choice?"

I looked to Andrew and Lexi, and neither seemed to know what to say, so I explained that they did have a choice and that it wasn't compulsory under Section 17 of the Children Act 1989, but I wondered what this meant at the same time – why did they feel that they were being forced into cooperating with us? I asked Rachel and Gareth why they would like to withdraw and what it was about our support that was deterring them. They both looked at Andrew and dropped their gaze. They seemed to look uncomfortable and I wondered if Andrew had said something about perhaps being reprimanded later if they didn't accept our intervention now. They laughed, a fake laugh, and told me not to worry about it and said that they just wanted to know, "that's all".

There was a moment when no one said anything and it felt awkward. I couldn't understand how the 'child in need' meeting had gone well, and now we were in the Smith's house things had changed. Rachel also seemed to find the silence uncomfortable and said, "It's just this space is private. It's our home and it feels strange having you lot coming round all the time"; she said it with laughter as if it was only joke, yet I sensed a note of seriousness, and I thought that they didn't really want us to be here with them after all. They didn't want us involved in their lives. However, our visit ended on a positive note, with Andrew asking them to think about whether they wanted our support or not. He concluded by saying that another option would be to "see how things go", and they seemed to like this.

Later, when I brought this up with Andrew, I was surprised to hear him express frustration with the family. He didn't know why they had said what they did, but he thought they had got cold feet momentarily. From being annoyed with them he then suggested that it could be a positive thing after all, as it was a situation that could be "easily fixed". However, I wasn't so convinced, and I suggested that this might not be as easy as we thought, and that perhaps we needed to think about Lexi holding this case alone. Lexi agreed. Andrew grimaced and I could tell that he wasn't impressed with this suggestion. He thought we were both imagining it. I got the feeling that he thought I was looking for things that weren't there, and he seemed a little short with me, as if he was irritated.

Andrew seemed to want to focus on the positive, and so I agreed with him that it had ended well. Yet even though I agreed, I had a niggle in my stomach that made me think that this case may be a problematic one for Lexi to pick up and for me to support her with. I got the sense that Andrew liked to be seen as the experienced senior social worker, the team manager who had everything under control and wasn't fazed by anything. He seemed to put on a front so as to keep up appearances. It led me to believe that he was the kind of character who was less likely to reveal how he genuinely felt about things.

When we got back to the office, I asked Andrew if he had found a space for Lexi to sit. She had been sharing my desk, and this hadn't been appropriate for either of us. Andrew told me that he had, that he had found her a desk downstairs. This shocked me as it appeared he wanted to remove her from the office where I and all the rest of the team were. I gently explained that it would be better for Lexi to be in and among the team and close to me so that I could support her effectively.

Andrew explained that he made the decision because there were no free computers in the room, which then made sense as to why he would want her to be in another place. I explained that Lexi wouldn't need a computer as she could use the laptop, and that there was a space on the table where the drinks were stored. Andrew considered my suggestion and then, after a few minutes, he agreed that Lexi could sit at the desk where we kept the tea and coffee. I envisaged Lexi sitting among the tea and coffee and being in a place which, although not ideal, was still where she could hear everything on the team, not being directly attached to one person, but being able to access everyone else in case she needed support. However, later on in the afternoon, Andrew told me that he didn't think Lexi should sit at the table after all because it was inappropriate to place a student at a table where everyone made their tea and coffee. I could see he had a point and

I felt foolish instantly. I should have thought about that before I suggested it, but I didn't, and I wondered why I had suggested it in the first place.

I asked Andrew where he thought Lexi should sit, and he said that he used to perch next to people on one of the rolling chairs when he was a student, so he couldn't see why Lexi couldn't carry on doing what she was doing: sitting next to me. It dawned on me that I hadn't enjoyed sharing my desk; it had been cramped, and I think I had been feeling resentful about not having time to myself to think. As I was always wondering if Lexi was okay and what I could do to support her I was getting tired of putting on a performance. I felt I was trying to be the amazing 'senior practitioner', but actually I wanted my own space and some time to myself. But rather than explain the way I had been feeling, I just said, "I don't think that is a good idea."

Andrew gave me an annoyed look that appeared to suggest that I was a difficult person to work with. I thought he must have been thinking I had been challenging his practice since we first started working together as a trio, and this made me question whether I had. However, I convinced myself that it wasn't me, it was him. He seemed to be the power hungry one; I was the one who was trying to make him see reason, I thought to myself.

We entered into a debate about where Lexi should sit without thinking about Lexi. We only became aware of her presence when she interrupted us both by saying she didn't mind sitting on the floor. Andrew immediately agreed that this would be a good idea, but I didn't think it was; the floor to me was a terrible idea. "When do you ever see students sitting on the floor in a social work office? This is not a children's home; it is an office for professionals", I blurted out. Andrew shook his head, looked dismayed and walked away. I felt horrified. I looked at Lexi and felt I was turning red; I couldn't believe I'd stormed ahead without thinking about where we were, who we were arguing in front of and worse still, what Lexi, Andrew and the others in the team thought about my performance.

Lexi came to my rescue. She told me that it wasn't a problem and that I shouldn't worry. However, I was worried. I felt I was losing face in front of both Lexi and Andrew, so I said nothing. I needed to leave it with the two of them for now, I thought to myself. This was, I realise, what Goffman (2008, p 16) would call a 'defensive measure', staying away from a topic that would lead to the expression of information, one that was inconsistent with the line Andrew was maintaining. I knew that I wanted to follow him and talk to him about it all again in his office, but I also knew that I didn't know yet what it was I wanted to say, so it was best that I let Andrew think too. He was my manager after all.

Reflection points

1. Have you ever been in a situation where your views have conflicted with your manager?
2. How did you manage the conflict?

Day 3

We were in a meeting with Lexi, her placement tutor Diana, and Andrew. The atmosphere was a little tense because Andrew and I hadn't cleared the air properly since the disagreement the other day over where Lexi should sit. We were going through the placement papers, and when we finished, Diana asked us for a tour of the office. We agreed, and Andrew said that we would all show her around. We walked around to Andrew's office and Andrew pointed out where he sat. He seemed to want to make it clear that he had been promoted and he was now the team manager, in charge of Lexi and myself. Although this annoyed me because it felt like Andrew was showing off (he has his own office, his own private space and is in a position that entitles him to this), I could see that Diana was impressed.

When we walked around to our office, Diana saw that one of our team was typing up an assessment. She was on the page 'The parent's story', which, Diana noted, was interesting, as the assessment process seemed to have changed from when she was in practice. Diana asked me why this social worker was sat separately from the others, and I explained that she was one of the assessment workers and, as a result, sat in another bay. I went on to share that her role was to carry out and complete the assessments that we then picked up. Diana looked bemused and asked how this affected continuity for families. I could see what she was saying and I agreed with her. I explained that it did pose issues, but that what we did was to try and deal with referrals more effectively. Without properly thinking, I then said, "It's our way of manipulating the Single Assessment – we try to complete it in 10 days, but if the case is too complex, then it will roll over to the long-term team. Basically, we have kept up the traditional way of working – Initial Assessment and then on to Core."

Diana laughed but Andrew turned to me and said that I was being assumptive. I, without properly thinking, immediately replied, saying that I was not, that this practice contradicted the aims and objectives of Munro's Single Assessment concept as she had introduced it to reduce bureaucracy and save time – "It clearly hasn't done either in this office!" I said. Me and Diana giggled, and Diana said that this was true and she hadn't seen it happen in another agency she had been to visit.

Andrew, however, looked less impressed. His face had fallen and he looked either annoyed or disappointed with me – again. I ignored this look, though, perhaps because I hoped it would go away or because I didn't want him to say any more about it in front of Diana, who I felt I had made a connection with, or Lexi, who I was trying to impress with my knowledge of Munro. Either way it didn't go away and as we continued the tour, I felt Andrew fall silent behind me as we proceeded through the rest of the building. The awkward silence felt unbearable and I started to feel sweat prick under my armpits and across my eyebrows.

Diana left, and as soon as we were alone with Lexi in the reception area, Andrew turned to me and said that I did things very differently to him. He brought up the comment I had made to Diana, and told me how unprofessional it was of me to say that in front of her. I immediately felt mortified. I was conscious of Lexi being present, and I was conscious again of losing face in front of both of them. Garfinkel (cited in Goffman, 1967, p 15) has suggested that when a person finds that they have lost face in a conversational encounter they may feel the desire to disappear or 'drop through the floor'. This may involve a wish not only to conceal loss of face but also to return magically to a point in time when it would have been possible to save face by avoiding that encounter. I felt all these things, but at the same time acknowledged that none of these things could happen.

I felt trapped in a moment where I was with my mentor and my student, both of whom I was trying to impress, knowing that the next move I made was crucial in avoiding further criticism or reinstating my credibility. I had to play the situation down. So I said, "Oh really? You're probably right. I think my positioning is confused and perhaps I've come across as too collegial." Andrew agreed, and suggested that I should have said, "Oh really? Tell me more about that." He didn't think I should give agency secrets away. I felt awful. I knew he was right and I should have been 'maintaining the line' that we were what we 'claim to be' (Goffman, 1959, p 166). I should have concealed the 'dirty work' that we do back stage to maintain the impression that we are doing the job as we should be (Hughes, 1962), and I wondered why I had charged ahead in the way that I had. The problem was that I didn't have time to think about the 'why' properly; I needed to think about how to reduce the embarrassment and shame I felt in that moment.

Lexi came to my rescue again. She said that we all say things that we regret, and she confessed to feeling embarrassed by finishing the placement meeting with "I am glad I'm doing well at placement. I know I make really good tea or coffee." I thought that this was lovely of her to detract attention away from me. However, I thought that her loss of face was nowhere near as bad as mine (see Goffman, 1967). The problem was, I couldn't comment on what she had said because I still felt like I was flailing, finding it difficult to grip on to anything that could hold me still for a moment to give me space to reflect and say the right thing next. I chose what Goffman (2008, p 15) calls the 'avoidance process', looking to change the subject away from this awkward moment, and asked Lexi if I could follow her to her visit. Andrew said that he would come with us and that he would go in my car. He explained to Lexi that this was because we rarely got to talk properly, so it would be good to catch up. I felt relief; relieved that he wasn't going to be talking to Lexi about me, and that this would give him the opportunity to explore any concerns he had about my performance with me 'alone', away from the rest of my team back at the office.

We got in the car but he didn't say anything. I drank some water; my mouth was so dry it felt like cardboard. I took a mint and sucked on it to try and reinstate moisture. I waited; he was bound to bring it up, I thought, but he didn't say anything. I couldn't bear the silence anymore, and so I said:

"Is everything okay Andrew? You seem worried." "Do I?", he replied, "No more worried than usual." "Are you concerned about my slip up?" I said. "We all make mistakes", he said.

I explained that I couldn't think why I had said what I had said, and I apologised. I apologised for my behaviour since I had arrived at the organisation, and for challenging him inappropriately in front of Lexi and the team. I waffled on for a good five minutes, not sure if I was making sense or if he was even listening. He didn't acknowledge what I said directly, but just nodded. Organisational cultures shape and reinforce socially appropriate roles for men and women (Lester, 2008), and part of me knew that I was taking up the role I believed Andrew, and my organisation, wanted me to take up – the stereotypical feminine gender role of apologiser, soother and rectifier of awkwardness. Although this would normally annoy me, at this point I didn't care, I just wanted to get out of the car. I couldn't, so I had to make the remaining part of the journey as stress-free as possible.

I tried to establish my credibility once more by bringing up the 'child in need' meeting when I introduced myself to the Smith family, and he finally said, "You were 100% in that meeting, spot on in every way." It worked. I suddenly felt relieved. He clearly hadn't completely lost faith in me. He then said, "I have to admit I don't even know the Munro review and I didn't even know what the Single Assessment was supposed to be for." This, I realised, was a big announcement to make, and alluded to the fact that Andrew had also lost credibility in 'that moment' with me and Diana. I felt the blood in my veins start to flow again; I could breathe once more. I wasn't a total fool or waste of space. I did have some use. I just needed to tone down my approach and blend in a little more, I thought to myself.

The conversation then moved on to Lexi, and Andrew told me that he found her annoying. He said that he thought she was far too passive in the placement meeting. I felt a little taken aback. I couldn't work out whether he was being mean or whether he was concerned about her. He answered this by telling me he was concerned about her and that I should keep a close eye on her. He said that he once overheard her talking to a few of the social workers, saying that she would like to "hang out" with them. He was worried that she was still in her 'student identity' and not in her 'social work' role. He added that he didn't want to say anything to her because he didn't want to knock her confidence. I told him that I saw it differently, that she was trying to fit in to a team, to be accepted, and that as she felt more comfortable she would adapt to the team and their cultural talk well. However, I was cautious; I had just apologised for challenging him, and here I was challenging him again.

Andrew then told me that it also annoyed him that she was always apologising and that she couldn't finish sentences. I wondered if Andrew was saying this to me because he was fearful that Lexi would let him or me down. But I also realised that I was beginning to learn how hard it was to live up to Andrew's ideals: I was too assertive and Lexi too passive. We both got on his nerves in one way or another. The only person who didn't recognise that they played a part in this interaction was Andrew. I explained that he had to remember who he was: Lexi's supervisor and manager. She would be feeling she had to work extra hard to impress us both, but especially him. I suggested that he should instead encourage her to finish her sentences with "Go on – that sounded interesting, tell me more." Although Andrew nodded and agreed, he ended by explaining that he was worried that if he prompted her she would have nothing more to say. I said that this was his fear, not hers, but she would be sensing this fear from him.

When we got to the visit I felt odd, like I was in a situation I didn't know how to handle. I didn't know the rules of this game and so I didn't know how to play. The visit went well nonetheless, but when it ended all I wanted was to go home. My head was banging and I felt exhausted. I didn't feel I could keep up my performance any longer. It had been hard trying to work out the right thing to say and making sure that before I said it I checked in my head that it wouldn't offend Andrew, humiliate me or embarrass Lexi. I dropped Andrew off at the office, sighing with relief when he had got out of the car. I drove all the way home feeling uncomfortable, anxious and confused.

Reflection points
1. What is your analysis of the events that took place on this day?
2. Have you ever felt you have lost face in a social work situation? How did you deal with it at the time?

Day 4

It had been a few weeks since Andrew and I had had that uncomfortable moment in front of Lexi. Since then I had been quiet around Andrew and tried to make sure that what I did with Lexi wasn't carried out in Andrew's presence. This meant that I hadn't been having the one-to-one mentoring sessions from Andrew, and this, in turn, meant that I hadn't been learning how to mentor Lexi from Andrew's guidance. But it also meant that I hadn't had to encounter more difficult moments, and this had allowed space for me and for Lexi to develop without Andrew. I wasn't sure if what I was doing was the right thing as a 'work-based supervisor', but Lexi and I had been learning from each other, and it had felt comfortable. Neither of us had ever talked about that moment again or about Andrew, but we had developed a good teamworking ethos between us. This had involved the two of us having supervision every day to go over Lexi's reflections on all her cases and her own development as a social worker. Each session ended with me highlighting the research that Lexi needed to read so that she had a better understanding of how each of her families functioned.

The one case that proved to be of particular interest was the Smith family. Lexi appeared to have built a trusting relationship with Rachel and Gareth, but in doing so, she had learned a lot more about their methods of parenting. Some of what they had told her had left her concerned. They admitted, for example, that they used their benefits to mainly buy alcohol. When Lexi asked them how they fed the children, they told her that when they had no money they went to the food bank and collected their weekly shop from there. Lexi was alarmed at first when she heard this, horrified that Rachel and Gareth would put their needs before those of the children. However, when she talked to me about it and we spent time thinking about the reasons why they did this, we realised that Rachel and Gareth's own childhoods and learned experiences of parenting may have had an influence. Both had come from difficult backgrounds: Rachel's father had been an alcoholic and Gareth had been brought up by his grandmother who suffered poor mental health and often struggled to provide him with the care he needed. We felt that both prioritised drink over food because neither had had experience of having their needs met as children. This may have been the reason why they were not equipped with the skills to parent their own children effectively.

Goffman (1967) may have argued, however, that Lexi's original view of the Smith family had been prompted by their spoiled identities, and the way in which they had not followed the rules on how to be effective parents. Goffman contended that the spoiled identity of a person was often stigmatising as it led to them being discredited by others. Being stigmatised can threaten the presentation of self, especially as Rachel and Gareth had to be understood against a backdrop of social care rules about what appropriate behaviour was and what was not. By being open with Lexi about how they managed their money, Rachel and Gareth had inadvertently blown their 'cover', acting in a way that contradicted the expectations of CSC.

Lexi decided to read into the situation further by doing a literature search on studies that had explored the impact parental alcohol abuse had on children. She learned that children of alcoholic parents were at increased risk of various childhood stressors such as abuse, neglect, witnessing domestic violence or growing up with other forms of household dysfunction (Windle et al, 1995; Sher et al, 1997). Yet what most concerned Lexi were the findings in a study carried out by Dube et al (2001), which stated that compared to no parental or single parental alcohol abuse, bi-parental alcohol abuse significantly increased the likelihood of children in the home experiencing all the adverse childhood experiences. Although Lexi was worried about what this may mean for Jane and John, she did bear in mind a limitation that the authors of this study ask readers to consider.

Dube et al (2001) admitted that they were not sure if the uncertainty of whether parental alcohol abuse or adverse childhood experiences were truly representative of the perceived exposure or outcome. Although they had identified strong associations between different forms of parental alcoholism and adverse childhood experiences, they realised that what they lacked was an understanding of the family dynamics. In other words, if we were to understand the impact that bi-parental alcohol abuse may have on Jane and John, we would need to properly consider what was going on in the family home first.

Lexi was clear that Rachel and Gareth had a loving relationship with Jane and John. She had observed the family together on a number of occasions, and did not feel that their interactions were forced or fake. Lexi had also spoken to Jane and John, together and separately, and both had talked about their lives being eccentric and chaotic, but not distressing. They felt that they led different lives to that of their friends, but they often argued that their home was "their home" and they didn't want to ever leave because they had a lot of fun with their parents. This had led Lexi to believe that even though Rachel and Gareth struggled to parent effectively in certain areas, they were meeting the emotional needs of their children rather well.

Reflection points
1. What are your views of the Smith family's case?
2. How do you think you would have proceeded and why?

Day 5

Andrew arranged to meet Lexi for a catch-up and apparently, when she told him about the Smith family, he was horrified. He immediately suggested that the case needed to be referred for a child protection conference so that we could monitor the situation for a while before starting legal proceedings. Andrew then started talking about how social workers have been criticised for ignoring neglect cases and allowing drift to occur, and that as a manager he could not allow that to happen. When Lexi told me, I wasn't surprised. Given that Pithouse (1998) has talked about the way in which managers have to consider pressing and contradictory issues if they are to avoid being blamed, I could understand why Andrew wouldn't want to take any risks. Lexi was shocked by what she heard, and tried to explain her rationale for keeping the case as 'child in need', but she became nervous, started stuttering and couldn't finish what she wanted to say. She felt Andrew wasn't impressed with her performance so she came and found me, and asked if I could join them. I was aware that defensive managers can generate a 'them and us' situation, especially when they fear their decision-making will be criticised, so I knew I had to tread carefully (Gibbs, 2009, p 295). I could see when I entered the room that Lexi looked worried and nervous and it was easy to see why; the atmosphere was tense.

Andrew didn't look impressed that Lexi had brought me in. He was frowning. I wasn't quite sure how to handle the situation in the best way, so I said "Let's all have a cup of tea first and think about what is going on here for the family. Lexi, you get your notes together and I'll make the tea." It was a tactic that gave me a few minutes to think about what I should do next and how I should play the next part.

When I returned to Andrew's office, I could see Andrew looked less irate and Lexi was sorting through her notes from the visit. I could see Lexi also had her action plan in her hands and was ready to talk it through with us. She also had the research articles next to her. "This might just work", I thought to myself. I gave Andrew his tea and offered him a chocolate biscuit. I then explained to Andrew that the last thing we wanted to do was act out of turn or appear as if we disrespected his decision-making. "All we want is for you to give us an opportunity to hear what we've been reading and thinking and to catch up on our recent observations." Andrew nodded but didn't say anything. I took this as a cue that we could continue.

I asked Lexi to go through everything and reassured her that she could take her time. This seemed to make her look less flustered and more relaxed. Lexi started by reading through the notes she had made from interviews with the children, the parents and also her own observations of watching the family interacting with one another. She paused and asked if we had any questions – Andrew shook his head. Lexi picked up the action plan and talked through the intensive support she felt we should provide Rachel and Gareth. This included drawing from the support of other professionals and groups such as the community mental health team, counselling service, drug and alcohol service, Home-Start, Triple P (positive parenting programme), young carers service and allocating the family their own support worker. The idea was to have a tight plan in place that addressed the needs of all the family, but to make sure Rachel and Gareth got the time and attention they needed so that they could care for their children properly.

Andrew didn't say anything at first. He looked at me and I took this as a cue that I could give my views. I felt nervous again, except this time, because we had done so much reading around the case, I also felt more confident. I picked up the research and went through the research findings. I explained the importance of the limitations of the research and highlighted how our role was to draw on the strengths of the parents because they clearly had some. I saw Andrew frown. I wasn't sure what this meant and I wanted to stop talking because I was worried that what I was saying was total rubbish. But then I remembered his comments about Lexi, how she couldn't finish her sentences and how this annoyed him, so I bit the bullet and saw it through. I then cited the parts of the *Working Together* document and the relevant bits of the Children Act 1989 and 2004, and explained how we could meet the requirements of both policy and legislation by working holistically and with the Smith family rather than against them. I stopped what I was saying when I heard myself start to waffle. I asked Andrew what he thought now that he had heard our explanation. For the first time, in what seemed a long time, Andrew smiled. He praised both of us for the thorough research we had done and said that we had reminded him what "good old-fashioned social work" was all about. We left the room, closed the door behind us, looked at each other and exhaled with a sigh of relief. It's going to be all right, I thought to myself.

Reflection points

1. What do you think about the approach Lexi and I took before and during the meeting?
2. What parts of that approach do you think worked well or not so well?

Reflection 'on' action

Gendered performances are derived from performativity theory and show how men and women use expressions as social norms within an organisation. Gender roles help us to understand how particular performances are favoured within organisations and how, in turn, individual gender identity is constructed and complicated by performances (Lester, 2008). By identifying the social norms and roles within social work we can define the expected gendered behaviours social workers perform or resist. These roles are always underpinned by the subtle organisational cultural practices that define how men and women in the workplace should behave. For women this includes nurturing, caretaking and exhibiting additional interest in the emotional health of students (Dallimore, 2003). Furthermore, women in leadership roles are expected to fit the leadership images of the organisation. Those who are promoted early in their careers traditionally perform male traits as their promotion is believed to have depended on their ability to act like men (Tedrow and Rhoads, 1999).

Linking gender roles to impression management is crucial in this case study as the struggle I faced in trying to make my performance credible was in part to do with what kind of role I should play as a newly promoted woman in a social work environment. Erving Goffman borrowed from performativity theory to explain how individuals shape their social realities. The theory of dramaturgy is therefore concerned with the theatrical elements of a performance such as acting, costumes, staging, masks, props, scenery and so on (Hatch and Cunliffe, 2006).

Applications of dramaturgy and performativity to the study of interactions that take place within the organisation explore how performances are played out between the different actors who form part of a particular scene. When thinking about why actors in an organisation behave in the way that they do, Goffman (1959) reminded readers that it was important to consider the purpose of the performance and not the characteristics of the performer. When reflecting on the way I had behaved in this situation, and drawing from Goffman's work, it became evident to me that both Andrew and I had been keen to impress those who were around us.

Narratives about gender and gendered traits support differences between masculinity and femininity, and generate a sense of an 'objective' reality. The narratives are not just the opinions of the storyteller, but also an indication of reality or 'the way things are' in the organisation (Lester, 2008). Initially this is what I had been worried about, the way in which the organisation worked and how this would affect my future as an individual and with my team. Yet, Andrew had just been appointed to a team manager role, and it became clear that he, too, wanted to be respected by those he was responsible for by making the right decisions. In my new senior role, I was trying to do the same for the team, but especially for Lexi. With both Andrew and I seeking to be experienced and credible practitioners, our views and actions often conflicted. Therefore, when Goffman (1959) suggested that the personal front of a performer was employed not because it enabled him [sic] to present himself as he would like to appear but because his appearance and manner could do something for a scene of a wider scope, it wasn't difficult to see how both Andrew and I were trying to present an image of ourselves that would impress a wide range of people.

The placement meeting with Diana was particularly relevant in exploring this dynamic. Both of us got caught up in trying to present an image that was both knowledgeable and demonstrated a form of seniority. Andrew did this by showing Diana where he sat – in a private office that overlooked the practice being carried out by his team. I didn't have my own space so I couldn't show Diana that I was in such a senior position, but I could demonstrate that I was aware of recent research activity such as the Munro report (2011). What I didn't anticipate was that my knowledge would inadvertently cause Andrew to lose face when I disclosed information to Diana that he wasn't familiar with, or had seen in that particular way.

Goffman (1959) often talked about organisations having a front and back stage. The front stage is used to present the organisation's public face to visiting outsiders. This forum can be where actors manage the impressions they wish to give to others through their appearance, language, knowledge and so on. It appeared as if Andrew wanted Diana to see that he was in a more senior position by showing her that he had his own office, and perhaps this action made me feel envious that I didn't have my own space. Research carried out by Jeyasingham (2014) and Leigh (2014) both deliberate the importance of practitioners having their own space in the social work setting, and if I had thought about it honestly, it was an aspect of practice that I valued greatly: having my own desk and having the room to think without obvious interruption. In this case, maybe the incident with Lexi and Andrew, where we had disagreed about where she should sit, instinctively reminded me that even my desk was not really mine.

In terms of my relationship with our visitor, I realised after the event that I had wanted to impress Diana with my knowledge of the Munro report. This may have been because I wanted to show that I was well read or because I was considering becoming a lecturer one day. Whatever the rationale, Goffman (1959) has noted that for a performance to be credible, the definition of the situation projected by that particular performer relies on the intimate cooperation of more than one participant. In this case, my performance was usurped by Andrew when he declared that I was being 'assumptive'. The embarrassment I felt emerge stemmed from the belief that Andrew had seen my behaviour as disloyal to the organisation.

Freidson (1986) recognised that the professional's attitude and their commitment to their career became that of their own identity because professionals were their areas of practice; they represented their profession through who they were and what they did. As Andrew and I spent time trying to carve out and present credible performances, what we didn't spend time properly considering was that Lexi was also seeking to establish her identity as a new social worker. Lexi was keen to pass her placement and qualify, and what should have been our priority was to ensure that the setting in which she was based was the ideal place to help her demonstrate her skills as well as accomplish her own social work identity. It was evident to see, on reflection, that our own personal feelings had interrupted how well this was managed, especially as disagreements were often carried out in front of Lexi.

Goffman (1959) identified that private conversations often take place back stage, a place where actors can shed their masks, relax and prepare for their next performance, and although Andrew and I did use the back stage on occasion, it wasn't always a comfortable place for us to share our views. This is probably because we were not well acquainted at the time, and perhaps we weren't sure if we could trust each other properly. The disclosures that Andrew made in relation to Lexi made me feel uncomfortable and perhaps anxious that I, too, wasn't meeting his expectations. Although the concept of feeling not 'good enough' is an inevitable human experience, in this situation, it felt as if Andrew was not prepared to tolerate any sign of weakness from those he was working with.

Yet the reason for this kind of behaviour may have been because of the role that others play in relation to inside social work practices. There are external influences that can bestow pressing and contradictory issues on to the organisational practices of social workers, and these need to be considered, especially as conflict, unpredictability and blame is now more pronounced than ever before (Pithouse, 1998). With the customary political game of criticising social workers, certain defensive organisational practices have, in turn, prompted many to develop the 'watch your back' narrative (White, 1997). These factors may have influenced Andrew's behaviour towards Lexi and his reactions to the Smith family.

Rather than showing others that working closely with families and taking risks can be a worthwhile activity, Andrew's role was compromised by considering the agenda of the organisation, an agenda that was shaped by a risk–averse narrative because of wider influences. His performance demonstrated that the desire to be well regarded by external agencies could lead to creative social work practice being stifled. Andrew's views supported Goffman's (1959) view that the authentic self is sometimes fragile and vulnerable, especially in instances when managers feel reluctant to challenge the performance culture they find themselves situated in. In this case, in an attempt to be seen as credible in the eyes of external others, Andrew felt it was necessary to follow the predicted rules because it felt the safest route to take. Yet following such rules of social interaction 'do not produce social order', they do not compel us to act; they instead exhibit a particular way of doing things in social work (Manning, 1992, p 10).

When people seek to do something against superordinate will, it is often considered as resistance to authority (Clegg et al, 2016). Authority is therefore seen as legitimate, but resistance is considered illegitimate. Obedience is a far more productive result of management control than resistance. Teamwork isn't usually seen as a mechanism of power, but recent theorists have identified that when people work together well, the rhetoric of empowerment, trust and enhanced discretion can give way to the power of superiors (Barker, 2002). In this case, with Lexi and me focusing on the needs of the family, and drawing from research to support our rationale for working in an emancipatory rather than an oppressive way, we were able to demonstrate to Andrew that social work practice can be flexible and co-productive with the support of his supervisory gaze. Despite Andrew and I trying (and often failing) to produce credible performances in front of others, one thing I believe we did, with the help of Lexi, eventually get right was providing the right service for the Smith family.

Summary

Goffman is not usually employed as a theoretical perspective for social workers to draw on when analysing practice situations; however, in this context, I believe it has been helpful to use his observations to explore how some practitioners might strive to accomplish credibility in the workplace. In doing so, I've examined just how micro–organisational practices emerged and unsettled the professional self of three individuals. This case study has shown how the professional self is not, therefore, an organic trait: it is a dramatic character performance that arises from social interactions and staged scenes.

The problems that have arisen in this chapter centred on the issue of rule-following in everyday social work life. The difficulty for all three of the actors in this case study was to find a way of acknowledging that, although rules guided their actions, they didn't determine what they did. Social work practice is an activity that is driven by rules, but these are not always made explicit, and are, instead, largely made up of background assumptions about what behaviour is acceptable. In this particular context, by exploring the more nuanced details of performativity, we have learned that accomplishing credibility in social work is not a straightforward process; it is not simply attained by putting on a good performance. It is an activity that can unsettle thoughts and feelings as it demands the social worker to question their values and loyalties to others. And although it is widely recognised that being respected is considered to be the hallmark of professional identity (White, 1997; Pithouse, 1998; Webb, 2017), what this actually means in reality is often confused in contemporary practice settings.

Goffman's dramaturgical approach to exploring everyday interactions has, over the years, faced criticism, not least from the theorist himself. Messinger et al (1962), for example, raised the question about when a performance ended for an actor, especially for those who suffer with mental health issues. They highlighted the pressure that service users face in having to perform in front of professionals, indicating that any intervention was an 'unwelcome interruption to their normal lives' (1962, p 105). Thus, there may be no back stage for those who are involved with social care. This critique may shed light on why the Smith family were reluctant to accept our intervention, a reluctance ignited, perhaps, by the fear of being perpetually on stage.

In addition, Sennett (1977) complained that Goffman offered a picture of society in which there were scenes but no coherent plot. He argued that Goffman's observational methods of everyday activity drew him into making inadvertent claims about the intentions of actors that his analysis couldn't substantiate. However, by drawing from Schön's (1983) reflective model and considering other relevant literature, this case study has been able to use Goffman's observations of the everyday and apply it to a set of scenes in this social work setting. In turn, this has created a coherent narrative that some may argue is deeply descriptive.

However, I would argue that this approach has highlighted the kind of social interactions that take place daily in social work organisations. Thus, in turn, demonstrates that social work life is far more complex than the dominant dichotomy of 'practice' and 'culture'. It involves a number of different activities (for example, practice, hierarchy, social interactions, status, decision-making and credibility) because social work life is in 'a state of constant flux' (Manning, 1992, p 19). In other words, the 'doing' of social work is remarkably difficult to describe because phenomena mutually affect each other. Apparently small actions prove to be highly consequential and nothing can be deemed as trivial until the actor has the benefit of hindsight (or has reflected on action). If anything is certain, then this case study has shown that while maintaining a good reputation is an activity all social workers try to achieve, accomplishing an image they are proud of in a culture that is preoccupied with performance is likely to encounter conflict and may, at times, be compromised.

Further reading

Goffman, E. (1959) *The presentation of everyday self*, London: Penguin

In this book, the author of *Stigma* and *Asylums* presents an analysis of the structures of social encounters from the perspective of the dramatic performance. He shows us exactly how people use such 'fixed props' as houses, clothes and job situations; how they combine in teams resembling secret societies; and how they adopt discrepant roles and communicate out of character. Professor Goffman takes us 'backstage', too, into the regions where people both prepare their images and relax from them, and he demonstrates in painful detail what can happen when a performance falls flat.

Pithouse, A. (1998) *Social work: The social organisation of an invisible trade*, Cardiff: Ashgate Publishing

This work sets out to shed sociological light on the realm of day-to-day childcare practice. It offers no conclusions other than demonstrating that the invisible world of practice cannot be readily understood or changed unless grasped through an interactionist sociology.

Webb, S. (2017) *Professional identity and social work*, London: Routledge
How are identities formed among social workers, many of whom perform complex, challenging and ambiguous public sector functions on a regular basis? This book, the first of its kind in the field, examines professional identity in relation to social work by asking how a practitioner thinks of themselves as a 'social worker', a professional self-concept often founded on a range attributes, beliefs, values, motives and experiences.

References

Barker, J. (2002) 'Tightening the iron cage: Concertive control in self managing teams', in S.R. Clegg (ed) *Central currents in organization studies II: Contemporary trends, Volume 5*, London: Sage, pp 180–210.

Clegg, S., Courpasson, D. and Phillips, N. (2006) *Power and organisations*, London: Sage.

Dallimore, E.J. (2003) 'Memorable messages as discursive formations: The gendered socialization of new university faculty', *Women's Studies in Communication*, vol 26, no 2.

Dube, S.R., Anda, R.F., Felitti, V.J., Croft, J.B., Edwards, V.J. and Giles, W.H. (2001) 'Growing up with parental alcohol abuse: Exposure to childhood abuse, neglect, and household dysfunction', *Child Abuse and Neglect*, vol 25, no 12, pp 1627–40.

Ferguson, H. (2011) *Child protection practice*, Basingstoke: Palgrave Macmillan.

Franklin, B. (1989) 'Wimps and bullies', in P. Carter, T. Jeffs and M. Smith (eds) *Social work and social welfare*, Milton Keynes: Open University Press, pp 1–14.

Freidson, E. (1986) *Professional powers*, Chicago, IL: University of Chicago Press.

Gibbs, J. (2009) 'Changing the cultural story in child protection: Learning from the insider's experience', *Child and Family Social Work*, vol 14, no 3, pp 289–99.

Gibson, M. (2014) 'Social worker shame in child and family social work: Inadequacy, failure, and the struggle to practise humanely', *Journal of Social Work Practice*, vol 28, no 4, pp 417–31.

Gibson, M. (2015) 'Shame and guilt in child protection social work: New interpretations and opportunities for practice', *Child & Family Social Work*, vol 20, pp 333–43.

Goffman, E. (1959) *The presentation of self in everyday life*, New York: Doubleday, Anchor Books.

Goffman, E. (1967) *Interaction ritual: Essays on face to face behavior*, New York: Anchor Books.

Greenwald, D. and Harder, D.W. (1998) 'Evolutionary, cultural and psychotherapeutic aspects', in P. Gilbert and B. Andrews (eds) *Shame, interpersonal behaviour, psychopathology, and culture*, Oxford: Oxford University Press, pp 225–45.

Hatch, M.J. and Cunliffe, A.L. (2006) *Organization theory: Modern, symbolic and postmodern perspectives* (2nd edn), Oxford: Oxford University Press.

Hughes, E. (1962) 'Good people and dirty work', *Social Problems*, vol 10, no 1, pp 3–11. doi: 10.2307/799402

Jeyasingham, D. (2014) 'The production of space in children's social work: Insights from Henri Lefebvre's spatial dialectics', *British Journal of Social Work*, vol 44, no 7, pp 1879–94.

Joseph, M. (1990) *Sociology for everyone* (2nd edn), Cambridge: Polity.

Leigh. J. (2013) 'The process of professionalization: Exploring the professional identities of child protection social workers', *Journal of Social Work*, vol 14, no 6, pp 625–44.

Leigh, J. (2014) 'Crossing the divide between them and us: Using photography to explore the impact organisational space can have on identity and child protection practice', *Qualitative Social Work*, doi: 10.1177/1473325014555442.

Lemert, C. and Branaman, A. (1997) *The Goffman reader*, Bodmin: Blackwell.

Lester, J. (2008) 'Performing gender in the workplace', *Community College Review*, vol 35, no 4.

Lewin, S. and Reeves, S. (2011) 'Enacting team and teamwork: Using Goffman's theory of impression management to illuminate inter-professional practice on hospital wards', *Social Science and Medicine*, vol 72, pp 1595–602.

Manning, P.K. (1992) *Erving Goffman and modern sociology*, Cambridge: Polity Press.

Manning, P.K. (2008) 'Goffman in organizations', *Organization Studies*, vol 29, no 5, pp 677–99.

Messinger, S., Sampson, H. and Towne, R. (1962) 'Life as theatre: Some notes on the dramaturgic approach to social reality', *Sociometry*, vol 14, no 2, pp 141–63.

Munro, E. (2011) *The Munro review of child protection: Final report*, London: Department of Education, HMSO.

Pithouse, A. (1998) *Social work: The social organisation of an invisible trade*, Aldershot: Ashgate.

Reder, P., Duncan, S. and Gray, M. (1993) *Beyond blame: Child abuse tragedies revisited*, London: Routledge.

Schön, D.A. (1983) *The reflective practitioner*, New York: Basic Books.

Sennett, R. (1977) *The fall of public man*, Cambridge: Cambridge University Press.

Sher, K.J., Gershuny, B.S., Peterson, L. and Raskin, G. (1997) 'The role of childhood stressors in the intergenerational transmission of alcohol disorders', *Journal on the Studies of Alcohol*, vol 106, pp 414–27.

Tedrow, B. and Rhoads, R.A. (1999) 'A qualitative study of women's experiences in community college leadership positions', *Community College Review*, vol 27, no 3, pp 1–18.

Webb, S. (2017) *Professional identity in social work*, London: Routledge.

White, S. (1997) 'Performing social work: An ethnographic study of talk and text in a metropolitan social services department', Unpublished PhD thesis, University of Salford.

Windle, M., Windle, R.C., Scheidt, D.M. and Miller, G.B. (1995) 'Physical and sexual abuse and associated mental disorders among alcoholic inpatients', *American Journal of Psychiatry*, vol 152, pp 1322–8.

3

Challenging decisions

Introduction

This chapter explores a situation the author encountered while she was working for an Out of Hours team. It follows the story of a teenage boy who was referred to the day time team but passed on to the author because no one could locate him. Known to the Youth Offending Team (YOT), this young person had been in trouble numerous times with the police as a result of drug dealing and burglary. His parents had had enough and had thrown him out of the home as they were tired of being threatened by his gang. They were also fearful of him stealing from them. It was a Friday evening in the midst of winter when the author received the referral and the snow was falling.

The case study examines how, despite carrying out a thorough assessment that identified that the young person needed to be accommodated for his own safety and because his parents refused to have him back home, the decision conflicted with the local authority's priorities. By discussing the wider contextual issues, the author explains how, as a result of the recent change in government, the agency was facing millions of pounds' worth of cuts. One way in which these savings could be made was to prevent children coming into care. Senior managers were therefore focused on reducing spending, and were adamant that no children were to be accommodated unless they were young and at significant risk of harm.

The case study goes on to explore how organisational ideals can often conflict with practice that occurs on the front line. It explores how the author appreciated the financial dilemma of the organisation, but felt that, at the same time, the needs of the young person came first. The way in which this was handled was not as effective as the author had hoped, and although the young person was accommodated, it was done so without the senior manager's agreement. This led to a complaint being made against the author. The author analyses how the situation unfolded as well as what she could have done to have approached the same situation from a more sensitive position.

Organisational conflict

Historically there has been extensive theoretical debate about how conflict emerges in organisations. Bissell (2012) has speculated that Taylorism, a philosophy that promotes a system where the 'science of productive efficiency and management' takes precedent over a discourse of care (Clegg et al, 2006, p 46), is still largely influential of managerial approaches within statutory social work today. Taylor's 'power over' approach emerged during the early 1900s and was better known for teaching managers how to improve worker productivity by reducing individual autonomy (Bissell, 2012). However, what Taylor failed to acknowledge was that a side effect of disempowering the worker was that it led to intra-agency conflict as workers felt subjected to a disciplinary system (Clegg et al, 2006).

After Taylor's inauguration, other organisation scholars began to argue that if managers were to avoid internal conflict, organisational directives needed to carefully consider the dynamic interplay between agency, structure and purpose (see Follett, 1918; Mayo, 1946). More recent studies of organisation have attempted to explore how intra-agency conflict affects its workers because it provides human relations scholars with an opportunity to examine how future progress could be made.

In Gabriel's (2012, p 1137) ethnographic study, he employed the term 'organisational miasma' to explain how internal conflict spread and impacted on professionals in a health and social care organisation. His concept of 'miasma' was used to describe 'a contagious state of organisational pollution', one that Gabriel argued was not only material but also psychological and spiritual (2012, p 1138). The miasma moved between the survivors who were left behind as they became affected by feelings of disgust, worthlessness and corruption following a series of dismissals of valued colleagues through downsizing or retrenchment.

In Fischer's (2012) ethnographic study of a mental health setting, he observed how conflict became a feature of the culture he observed and, in turn, produced widespread organisational turbulence as it impacted on the internal dynamics between practitioners and service users. However, Fischer argued that there were advantages and disadvantages to this: it could produce formative spaces that were creative and useful for productivity and perverse spaces that, in contrast, were destructive and led to organisational dysfunction, crisis and even collapse.

This notion of organisational dysfunction is a concept that was also studied by Fotaki and Hyde (2014). Through the use of vignettes they identified how different organisational tiers in the NHS developed 'blind spots' (Fotaki and Hyde, 2014, p 1). Because all staff members were unable to acknowledge that they were working with unworkable strategies, the authors argued that conflict led to poor communication and destabilised all working processes within the agency, at organisational, systemic and individual levels.

Collectively, these studies assert that although organisational issues are often exacerbated by wider contextual issues because of regulation, governance and change, organisational conflict is often encouraged by those who recognise, endorse and pass on the problematic practice. This not only leads to troubled social interactions but also contributes to the mobilisation of intra-agency affected activity.

But what this brief review also shows is that although conflict is constructed within discursive contexts, it is also recognised that individuals will respond to, negotiate and shape these contexts in different ways depending on the situated activity (Clegg et al, 2006; Froggett et al, 2015; Ferguson, 2011; Fischer, 2012).

Organisational conflict can therefore emerge between people, but it is not always limited to direct social interaction. It can also be influenced by processes, structures and wider society (Kenny, 2012; Fotaki and Hyde, 2014).

Case study

Context

This event occurred shortly after the coalition government had been elected and all local authorities across the country were faced with having to reduce their spending. Jordan (2011) has contended that the sudden reduction in council resources left organisations struggling to deal with reduced budgets and mounting care costs. Residential placements are expensive and charge anywhere in the region of £2,000–£5,000 per week (McNicoll, 2014). One primary way in which the authority in this case study attempted to make savings was by reducing the number of young people being accommodated. These stringent measures left social workers in a difficult position as they often felt that they had to hold potentially risky cases for much longer than they would have done previously. This is what happened with Dan, 14, who was referred to the Out of Hours team by his allocated social worker in the YOT one Friday evening.

The referral expressed concerns for Dan's welfare. Dan had come to the office on Tuesday the same week asking for food as he was hungry. He told his social worker that he had been chucked out of his home and had no money. The social worker asked him to go home and make friends with his parents, and if that didn't work, to give her a call and she would visit them. Dan left the office and didn't return. His social worker called his parents, but they hadn't seen him. They confirmed that they would not allow Dan to return home because they felt unsafe and couldn't cope with Dan's behaviour any longer. The social worker had tried calling Dan's mobile but it was constantly switched off. She was worried for his welfare and had asked his parents to report him missing from home. She asked me to carry out a safe and welfare check in the home that evening and to talk to the parents.

From his case notes I could see that Dan had a 'youth caution' for burglary. His case had proceeded to court but because Dan had admitted guilt, the prosecutor had decided that a youth caution was justified if the YOT was able to support him appropriately and prevent recidivism. Since then, however, Dan had not been attending meetings with his support worker or his social worker, and there were concerns that he had been hanging around with the same friends who were a lot older than him and known to the police for serious criminal activity.

I could also see on the case notes that the parents had been asking for Dan to be accommodated as they found his presence in the home untenable. The Family First Team (FFT) had been involved, but even their attempts to prevent a breakdown between Dan and his parents had been unsuccessful because he had refused to engage with workers. After six weeks of attempting to intervene and build the relationships that had deteriorated in the home, FFT had closed the case. This had left his parents even more frustrated and annoyed with social care.

Visit to the home

I called ahead of my visit to speak to Dan's mother, Rachel, to find out if she had heard from Dan. She had not, but she welcomed my visit because she was annoyed that she had not seen anyone from the YOT despite requests for Dan to be taken into care. I was not surprised to hear this news, but I still felt irritated. From my perspective, this was a task that Dan's allocated social worker should have dealt with much earlier in the day. Because she had not responded to the case, it led me to believe that she was trying to avoid the confrontation that this kind of case would lead to, which is why she had passed it on to the Out of Hours team.

I was aware that everyone across the authority had been given the message that 'unnecessary accommodation' should be avoided. In this case, which from the outset appeared to be one in which accommodation was required, few social workers would want to have to deal with a situation where a parent is asking for their child to be accommodated. Wittgenstein (1953) identified that in some organisations 'language games' can be played, where words take on meaning in relation to the rules of specific communities. In this organisation, although the message being relayed was that only young people at high risk of harm should be considered for accommodation, what was actually meant was that no young people (teenagers) should become looked after because the cost of care was too high.

These kinds of situations were not just emerging in our service but also nationally. For example, Klonowski (2013, p 44), a reviewer for the report into child sexual exploitation issues in Rochdale, found that although an organisational policy was formally entitled 'Supporting children and young people to remain within their family', it was often referred to by social workers as the 'non-accommodation policy'. This was because one of the lines in the report stated:

> Apart from situations where children and young people are very vulnerable and cannot live with their own families, the Authority will NOT LOOK AFTER children/young people on a long-term basis. (Klonowski, 2013, p 45)

Although no such policy emerged in written format in our agency, the term 'unnecessary accommodation' still carried significant power verbally, and was leading to conflict across the organisation between different teams as managers refused social workers' requests for accommodation. This, in turn, meant that relationships between families and social workers were being affected as parents felt they were being left to fend for themselves, with the responsibility that they were the ones who needed to 'work it out' with their child.

Although FFT had closed the case I knew from working closely with them on Out of Hours that they were a supportive team and, if needed, would become involved again. I therefore asked a member of their team to come with me on the visit, and I was fortunate that the worker on duty that evening was familiar with the case and had met the parents previously. When we arrived at the house we were both greeted by Rachel and her partner, Liz, and it soon became apparent that they were not only frustrated but also distressed.

They began by showing me around their home and pointing out the damage that had been caused to the house and their belongings. Due to Dan's recent criminal activity they had felt it necessary to put padlocks on the outside of all the doors and secure locks on the inside of the doors. This is because Dan had not only burgled their neighbours, but also his own home. Rachel told me that Dan had stolen items such as a TV, Xbox, camera, jewellery and other small, personal but valuable items that meant a lot to them. She said that when these items were replaced Dan would do the same again.

Dan was the eldest child of three, and Rachel and Liz were clearly struggling to cope with the situation, especially as Dan had been physically threatening to the two younger children when they had refused to let him into their rooms. They both told me that although the current situation was difficult, it had become traumatic when the weekend before they woke to find they were being broken into again. They came downstairs to find three men with balaclavas on turning their sitting room over. It emerged that Dan owed them money so they had come to the home to seek their overdue payment through other methods. It had been this incident that had been the final straw for Rachel and Liz. They called Dan's social worker and said that they wanted Dan accommodated. They told me that they had been told this was not a possibility, and that they should instead try to restore harmony in the home.

This was a situation, however, that neither Rachel nor Liz felt equipped to handle. It emerged during the visit that they also felt fearful of Dan. Rachel told me the history of her relationship with Liz, which she felt had been the cause of recent events. Rachel had been married to Dan's father until Dan was nine years old when he had left the home, moved abroad and the children had not seen him again. It was about six months afterwards that Rachel met Liz and they fell in love. Dan had been very fond of Liz when he was younger and had been happy for his mother when she had found a partner who had made her happy and got on well with the children. However, they informed me that as Dan grew older and started to hang around with different people, he changed. He had become distressed by the lack of contact with his father and angry with Liz for taking his place. He was also ashamed that his mother was living with a woman and had, on several occasions, physically threatened Rachel.

Reflection points
1. What are your views on the chain of events?
2. What would you have done in this situation?
3. What do you think Dan's allocated social worker should have done?

Although neither knew of Dan's whereabouts, both felt that he could not return to the home without some kind of intervention from social care services. They felt he needed therapy and that he was struggling with issues that had come back to haunt him. Rachel, however, also had her own issues. She had recently been diagnosed with General Anxiety Disorder, and felt unable to leave the home, although she was frightened when she was at home in case Dan, or those coming after Dan, would break in. Liz also described herself as "stressed" and was close to leaving. She felt she could no longer cope with the situation and had started to believe life would be easier for Rachel if she did leave. Dan's younger siblings also told me that they were frightened at night and didn't want to go to school in case something happened at home while they were away.

Something else emerged during the visit that wasn't obvious to begin with but was evident in the nature of what was being said by the whole family. All of them missed Dan – the child they had once known but no longer recognised. They all clearly loved him and were worried for him. The problem was that they couldn't get through to him and didn't know what to do anymore.

The problem I had was that I needed to find and talk to Dan. After meeting the family and hearing the details of their dilemma I was worried for Dan and wanted to resolve the situation as best as I could. Seeing Rachel and Liz had made the situation more emotive, and I realised that perhaps this was one of the reasons why Dan's allocated social worker had avoided visiting the family – it is likely to be easier to make an objective decision on what a family should do when you feel removed from the situation. It also occurred to me that this same view could be applied to our authority that had issued a statement that young people should not be accommodated without properly considering what that might actually mean for the families who were experiencing trauma and distress. Remaining distant from clients may be appropriate in some occupations, but in social work, it can lead to professionals becoming alienated from the service they are meant to be providing. Social work is the kind of labour that calls for 'a coordination of mind and feeling', and it sometimes even draws on 'a source of self that we honour as deep and integral to our individuality' (Hochschild, 2012, p 7).

Listening to Rachel, Liz and their children I could tell that they had been traumatised by the events that had occurred with Dan. This had been exasperated by the lack of support they had received from Children's Social Care (CSC). Indeed, trauma is a trigger that can affect a person in different ways. Traumatic events are recognised as such because they have disrupted, overwhelmed or destroyed a person or community's sense of wellbeing, safety and capacity to cope (Harms, 2015). This definition of trauma could have been applied to Dan's family but also the area in which they lived – not only had the home become an unsafe place but so had the community. Both Rachel and Liz felt ashamed for what Dan was doing, and the fact that they felt they had little control to prevent him from doing it again. Rachel and Liz also felt embarrassed of what their neighbours thought, so I was aware that I also needed to consider how emotions of trauma, such as shame, guilt and anger, could further lead to the family's expressions of anxiety (Tedeschi and Calhoun, 1996; Harms, 2015).

However, I was also mindful that for Dan to behave in such a way, with scant regard for the people he had once loved and cared for, he, too, must have been experiencing trauma of some kind. With both Dan and his family facing trauma and it having an impact on them in different ways, the idea of putting them all back together under the same roof and being told to 'work it out' left me feeling frustrated with my own service and with the allocated social worker. From my perspective, the family would not be able to recover from their trauma until they had learned to adapt to the new situation they had found themselves in and come to the realisation that they could survive it. However, as Herman (1992) has argued, resolution of trauma is never final and recovery is never complete. Therefore, the impact of a traumatic event doesn't end once the situation is over; it continues to reverberate throughout the survivor's lifecycle. What makes positive adaptation possible is when a person feels a sense of security, and this can only be achieved once they have become resilient (Payne, 2011). Feeling secure is a person's belief that they will be safe from harm and exploitation in their home and social environment.

In my opinion, if Dan's family were to achieve resilience and the feeling of being secure once again, they would need space away from Dan. Dan would also need to have time in a safe place to consider his actions and to think about what he should do next. To do this, he would need to engage with the services that could provide him with support. I therefore felt that initially Dan should be temporarily accommodated under Section 20 of the Children Act 1989 so that we could ensure that he had somewhere to stay that would keep him safe. Section 20 requires a local authority to provide accommodation for a child where there is no person who has parental responsibility for the child; the child is lost or abandoned; the person caring for the child is prevented from providing them with suitable accommodation or care; or the child is over 16 and their local authority considers their welfare likely to be seriously prejudiced without accommodation.

If Dan agreed to being looked after, we might be able to work with him more closely as he would be assigned a key worker at the residential home who would try to build a relationship with him. Part of the problem that the FFT and YOT had encountered was that Dan didn't turn up for meetings. If he was in a residential home, both these services would find it easier to contact him and initiate those initial connections that are required to build a relationship.

During my visit, Rachel and Liz told me that they had heard a rumour that Dan was sleeping in people's sheds around the estate they lived on, so me and my colleague thought we would begin by knocking on neighbours' doors to see if they had any information on Dan. It was January and it was very cold outside. It had started snowing and the area where they lived was prone to being closed off when there was a heavy downfall. I was worried that if Dan was sleeping in someone's shed, he would freeze to death. It turned out that I wasn't alone. The neighbours I approached were all aware of the situation, and some had even had their sheds burgled by Dan! However, what was apparent was that although they were annoyed with Dan, they cared for him and were also worried for his welfare. That evening it wasn't just me and my colleague who were walking the streets and calling for Dan, but also 10 or more of his neighbours. Unfortunately, we didn't find him.

Reflection point
1. What do you think you would have done in my situation?

Although we didn't find Dan, it became apparent that the neighbourhood was a close community. I therefore asked the neighbours to pass a message on to anyone who might know where Dan was, and to ask him to go home to let his mother and Liz know he was alright. We then returned to the home, and I asked Rachel and Liz to let Dan come in if he did return and to then call me. It was now around midnight, so I thought it wise to contact the manager on call, the person in charge of authorising my requests for accommodation, to see if we could accommodate Dan if he did call in.

The service unit manager who was on call that evening, Hermione, was someone I had always considered to be a fair and wise person. Although she sounded sleepy when I called, once I had briefly explained the situation, she agreed that Dan could be accommodated. I relayed this message to Rachel and Liz, who were both sat with me when I made the call, and I could see the relief on their faces. I then called the police to explain the events of the evening and asked for them to alert all on patrol of the concerns I had regarding Dan's welfare.

At around 4am I received a phone call from the police. They had found Dan walking the streets so they had picked him up and taken him home. They wanted to let me know that because it was late, Rachel and Liz had said that he could sleep on their sofa, but that, in the morning, he would need to leave. They said that Dan had agreed to return to the home on Saturday evening when I was back on duty, to meet me and be taken to a residential home.

When I started back at work the next day I drove straight to Rachel and Liz's house to meet Dan who was waiting for me when I arrived. He didn't look like I had expected him to. I imagined that I would encounter a young man who would be abrupt, rude and aggressive. Instead, I found a boy who looked lost and furthermore, confused. With Rachel and Liz present we all talked about what had been happening. Dan was silent at first, but when I asked him for his views, he slowly started to talk. He told me that he had been staying in the 24-hour Tesco's baby changing room until a security guard had caught him and thrown him out.

I noticed that once Dan started talking he couldn't stop. It was as if he had finally made some connections between his behaviour and his recent actions, and he was keen to explain what these were. He talked about his disappointment in his father, his anger with his mother and Liz, who he blamed for "making mum gay", and his drug use that had led to him getting in with "the wrong crowd". He knew Rachel and Liz had had enough of him and he could understand why. He'd always hoped that he'd find his father and that once he had, everything would go back to the way it once was. He'd come to the realisation that this was unlikely to happen and he had learned that he wanted to change and undo what he'd done; the problem was he didn't know how.

I asked Dan what he thought about moving into a residential home for a short time while the right services got established and helped him resolve the issues he and his family faced. Dan agreed. He said he was tired and he just wanted a warm, dry bed to sleep in. It seemed that Dan's recent experience of displacement had forced him to appreciate the 'depth and strength' of relationships that already existed (Harms, 2015, p 19). This conversation was not only powerful in that it provided Rachel and Liz with some answers as to why Dan had behaved in the way he had, but it was also apparent that Dan was in a position where he was ready to move on. What he needed was the support to do so. We agreed that I would call ahead and let the residential home know he was coming, and Rachel and Liz would help Dan pack his things.

I went outside the house to make the call and to let Dan have some private time with his mother. The snow was still falling and it was freezing cold. After calling the residential home to ask them to get his room ready, I then phoned Hermione, who I was relieved was on call again that evening, as I knew she was aware of the situation from the night before. From the moment Hermione answered the phone, however, I could tell from the sound of her voice that something had changed. She sounded different, more business-like and less compassionate. This feeling of change was supported when Hermione said that she no longer felt that Dan should be accommodated and that it was my duty to tell Rachel that she was responsible for Dan's welfare. Hermione used the fact that Rachel had let Dan stay the night before as evidence that she was willing to "work things out", and she described my request as "an unnecessary accommodation".

When I explained to Hermione the circumstances behind Rachel's decision to let Dan stay, and supported this with the fact that Dan had been sleeping in the baby changing room of the nearby 24-hour Tesco's, Hermione refused to change her mind. She instead asked me to stop what I was doing and to go to Tesco's. Hermione felt it was important that I find and speak to the manager about the way in which the security guard had handled the situation with Dan. She suggested I challenge them on why they were not following the correct safeguarding protocol, and after doing so, I should inform the police about the security guard's conduct.

While Hermione was still talking to me on the phone, Dan came out and joined me in the snow. I noticed he had a bin bag with him, which I guessed contained his belongings. My heart sank. I felt terrible. I had promised him and his family a way forward and yet, as I stood there, in the white soft powder, Dan and his family were unaware that I was listening to my manager tell me that this was no longer an option. I knew that I had let them down, but I also felt unable to challenge Hermione appropriately because Dan was stood next to me with his belongings. He wanted to get in the car, go to his new home and get into his dry bed, but all he could see was me saying nothing to someone who was rather loudly telling me that he wouldn't be accommodated. I was worried Dan could hear what Hermione was saying, and I didn't know what to do.

Reflection points

1. Do you agree with Hermione's decision-making?
2. Do you understand why Hermione changed her mind?
   The recent policy stating that accommodation should be avoided given the financial constraints had clearly affected Hermione's decision-making.
3. What would you have done in my situation?

I eventually stopped Hermione talking by telling her that Dan was stood next to me and that he could hear everything she was saying. I explained that he had with him a bin bag with his belongings and all he wanted was to go to his new home. Dan looked at me despairingly; I could see he was worried that this placement was not going to emerge after all. I felt uncomfortable once more, and so I asked him if he wouldn't mind sitting in my car and waiting for me. I knew that Hermione would hear this and would object, but I didn't want Dan to hear what I was planning to say to Hermione next. As Dan went to sit in my car, Hermione started objecting and told me that she would not agree to Dan being accommodated and that I needed to follow her instructions. The feelings of frustration, annoyance and disappointment welled and I knew it was time I let Hermione know what I felt about her decision-making.

Part of me knew that this was not a good idea and that it could go badly wrong, but the other part urged me to go ahead. So, when Hermione told me to go to Tesco's again, I simply said "No". I then proceeded to tell her that I did not think that it was my priority to do that right now, but that if she were interested in pursuing the matter on Monday, then she could go and talk to Tesco's herself. I heard Hermione gasp, most probably from shock that I had spoken to her in such a way, but once the words had been said I also knew that there was no way back, and so I continued.

I explained to Hermione that I felt my priority was to make sure that Dan was safe and that what annoyed me was that only the day before she had agreed with me. My heart was pounding as I was talking, but at the same time it felt so good to get these feelings out, rather than keeping them bottled up inside. Even though I was well aware I was going to later face criticism and possibly be reprimanded for what I was saying, I found I couldn't stop. I went on to tell Hermione that I was not going to follow her current instructions but proceed with the agreement I had made with her yesterday. I was therefore going to take Dan to his residential home whether she agreed with that decision or not. At the end of my speech, I ended the call so I didn't have to spend time listening to anymore of Hermione's objections.

When I got in the car, Dan asked me if everything was alright. I looked at him and could see that he was confused about what had happened, so I reassured him that there was nothing to worry about. I then took him to the residential home and got him settled in. I signed the paperwork and headed back to the office. I could hear my phone pinging all the way there and I had a good idea who might be attempting to contact me. I also knew that I would face a few emails from my own manager on my return who would have probably been informed of the matter by Hermione. But as I drove to the office that evening, I also knew that deep down I had done the right thing, and that if I felt convinced I was right, I had to go along with the decision that I had made, no matter who I upset in management along the way.

When I reached the office, I was surprised to find my manager, Tom, waiting for me. He had, indeed, been informed of my misconduct and had come to the office to find out my side of the story. Although Tom appreciated why I had overruled Hermione's change in decision-making, he felt the way I had done so was inappropriate. I recognised that Tom was also under pressure to prevent unnecessary accommodations, but I also knew that he was the kind of manager who remained closely connected to practice issues by continuing to carry out visits with families. Although I didn't completely agree with his views, I did listen to what he had to say and agreed to send Hermione an apology.

However, when I logged on to the computer there were several emails already waiting for me from Hermione complaining about my behaviour and the fact that I had acted against her instructions. What was particularly upsetting was that I could see that Hermione had copied in other more senior members of the organisation. This action infuriated me as I felt it was an attempt to protect herself and demonstrate to her peers and seniors that she had not agreed to an 'unnecessary accommodation'; it was therefore presented as a practice issue of mine, not hers. Rather than think through what I should do next, I replied rather tersely to all the emails outlining my rationale for making the decisions that I had. Although I knew this would make the situation worse between me and Hermione, it left me feeling satisfied that I had told her, and her peers, what I thought of her.

Reflection 'on' action

Although conflict is normally seen as being dysfunctional, Mikkelsen and Clegg (2016) contend that the most common lay view deplores the idea that people at work cannot get along with each other. The talk of teamwork and working together in harmony are normative views that believe conflict should be avoided at all costs and these concepts create issues. Mikkelsen and Clegg instead (2016) propose that organisations should accept that they will encounter and have to handle conflict at some point. What matters is the way in which conflict is dealt with. If it is treated as a negative phenomenon it can be destructive or disruptive, but if it is seen as a constructive process it can produce positive consequences.

Putnam and Poole (1987) suggest that there are three levels of conflict: interpersonal, intergroup and inter-organisational. These three levels have been deconstructed further by de Dreu and Gelfland (2008) and are shown in the following table:

Table 3.1: Sources of conflict

Conflict	Disputants	Sources of conflict
Interpersonal	Individuals – often dyads	Competition, incompatibility
Intergroup	Teams or informed groups	Work-related disputes due to ambiguity
Inter-organisational	Different organisations	Different organisational interests; different national cultures

Drawing from this table and applying it to this case study, it would appear that the conflict that arose between me and Hermione had developed because of different organisational interests. As a service unit manager, Hermione was concerned with how resources would be spent. She wanted to prevent money being spent on services that were costly and could potentially be avoided if the situation between Dan and his family were to turn around. The reason Hermione behaved in this way was because we had all received the same message from the assistant director about avoiding the unnecessary accommodation of young people. But in this situation, the meaning this directive had in reality was entirely different for me than it was for Hermione because of the different positions we were in.

Hermione was in a more powerful position, but also one that was far removed from frontline practice. I was of the view that she was blindly following the 'unnecessary accommodation' strategy so that she could impress senior management. However, as Fotaki and Hyde (2014) have pointed out, working with unworkable strategies can lead to communication breakdown and destabilise working processes at organisational and individual levels. This lack of insight, as Gabriel (2012) and Fischer (2012) have identified, can create incidents that may lead to intra-agency conflict. I certainly felt devalued and disempowered that evening when Hermione changed her mind, but I knew that I also needed to make sense of why she had altered her decision and refused to take my views into consideration. It wasn't long before I realised that it was easier for Hermione to make the decision she had because she hadn't met the family, listened to their stories, seen their home and hadn't experienced the impact that Dan's behaviour was having on their mental health and emotional wellbeing. Hermione was therefore less affected by the visit than I had been – she was able to stay detached and focused on the role of saving the authority money.

Social psychologists French and Raven (1968) argue that power is relational. They use the concept of positional power to demonstrate how an individual's position within an organisation can mark the difference between whose opinion actually counts. Therefore, in this context, it distinguished who could and should make the final decision in relation to Dan and whether he should be accommodated or not. However, it is important to remember that social workers are not powerless because, according to French and Raven, I also had power, expert power, in that I had the skills and specialist expertise to convince Hermione what that right decision should be. The problem I faced was that in this situation, most probably because of the way that I had responded to Hermione, I was about to experience how Hermione also had coercive power at her disposal. In other words, by informing my manager and her own peers of the situation, Hermione would be able to use fear and reprisal to try and ensure that I would be more obedient in future.

I have to admit that had this event happened at a different time of my career I would not have spoken to or responded to Hermione in the way that I did because I would have been fearful of reprisal and what this might mean for my career and my financial income. I had observed the culture in my organisation change in recent years and rather than, as Mikkelsen and Clegg (2016) suggested earlier, welcome conflict or critical debate to produce positive outcomes, the organisational culture had appeared to morph into one that drew from a more Tayloristic approach to practice (see Clegg et al, 2006, p 46). But when this event between me and Hermione did occur I had reached a time in my life where I was ready to leave social work practice. Due to the recent financial cuts, I was aware that redundancies were being offered to practitioners to reduce staff numbers. I therefore concluded that if the organisation did want me to leave because of my misconduct, they would be likely to offer me a way out with a redundancy package.

This doesn't mean that I would recommend others who are reading this chapter and find they are in a similar situation to do the same. The reason why I have chosen to reflect on this case study in particular is so that I could explore how I could have handled the situation differently. As mentioned earlier, although social workers can often feel powerless in situations such as these, they do have individual power tactics that they can refer to and draw from to persuade senior managers of the decision they should be making. For example, Kipnis et al (1980) identified some of these strategies as friendliness, reasoning, coalition- forming, bargaining and making the other person feel important.

I recognise now that I could have used any, or all, of the above to have dealt with the situation differently. Therefore, on sensing that Hermione had changed I could have, in a friendly manner, asked much earlier on how she was feeling. By perhaps checking how she felt and reassuring her that I valued her opinion, I could have used reason to have reached a decision we both felt comfortable with. Mintzberg (1983) has identified that players can exert influence on organisations from the inside and the outside depending on the strategy they choose. In this case I could have identified that the reason we were disagreeing was because central government had reduced funding for all social care services nationally, and that collectively, we both felt the strain of these cuts. By being transparent and including the wider structural issues in the discussion, the way in which this situation developed could have been completely different.

Summary

What is interesting about using reflection to analyse case studies is that it can provide an opportunity for practitioners to explore how wider structural issues affect internal organisational dynamics and lead to, in turn, a wide range of contradictions. In current social work practice, there is growing recognition that clear tensions between increasing managerial regulation and social work practice are emerging (Fook, 2012). The way in which we reconcile and integrate these tensions is what produces meaningful approaches to moving forwards when conflict occurs.

Reflection is a process where we can consider events or situations in depth so that we can understand beyond what happened, to why it happened and how different people within that context might have felt about it (Bolton, 2010). By reflecting on this event, it has emerged that increased managerialism and reduced funding arrangements challenged the social work values and ethos of those who worked for the organisation. Money is crucially important in social work practice, but it can become the central cause for some social work agencies to such an extent that it can override consumer need and question the legitimacy of practitioner expertise. For social workers, these issues are perhaps particularly important because they view their position as representing the interests of the individual (Fook, 2012). Yet these positions can present their own challenges when practitioners are faced with a managerialist discourse that can decontextualise a situation and devalue the skills and knowledge of the social worker.

However, by simply positioning managers as cold-hearted, objective authoritarians, an in-depth and nuanced understanding of why managers do what they do and what they need to do to change cannot be achieved. This approach can also pile all the responsibility of 'making change' on to the manager and leave the social worker in a position without responsibility. What can easily be forgotten when professionals become engaged in conflict are the needs of the service user, and this is an issue that remains everyone's responsibility.

There have been a number of scandals recently where social work organisations have made headline news because they have been too caught up in the processes of doing social work, or saving money, that they have overlooked the needs of those they are working with (see Jay, 2014; Casey, 2015). By drawing from Argryis and Schön's (1974) proposed model of single-loop and double-loop learning, the rational technical approach to understanding why different people respond to the situation in the way that they do, has enabled a critique of all who were involved in this case to take place. It is the process of seeing things from a different perspective that has led to a more balanced and considered understanding of the events that occurred in this case study.

Self-organising systems develop to learn and thus become intelligent enough to define their own fundamental operating criteria, behaviour and identity (Hatch, 2006). If social workers and managers adopt a double-loop learning approach, this method can diffuse throughout an organisation and in turn create new organisational orders that rely on strong internal relationships rather than top-down management processes. This kind of organisation style doesn't rely on managers doing it first; it can begin anywhere in the organisational hierarchy. All that is required is openness and a willingness to take part, since questioning underlying assumptions, values and risk is the fundamental key for an organisation to change its approach to care.

Further reading

Hatch, J. (2006) *Organization theory*, Oxford: Sage
  This book is theoretically accurate and gives a comprehensive and up-to-date view of organisation and management theory in a quickly developing field. In addition, it is written in such a way that it encourages a reflexive stance towards both academic theory and organisational practices.

Bissell, G. (2012) *Organisational behaviour for social work*, Bristol: Policy Press
  This book unites the well-established study of behaviour in organisations with the special, and sometimes unusual, organisational settings or social work practice. In doing this, the gendered nature of social work organisations is explained.

Clegg, S., Kornberger, M. and Pitsis, T. (2015) *Managing and organizations: An introduction to theory and practice* (4th edn), London: Sage
  This textbook is a classic in the field of management and organisations. The key issues are clearly articulated in ways that introduce difficult concepts without using simplistic or jargonistic language.

References

Argryis, C. and Schön, D. (1978) *Organizational learning: A theory of action perspective*, Reading, MA: Addison Wesley.
Bissell, G. (2012) *Organisational behaviour for social work*, Bristol: Policy Press.
Bolton, G. (2010) *Reflective practice: Writing and professional development* (3rd edn), London: Sage.
Casey, L. (2015) *Report of inspection of Rotherham Metropolitan Borough Council*, London: Department for Communities and Local Government.
Clegg, S., Courpasson, D. and Phillips, N. (2006) *Power and organizations*, London: Sage Publications.
de Dreu, C.K.W. and Gelfland, M.J. (eds) (2008) *The psychology of conflict and conflict management in organizations*, New York: Taylor Francis.
Ferguson, H. (2011) *Child protection practice*, Basingstoke: Palgrave Macmillan.

Fischer, M. (2012) 'Organizational turbulence, trouble and trauma: Theorizing the collapse of a mental health setting', *Organization Studies*, vol 33, no 9, pp 1153–73.

Follett, M.P. (1918) *The new state: Group organization the solution of popular government*, University Park, PA: Pennsylvania State University Press.

Fook, J. (2012) *Social work: A critical approach to practice*, London: Sage.

Fotaki, M. and Hyde, P. (2014) 'Organisational blind spots: Splitting, blame and idealization in the National Health Service', *Human Relations*, 14 June, doi: 10.1177/0018726714530012.

French, J.R.P. and Raven, B. (1968) 'The bases of social power', in D. Cartwright and A. Zander (eds) *Group dynamics*, New York: Harper & Row, pp 150–67.

Froggett, L., Manley, J. and Roy, A. (2015) 'The visual matrix method: Imagery and affect in a group-based research setting forum', *Qualitative Research* (www.qualitative-research.net/index.php/fqs/article/view/2308).

Gabriel, Y. (2012) 'Organizations in a state of darkness: Towards a theory of organizational miasma', *Organization Studies*, vol 33, no 9, pp 1137–52.

Harms, L. (2015) *Understanding trauma and resilience*, Basingstoke: Palgrave Macmillan.

Hatch, J. (2006) *Organization theory*, Oxford: Sage.

Herman, J. (1992) *Trauma and recovery: The aftermath of violence*, New York: Basic Books.

Hochschild, A.R. (2012) *The managed heart: Commercialization of human feeling*, Berkeley, CA: University of California Press.

Jay, A. (2014) *Independent Inquiry into child sexual exploitation in Rotherham (1997–2013)* (www.rotherham.gov.uk/downloads/file/1407/independent_inquiry_cse_in_rotherham).

Jordan, B. (2011) 'Making sense of the "Big Society": Social work and the moral order', *Journal of Social Work*, vol 12, no 6, pp 630–46.

Kenny, K. (2012) '"Someone big and important": Identification and affect in an international development organization', *Organization Studies*, vol 33, no 9, pp 1175–93.

Kipnis, D., Schmidt, S.M. and Wilkinson, I. (1980) 'Intraorganizational influence tactics: Explorations in getting one's way', *Journal of Applied Psychology*, vol 65, no 4, pp 440–52.

Klonowski, A. (2013) *Report of the Independent Reviewing Officer in relation to child sexual exploitation issues in Rochdale Metropolitan Borough Council during the period 2006 to 2013* (www.rochdale.gov.uk/pdf/2013-05-23-independet-reviewing-officer-report_into-csc-issues-v1.pdf).

Mayo, E. (1946) *The human problems of an industrial civilisation*, Cambridge, MA: Harvard University Press.

McNicoll, A. (2014) 'Cuts to safeguarding teams and looked-after children services as council spending drops', *Community Care*, 16 April (www.communitycare.co.uk/2014/04/16/cuts-safeguarding-teams-lookEd-children-services-council-spending-drops/).

Mintzberg, H. (1983) *Power in and around organisations*, Englewood Cliffs, NJ: Prentice Hall.

Mikkelsen, E.N. and Clegg, S. (2016) 'Managing conflict', in S. Clegg, M. Stewart and T. Pitsis (eds) *Managing and organizations. An introduction to theory and practice* (4th edn), London: Sage Publications.

Payne, M. (2011) *Humanistic social work: Core principles in practice*, Chicago, IL: Lyceum Books.

Putnam, L.L. and Poole, M.S. (1987) 'Conflict and negotiation', in F.M. Jablin, L.L. Putnam, K.H. Roberts and L.W. Porter (eds) *Handbook of organizational communication*, Newbury Park, CA: Sage, pp 629–52.

Tedeschi, R.G. and Calhoun, L.G. (1996) 'The posttraumatic growth inventory: Measuring the positive legacy of trauma', *Journal of Trauma Stress*, vol 9, p 455, doi:10.1007/BF02103658.

Wittgenstein, L. (1953) *Philosophical investigations*, London: Blackwell.

4

Dealing with a colleague's suspension

Introduction

This chapter explores a situation where the organisation was going through a difficult time and a long-standing member of the team was suspended. The way in which this was carried out was disturbing for all who were present because of the lack of information they were provided with.

I begin by exploring the theory of affect and emotion, and discuss how it can emerge in situations such as these. I go on to unravel the sequence of events that occurred through a psychodynamic lens, using the processes of splitting and blame to explain how turbulence manifested itself in the team. This period of instability did little to reassure the team members who remained. Instead of feeling informed and aware of what was happening, the way in which the organisation dealt with the matter was to remain silent and not answer any questions. This led to the suspended social worker being cut off from contact with others, and left social workers in the team feeling paranoid that they were going to be suspended next.

The chapter concludes by explaining how it was only through reading the relevant departmental policy that I began to realise the way in which this suspension had been handled was unethical as it contradicted the suggested recommendations. In the following narrative, I explore how difficult situations such as these should be handled sensitively by managers in order to prevent atmospheres of mistrust and suspicion developing inside the workplace.

Background

In order to understand why the events in this narrative unfolded in the way that they did, it is important to consider the context within which the organisation I worked for was situated. At the time this event happened the coalition government had just been elected and all local authorities across the country were faced with having to reduce their spending (Jordan, 2011). Under the New Labour government, our organisation had been able to create and implement new services that were targeted at improving early intervention measures. However, with the impending loss of a significant amount of money, the agency realised it was about to enter a new era, one that would see the implementation of cuts and job losses.

Our agency consisted of four safeguarding teams that had in total 36 social workers, 10 middle managers (team managers and assistant team managers) and 3 senior managers (2 service unit managers and 1 assistant director). The agency dealt with both 'child in need' (low-level intervention) and 'child protection' referrals

71

(when a child is at risk of significant harm). In recent years the organisation had increased staff numbers in order to make stronger links between services and practice. These changes had consequently led to a 'good' Ofsted rating. However, when this situation occurred, our organisation was awaiting another visit from Ofsted. This time the feeling in the agency was far more anxious due to the fact that the impending cuts would undoubtedly affect service delivery and perhaps affect the agency's 'good' Ofsted rating.

Before I go on to explain what happened to my team, I want to begin by setting the scene and describing how three different events affected activity within the department. The first event was linked to our agency trying to adapt to a new identity, one that was influenced by the new coalition government's austerity rhetoric. In our agency, the period under New Labour became colloquially termed 'The golden era'; this referred to a time when our organisation didn't have to worry too much about resources. However, when this event occurred, our department was about to enter a new era, the 'era of austerity'. Although everyone was aware that there would be 'cuts', it wasn't until we received an email from the assistant director announcing that we had gone over budget by a few million that we were fully informed as to the extent of these cuts.

What was particularly interesting about the way in which this information was distributed was just that, how it was distributed. Normally members of staff were invited to a consultation meeting where the impact of such a serious issue would be discussed with senior management. But this time, perhaps due to the emergency of the situation, the purpose of the email was to quickly highlight to all employees the huge debt that our agency had suddenly accrued, a debt that could have emerged as a result of systemic failure or that could have materialised from the sudden cut in resources. But with no explanation of how this debt had occurred, or how this predicament might affect the future of the department, what followed was a situation of panic.

This is most probably because before anyone had the chance to properly digest the email, it was quickly followed by an announcement that we were soon to expect a visit from Ofsted for another agency inspection. Within a relatively short period of time, what immediately became apparent was the way in which managers attempted to deal with both of these situations. Rather than pulling together to overcome perceived adversity, the opposite occurred. Team managers started to panic and team members saw regular demonstrations of distress or anger. Managers' feelings of panic were most likely provoked by the worry that Ofsted would be assessing the performance of each individual safeguarding team. This was no more unusual for any other visit from Ofsted; however, this time, there was a different fear to contend with, a fear that was underpinned by a perceived certainty that job losses would ensue if performances didn't meet Ofsted expectations. As a department we had accrued a growing number of managers and frontline staff over the years, which led people to believe that redundancies would be related to Ofsted performance ratings.

During this new era of austerity, these two events, although separate, were actually intimately connected, and collectively created concern for all involved, but more so for team managers who struggled to keep up appearances in front of their superiors and their teams. Team managers were often heard describing their position as being stuck between 'a rock and a hard place' as they had to deal with the stresses and strife of individual team members as well as meet the demands of senior management.

The third event that was not obvious at the time but that is always significant in child protection practice was the notion that someone was holding a case that could be the next 'Baby P', also known as Peter Connelly. In 2009, social workers across the country watched in horror as Gillie Christou, Maria Ward and Sharon Shoesmith from Haringey Local Authority were publically vilified for the death of Peter Connelly. The extent of this condemnation generated more hate and revulsion for social workers than had ever been seen before (Warner, 2015). Although no such case had (yet) occurred at our agency, we were still affected by this traumatic event, in a number of different ways. This fear was compounded by the fact that the imminent cuts would mean there would be less resources available to manage 'the risky' cases. It would also lead to a reduction in staff, which would mean an increase in workload for others who were already at or above their recommended case limit of 25 children.

When discussing how negative affects emerge, Tomkins (1963, p 48) has suggested that it is done so through 'three general sources of human suffering: the ills of the body; the frustrations of interpersonal relationships; and the recalcitrance of nature to human striving and achievement.' As we will see shortly, these sources of human suffering surfaced in my agency and were underpinned by the three events outlined above.

The theory of affect and emotion

The notion of affect first emerged as a theory in 1677 when Dutch philosopher Baruch Spinoza highlighted the difference between an 'affect' and an 'emotion' in his work on *Ethics*. An affect, for Spinoza, was different to an emotion because it was something that was produced by the body, or the mind, when an interaction occurred with another body or mind. This interaction subsequently increased or diminished the body's power of activity.

Affect has been described as that feeling a person gets when they walk into a room and sense an atmosphere (Brennan, 2004). Affect doesn't mean that the mind can determine the body to act, or that the body can determine the mind to think (Hardt, 1999). Quite the reverse; Spinoza identified that the body and the mind are independent of one another, but the powers of both are constantly corresponding with each other in some way that becomes so obvious others can sense an atmosphere in the room.

Since Spinoza, a number of alternative connotations of affect have emerged. Some scholars have used affect to focus towards a more vitalist, 'post-human' and process-based perspective (see Hammed, 2004; Blackman and Venn, 2010) or on becoming, potential and virtual (see Froggett et al, 2015). Whichever perspective is adopted it is collectively agreed that affect can be considered a psychosocial concept because it interferes with our emotions and our interactions with others (Brennan, 2004).

However, Wetherell (2012, p 3) contends that ordinary 'basic emotion' terms such as sadness, anger, fear, surprise, disgust and happiness don't adequately describe the range and variety of affective performances, scenes and events that take place in life. Instead, she proposes that social analysis should focus on the 'affective practice' of an individual and their wider group so that researchers can attempt to understand how people are moved, attracted to or pained by certain social interactions (2012, p 78). She settles therefore on the concept of affective practice as the most promising way forward for understanding affect and emotion as it tries to follow what participants do and feel. It is this particular perspective of affect that is drawn on in this chapter when attempting to explore the accounts of different social workers' interactions inside this organisation.

Object relations theory: splitting, blame and idealisation

Psychodynamic theory can offer a helpful method of exploring unconscious aspects of individuals who interact with organisational and social structures through various psychological mechanisms (Fotaki and Hyde, 2014). Psychoanalytic theories recognise individual tendencies for self-deception that originate from the desire to repress undesirable feelings and/or realities. Object relations theory (Klein, 1952) suggests self-deception processes involving projecting the unwanted aspects of self on to other objects/people/groups. Isabel Menzies Lyth (1960) built on the concept of the 'social defence' against anxiety, originally developed by Elliot Jacques (1956), to transfer attention from the individual to the organisation. Menzies Lyth argued that socially sustained defence mechanisms occurred when anxiety was evoked in an individual by the undertaking of a specific work task. In her study of hospital wards, the fear of death experienced by nurses led to them avoiding closeness with suffering patients.

Menzies Lyth's theorising was helpful as it explained why organisations develop defences and how these, in turn, enabled staff to avoid work-related anxiety by depersonalising care, avoiding responsibility and giving slavish attention to routines and rituals (Menzies Lyth, 1960). The psychological notion of 'splitting' refers to a defence that is employed by people to cope with doubts, conflicting feelings and anxiety (Fotaki and Hyde, 2014). Splitting therefore enables the individual to separate their negative feelings from their positive ones. When splitting occurs, objects are not seen as wholes, but as separate 'part' objects: the 'good' part is idealised and the 'bad' part has the potential to cause harm (Klein, 1952). During periods of extreme stress, adults may regress to a developmentally earlier state of splitting and projecting in order to temporarily relieve anxiety.

The idealisation of wholly good objects and the blame of wholly bad objects has been associated with splitting and can enable the individual to detach from reality (Fotaki and Hyde, 2014). Although defences help the individual to survive in the organisation, they do not resolve the original source of anxiety, and therefore further anxiety is generated from fear of attack from the 'bad' object (Klein, 1952). When this occurs, splitting results in a spiral of increasing threats towards a person, and the person has the reduced capacity to deal with such threats effectively. As a result, it becomes increasingly difficult to challenge as any resolution involves the reintegration of unpleasant elements.

Splitting can also occur when organisations go through a period of change and new elements of organisational learning threaten previously established team identities (Gabriel, 2012). Unconscious and socially sanctioned mechanisms become embedded in organisational structures and cultures, obscuring problems and interfering with change. This occurs when problems are too difficult and painful to confront and established organisational practices may be too precious to relinquish (Fotaki and Hyde, 2014). To defend against failure, the problems that are experienced are then projected onto the departments or people who are wrongly identified as being problematic (Gabriel, 2012). Denial and displacement of unworkable strategies leads to the creation of organisational blind spots and the ultimate failure of projects (Fotaki and Hyde, 2014).

Case study

Day 1

It was 7pm at night and I got a telephone call from my manager, Shelly, asking if I could do overtime. I asked what had happened to Kenny as he was supposed to be on shift but she said she couldn't say. I called Kenny but there was no answer. I left a message asking him if he was okay. As soon as I put down the phone, Kenny called. He said he wasn't supposed to speak to me because he had been suspended. He said he had gone into work to have supervision with Shelly. Supervision had just started with Shelly, when Shelly's manager and another service unit manager arrived. They explained that they were suspending him on full pay for three weeks. He asked them why and they said that all he could know is two names – they gave him the two names of the children in a case he had been working with. He asked them what he had done and they told him that they couldn't tell him. They asked for his computer, ID and for his phone. He asked if he could bring these items to their office so he could be spared some humility in front of the rest of the duty team. They said "No", and then took him into the main office where the others were. He handed over his computer and his ID but he had forgotten his phone, he had left it at home, so they told him not to contact anyone and then they marched him off the premises. Kenny sounded in shock and said he couldn't decide whether he should laugh or cry. He told me that his head was spinning and that he couldn't think straight.

Reflection 'on' action

Emotions, such as the ones Kenny was experiencing at this time, are what Reddy (2001) refers to as speech acts in that they have performative and constative features. An emotive is constative in the sense that it has the appearance of a description. Emotives are also performative because they perform an act that changes the meaning of the situation. Kenny's subjective experiences transformed what happened to him in that supervision meeting from a terrible situation into a highly emotionally charged encounter. But Wetherell (2012) would argue that such emotives are also relational because they affect the person who is addressed, who, in this case, was me. The performative effects of emotives are thought to have the capacity to 'arc back and reconstitute subjective experience' (Wetherell, 2012, p 69).

This means that those involved in that encounter (me and Kenny) may not even have been aware that the particular emotive has altered the affective flow in the social interaction. This is understandable given that as human beings we are prone to empathise with those who have experienced a traumatic experience (Ruch and Murray, 2011). This is also relevant in terms of splitting because although Kenny felt guilty for contacting me, talking to someone who could sympathise with him had left him feeling better, momentarily. Yet in listening to Kenny's trauma, I had inadvertently become affected by the distress he had experienced.

Reflection 'in' action

Kenny said that after his suspension he had gone home immediately, found his phone and immediately contacted his Union representative to tell them what had happened. He was shocked to learn that they already knew. It materialised that his managers had contacted the Union representatives during the day to inform them that they would be suspending Kenny later that day. They warned them to be ready to support Kenny when he called them later. As Kenny was a Union representative they wanted to warn his colleagues in advance of what he had done. Kenny ended the call by asking me not to tell anyone he had called me. I found myself agreeing I would not.

Reflection points
1. What does your in-house procedure say about suspension of colleagues and contact with other members of the organisation?
2. What information does your policy state that Kenny could have been provided with that would have helped him in this situation?

Reflection 'on' action

Wetherell (2012, p 74) has suggested that individual bodies and minds constitute one place where diverse affective flows become organised into what she calls 'a situated activity'. If we are to make meaning of how affect and emotion emerged in this encounter, then Wetherell argues that we need to explore the dialogic exchange between me and Kenny more closely. Intersubjectivity develops through projective identification, a complex mechanism in which, in this case, Kenny has unconsciously projected impulses or mental representations on to me. Through social interaction, and knowing Kenny well, I identified with his projections, I felt his distress and thereby empathised with how he was feeling and experienced those feelings of panic for myself.

Reflection 'in' action

Wetherell's exposure of the importance of the dialogic exchange is important given that when the call ended, I started to feel sick and anxious. This is most probably because when I had heard the names of the children Kenny had mentioned, I realised that it was a case I was also involved in. My first reaction was to look at the case notes to see if I had also made a mistake. However, I knew from past experience that I couldn't look at the ICS (Integrated Child System) to see what was happening because the IT department would have been able to trace my steps, and this could get Kenny into trouble. I was also concerned that I would implicate myself.

Instead, I started to mentally analyse everything from the beginning, the moment we had first become involved in the case. I went over my handwritten notes again and again to see the role I had played in the events that had led up to Kenny's suspension. From what I could see we had not done anything wrong, but at this stage I was aware that we didn't know what they knew. Had something gone wrong after our involvement? Was Kenny being blamed for an action he did or didn't do? And how would this affect me? As I started to panic I became consumed with the thought that I would be next. I couldn't stop checking my phone, waiting or looking for a text or telephone message that was going to tell me that I needed to come in to attend a meeting that might, perhaps, lead to my own suspension.

Reflection points
1. Pause and think about why I felt frightened. Have you ever been in a situation like this?
2. Who do you think I should have talked to about this dilemma?
   The difficulty I faced was that Kenny had shared the details of a situation with me that I was not supposed to be aware of. I couldn't talk to other team

*members or my manager about this. When I spoke to family or friends they
didn't understand why I felt anxious.*

An email eventually popped up on my phone. It was from my manager. She asked
whether we (the whole team) could all have an emergency team meeting at IKEA
the next day. She suggested IKEA because "it is away from the office". Originally
the affective activity that I had been talking about had been situated with just me
and Kenny, an interaction that had taken place over the phone. However, as soon
as I saw this email I realised the affect had spread and was moving quickly. Situated
affective activity moves when an individual interacts with others who recognise,
endorse and pass on the affected emotions and feelings (Wetherell, 2012).

I started to recall the actions that Shelly had carried out the day after Kenny
was last in work, and I realised that what had happened had also clearly affected
Shelly as she had made the suggestion that we all meet away from the office. She
must have been feeling suspicious, I thought, if she didn't feel it safe for us to all
meet at work. But her suspicious behaviour soon led to me feeling paranoid as I
started to recall how Shelly had behaved in work the last time we were together.

We had been on duty and I had picked up Kenny's work from the day before and
looked through the notes he had made. Shelly and I were dealing with the tasks
that had still not been completed and needed attending to so that we could agree
on what needed to be done next. It was when we were looking through Kenny's
notes that I had heard Shelly tut a few times. Then, without saying anything, she
had gone into her office, and closed the door and the blinds. I then heard her
talking on the phone to someone, and I remembered thinking at the time that
it was strange that she would make such an effort to conceal her conversation.

During that phone call, Shelly kept coming out and asking me questions about
Kenny, questions that I didn't understand properly. For example, had Kenny
spoken to me about why he had not gone to the hospital? Had he spoken to
anyone in health? She also asked if I would cover for him on Friday – the day I
now knew would be the day he would go into work and be suspended. Once I
put the events in order and digested the information, I felt convinced that Shelly
was involved in some way and that she must have been planning his suspension
over the phone with her own manager.

Reflection 'on' action

Although the flow of affect is located in the body, it is also located within the
flow of ordinary life (Wetherell, 2012). It becomes part of social interaction
when it gets caught up in social business. The events that had happened so far
had triggered physical reactions, both emotionally and mentally. I was feeling
scared, anxious and paranoid. I knew that Kenny was feeling the same, and from
Shelly's behaviour she must have been too. But it became most apparent that

these affective activities were, indeed, social business when Mary (a colleague and team member) called me.

Reflection 'in' action

Mary had seen the email from Shelly and had called me to find out what the email meant. Unable to keep the feelings of anxiety to myself I told Mary about what had happened to Kenny. Mary's reaction was different to mine; she sympathised with him but recounted a time when she had been suspended over sickness. The problem had been that she had not been sick at all; she had called in sick because her mother and father had died in quick succession of one another and she was grieving. Mary had told me that she had taken a month off to deal with their deaths, but that this time away from work had triggered a notification on the system that she was taking too much time off sick. Rather than talk to her about the situation, her manager had called her into a meeting and Mary had been suspended by another senior manager. Mary informed me that this was the culture of the organisation, and that I had best be prepared for this kind of activity as it was likely to happen again.

Although I recognised that Mary was telling me this story to demonstrate how the organisation functioned, this information distressed me further as I started to feel sure that I, too, would be suspended when I returned to work. Even though Mary had tried to reassure me, it didn't work. Instead, I felt annoyed with her and believed that the only reason she felt calm about it all was because she hadn't been on duty on any of the same days as we had been, she could feel relieved because she wasn't involved in this particular case. This soon changed when I gave her the names of the children in the case.

Reflection points
1. Pause for a moment and think about what is happening here. Although I talked to Mary to seek reassurance, what did we end up doing together? *We made each other panic. Critical reflection and questioning about what could be done to resolve the situation became impossible.*
2. What did Mary contribute to the conversation that provided more information about how our organisational culture functioned? *Mary's news highlighted that this organisation had blind spots. It could be so focused on following processes, it might neglect to communicate effectively, overlook individual situations and create further distress.*

Mary suddenly remembered that she had carried out an initial assessment for them some months earlier, and once she realised who they were, she also started to panic. She recalled closing the case because she felt there was nothing more we could do, but now she was worried that she had made the wrong decision.

The situated affective activity that had originally emerged between me and Kenny had spread and in turn affected other members of the team.

Day 2

The next day we all met at IKEA as planned. Shelly explained that Kenny had been suspended and that she couldn't tell us anything about the case apart from the fact that we "need to tighten things up" as they were now looking at everything we were doing. I asked Shelly who she meant by "they" and she said, "senior management". Shelly warned us that they wouldn't tolerate any mistakes, no matter how small, because Ofsted inspectors were due to arrive at any time and as a result, they would be scrutinising our performance.

I asked Shelly if she knew that Kenny was going to be suspended, and she immediately became defensive. She stated that she was not brought in to be "a cleaner", and that it was not nice watching what had happened to him. She then went on to remind me of another 'moment of affective action' where something distinct and recognisable had happened (Wetherell, 2012, p 78). She referred to a disagreement me and Shelly once had over another case where she had recorded on the case notes that she hadn't approved of what I had done. I had challenged her about this at the time as I had felt it was inappropriate to use a child's case notes to discuss my practice, and I had asked her to remove the comment. She did remove the comment but she told me now that she had written that comment because she was covering her own back. Shelly then told me that she had never been suspended but has watched it happen to other people, so she always covers her back.

Shelly then disclosed that although Kenny might have said he was doing a lot of work, the system showed that he hadn't actually done that much and that he had left it for the rest of the team to pick up. I started to feel my skin prickle when I heard this. I couldn't decide whether she was telling the truth or whether she was trying to turn us against Kenny. I tried to explain the situation by describing the sheer volume of work we were faced with on that particular day, but Shelly refuted this by arguing that a number of jobs that should have been completed by Kenny hadn't been.

This revelation made me wonder if I had been the gullible one and that maybe I was protecting the wrong person. Shelly said that she told her manager that she was going to address this with Kenny in supervision. I realised when I heard this that this must have been why Shelly had been making private phone calls in her office. Shelly said that she had spoken to her manager about her concerns and had agreed that she would go into supervision with Kenny to try and resolve them. However, she wasn't prepared for her own manager to arrive with the service unit manager and suspend Kenny. Shelly promised us that she had had no idea that they were going to do that.

We all started to realise at this point that something wasn't right and together we tried to work out what was happening. It felt like we were playing a game of Cluedo as we tried to reveal who the perpetrator was in this scenario. Who was the victim? And why? Although this activity brought us closer together that day, on the drive home the doubts I had about Shelly and her intentions started to resurface once more. They led me to believe that I needed to distance myself from Shelly as I still felt she was a manager I couldn't trust.

Reflection points

1. If you were a team manager in this situation, what would you have done?
   The role of the team manager should be to remain calm and reassure the others in the team. However, Shelly was unable to do this because she felt uncertain of her own position. She had planned on talking to Kenny about her concerns, but her own manager and senior manager had used that meeting to suspend Kenny, an action she wasn't prepared for.
2. How was the situation made more problematic?
   Although meeting in a building away from the office enabled Shelly to share her fears and talk to the team without fearing that she would be overheard, the conversation fuelled feelings of paranoia and panic.
3. What should have happened to reverse the panic and paranoia that everyone in the team was feeling?
   If Shelly had perhaps called a meeting with her own manager, the senior manager and the team, then these feelings could have been discussed with those responsible for Kenny's suspension. If they had realised how the remaining team members were feeling, they may have been able to provide information and reassurance.

Reflection 'in' action

Later that afternoon I got another call from Shelly. She was crying on the phone and it took me a while to work out what it was she was trying to say. She eventually managed to tell me that when she had returned to work after our IKEA meeting, she had been called into a meeting with her own manager and the service unit manager. She had been informed by them both that she would be receiving notice for "poor decision-making".

When I heard her say this my head started to spin and I felt sick again. I couldn't believe what was happening. I had thought that she was "in on it", but now I could see that I was wrong. I had no idea who to trust and I asked her if she thought we, the rest of the team, were safe. She said she got the feeling that Mary was next because those above "just don't like her". She then told me that I, too, should look for another job to be on the safe side. Shelly also advised me to download all my files in case they called me in and suspended me. If I did get suspended, then when I got called back I would at least be able to defend myself as I would know from the downloaded case notes what they were referring to. Shelly warned me to be careful because she thought there was "a hidden agenda".

Reflection 'on' action

Affect is lodged within embodied sequences of action that, in turn, shape future events (Goodwin, 2006). The stories I had been told by Shelly, Kenny and Mary had physically affected me and emotionally disturbed me. These feelings didn't disappear when I stopped talking to them; they stayed with me like a form of embodiment, and significantly affected my own behaviour. The trouble that was situated in the team had emerged from relational tensions. The relational turbulence that had emerged originally between me and Kenny had escalated beyond the original scene, and in turn produced contagious 'ripple effects' (Barsade, 2002) across the boundaries of individuals, our team and the organisation.

Day 3

That night I couldn't sleep. I tossed and turned thinking about Kenny, Mary and Shelly. I woke up sweating, worrying that I was going to be next and wondering what I would do if I were suspended or dismissed – how would I look after my family? Pay the mortgage? Find work again?

The next day, it was my turn to return to work. I hadn't been back since Kenny and Shelly had been suspended. I didn't know what would be waiting for me when I walked in the door. As I drove to work, I realised I was physically shaking. I hadn't eaten properly the day before and I realised that I had also missed breakfast. I was tired and frightened.

When I got to the office I looked down to feel my knees knocking. I was trembling so much I struggled to walk towards the door. Before I entered, I stopped and peered in the windows to see if anyone was waiting for me. There was no one there. I went inside and into our office, but there were no managers waiting for me. I walked around the whole building to see if there were any members of senior management hiding in one of the other offices somewhere, waiting for me to start work before they called me in and suspended me. The building was eerily quiet. People were sat at their computers working, like any other normal day, except it didn't feel like a normal day. No one was talking; there was no hubbub in the office like there normally was. The whole department felt different.

Reflection 'on action'

Morrison (2007) has argued that it is increasingly apparent that the most troubling and intractable situations exist when performance difficulties occur in the context of staff who lack accurate empathy, self-awareness and self-management skills.

Morrison's use of the word 'accurate' is especially poignant in this context. As social workers, we are trained to demonstrate empathy, be self-aware and develop our self-management skills when we are working with service users and their families. However, what is clear from this case study is that these insightful skills were absent when it came to relating to each other inside the workplace. Given that emotions are often generated around power, status interactions and the presence of anxiety (Morrison, 1997; Kemper, 2000), it is important that social work organisations make it a priority to pay attention to the emotive and affective states of not only their service users but also their own staff. The turbulence that had emerged within our team had developed from the organisation's tendency to scapegoat underperformers or perceived troublemakers. At times of intense frustration and exhaustion, rather than use democratic decision-making that could have repaired team tension, the practice was to suspend anyone who generated concerns. This defence enabled senior managers to cope with doubts, conflicting feelings and anxiety (Fotaki and Hyde, 2014). They were expecting Ofsted inspectors to arrive at any moment, and didn't want to be blamed for staff malpractice.

However, their blame of wholly bad objects versus their idealisation that without them the team would thrive was misjudged and instead created anxiety and panic. When senior managers suspended Kenny they felt that the malpractice issue had been instantly resolved and probably felt relieved of it, momentarily. By drawing from the theory of affect and emotion we have been able to see how the situation unfolded between an individual and their wider group. It is through this process that we have also learned just how people are moved, attracted to or pained by certain social interactions (see Wetherell, 2012).

Although it became apparent that management held concerns about Kenny's practice, at the same time they failed to recognise that he was also a valued member of the team. This lack of emotional competence can render specific performance problems all but unmanageable. In fact, Morrison (2007) has argued that in the worst cases, this form of emotional incompetence can become almost 'toxic' as whole teams or even agencies become enmeshed in the distorting dynamics surrounding the individual staff member.

This is evident in this situation as the way in which Kenny's suspension was handled meant that it was not just Kenny who was affected but also other members of the team. As we picked up on each other's anxiety, rather than reassure each other, the panic spread and distorted our team's dynamics. As Ruch and Murray (2011) have argued, what seems to be lacking in political responses to childcare tragedies is a reluctance to acknowledge the role played by anxiety, and the impact this has on the emotional aspects of practice.

Fook (2012) has suggested that power is something that people use or create, rather than simply possess; it is a factor that is given life through processes and structures of social interaction. Different contexts can affect the types of power used, how it is practised and thus exercised (Healy, 2000). Although Down and Reveley (2009, p 380) highlight that managers are on 'the sharp end of organisational change', this doesn't necessarily mean power will be used in a positive way all of the time.

In defence of managers, Watson (1997, 2001) has highlighted the difficult situation that they often find themselves in. He argues that managers are never easy with the notion of themselves because they are conscious of an ever-present, if implicit, division between an insincere person and a sincere one, or a manipulator and an honourable individual. As a team manager Shelly may have felt like a constituent part of two teams, someone who tries to lead on behalf of the senior managerial audience while translating what she knew about their beliefs to the team she was there to support.

This was most apparent when Shelly explained that she was trying to raise concerns about Kenny's practice to her own managers. As a manager, she was responsible for the way in which her team practised, but she wasn't prepared for the way in which her own managers responded to her concerns. This is hardly surprising because the way in which Kenny's suspension was handled actually contradicted the recommendations made in the organisation's own policy. These recommendations were informed by the *Code of practice for disciplinary and grievance procedures* issued by ACAS to local government agencies. The following extract is taken from recent guidance (2015, p 5):

> Inform the employee of the problem
>
> 9. If it is decided that there is a disciplinary case to answer, the employee should be notified of this in writing. This notification should contain sufficient information about the alleged misconduct or poor performance and its possible consequences to enable the employee to prepare to answer the case at a disciplinary meeting. It would normally be appropriate to provide copies of any written evidence, which may include any witness statements, with the notification.
> 10. The notification should also give details of the time and venue for the disciplinary meeting and advise the employee of their right to be accompanied at the meeting. The statutory right of the employee is to be accompanied by a fellow worker, a trade union representative, or an official employed by a trade union.

In this case study, these key points were clearly not followed by senior management, and there may have been a number of reasons for this. As mentioned previously, the agency was trying to deal with three previously identified issues: the significant reduction in resources; the imminent Ofsted inspection; and the fear that, as a result of these two factors, safeguarding teams would not be able to respond to the needs of children at risk effectively. It was perhaps because of the latter issue that Kenny's situation was handled in the way that it was.

Rather than follow their own in-house guidance and perhaps ensure that Kenny was prepared for a disciplinary meeting, it would seem that the managers in this case were unsure of how to deal with the situation for the best. As a result of poor communication, a distinct lack of trust materialised and it wasn't long before the entire department felt affected by Kenny's suspension. These feelings were further exacerbated when we learned that Shelly had also been suspended for poor decision-making.

Affective practice is relational, and affect performances come in conventional pairs (Wetherell, 2012), which, in this case, divided members of our team into positions of either accusation or defence. These binary positions subsequently contributed to the development of derisory organisational narratives that promoted and nurtured discourses of disempowerment, blame and suspicion. With no one from senior management stepping in to resolve the conflict, their actions appeared instead to be contributing to a turbulent atmosphere, which, in turn, produced wider destabilising effects. What emerged in its place was a toxic culture, which Morrison (2007) referred to earlier, as a context where feelings of uncertainty and apprehension can arise and unsettle all those present.

Summary

When we consider the notion of 'power' we often split the context into two oppositional groups – 'the powerful' and 'the powerless' (Fook, 2012, p 57). An understanding of power inequalities in the workplace needs to be explored if we are to examine how this situation could have been handled differently by all involved.

First of all, it is clear that the situation could have been handled differently if the team manager and the senior managers had been properly aware of and subsequently duly followed the correct policy. If this had happened, then Kenny would have been informed in advance of his supervision what his meeting was going to address. He would have had the time to have sought support from a colleague or his Union representative. He would also have been provided with the reason for the meeting, and further details relating to why there were particular concerns about his practice could have been relayed. Kenny would have seen the notes relating to the case in question and he would have had the opportunity to respond to these appropriately.

If the appropriate procedure had been followed correctly, then perhaps the hasty and unexpected removal of Kenny, which took place in front of his team, would not have been deemed necessary. This action also contradicted with the procedure that recommends that such situations be handled respectfully. A calm and informed departure would have been less dramatic and perhaps prevented feelings of uncertainty and apprehension to escalate within the team and later, the department. Social workers who witness these kinds of situations may feel let down by their organisation because those they rely on to lead the service effectively don't always behave as practitioners would hope or expect them to. By taking a critically reflexive approach to organisational functioning, social workers can become aware of the hidden influences of assumptions that emanate from such cultural contexts.

Fook (2012, p 167) refers to this form of critical thinking as 'contextual competence', which means having the ability to read the cultural climate of contexts and then being able to practice effectively with and within this climate. Attending to these aspects of practice can help explain why organisational changes are sometimes unsuccessful, and why alternative approaches to the barriers encountered in the workplace are sometimes required (Ruch and Murray, 2011). This doesn't mean that social workers should adapt to a 'toxic' culture and thus perform in oppressive ways; rather, they should pause and consider why people are behaving in the way that they are, and then contemplate how their own behaviour is affecting the cultural context within which they are situated.

In this situation, it is evident that I wasn't contextually competent. It was a while before I realised that what I needed to do was to read the in-house disciplinary and grievance policy. Once I did, I became informed about how the situation should have been handled and I felt more aware of what needed to happen next. I was able to inform Kenny of what his rights were, and when I showed him the document he was able to understand how the situation should have been dealt with. Kenny was then able to use this information when talking with his Union representative, and together they resolved the issue with the organisation by following the recommended guidelines.

While conflict between organisational members is natural, indeed, inevitable, direct approaches to dealing with this fact of organisational life are not. The way in which policy and procedure is interpreted into practice can create intra-agency conflict and leave a residue of interpersonal antagonisms (Walton, 1987). The scapegoating dynamics evident in this organisation can be observed through object relations theory. The paranoid-schizoid forms that were apparent strengthened projections on to the group: there were good workers and bad workers, those who were seen to be 'bad' were removed, externalised and thus controlled by their removal (Fischer, 2012).

In social work, this is relevant with regards to the practice that takes place outside of the office with service users and families as well as the practice that takes place inside the workplace. Change in cultural patterns depends not only on what is said, but who that dialogue is with and the feelings that can be generated from that dialogue (Warner, 2015). Cultures that appear to thrive are those where although there are still organisational leaders and middle managers, their authority is decentred (Clegg et al, 2006). When organisational leaders are part of the frontline working environment and take part in discussions, meetings and social care practice, communication is less inhibited as better relationships are encouraged between the organisational tiers (Whittaker, 2011). It is then that practitioners are able to share their thoughts, feelings and experiences with all senior managers, and managers are in a good position to understand what frontline practitioners face.

Further reading and information

British Association of Social Workers Union, www.basw.co.uk/swu/
  BASW Union advisers are trained social workers who also have legal training and are often able to provide members with the right sort of advice and direction.

Wetherell, M. (2012) *Affect and emotion: A new social science understanding*, London: Sage
  The book is about how affect is situated: through interaction or accountability in any given moment. Wetherell uses affective practice to focus on the emotional in social life, and tries to explore how using this approach enables readers to challenge emotive states.

Kenny, K. and Fotaki, M. (2015) *The psychosocial and organization studies: Affect at work*, London: Palgrave Macmillan
  This book brings together psychosocial approaches with the field of management and organisation studies. It distinctively represents a collection of important and well-regarded theories and methodological approaches from leading authors within organisation studies and also from broader social science disciplines including critical psychology, social policy, cultural studies, gender studies, feminism and postcolonial theory. By drawing attention to the implications of psychosocial theorising in the workplace, the book adds to the core debates within organisation studies and critical management studies, and illuminates key concerns within psychosocial studies.

References

ACAS (2015) *Code of practice on disciplinary and grievance procedures* (www.acas.org.uk/mEdia/pdf/f/m/Acas-Code-of-Practice-1-on-disciplinary-and-grievance-procEdures.pdf).

Barsade, S. (2002) 'The ripple effect: Emotional contagion and its Influence on group behavior', *Administrative Science Quarterly*, vol 47, issue 4, pp 644–75.

Blackman, L. and Venn, C. (eds) (2010) Special Issue: *Affect, Body and Society*, vol 16, no 1.

Brennan, T. (2004) *The transmission of affect*, Ithaca, NY: Cornell University Press.

Clegg, S., Courpasson, D. and Phillips, N. (2006) *Power and organisations*, London: Sage.

Down, S. and Reveley, J. (2009) 'Between narration and interaction: Situating first line supervisor identity work', *Human Relations*, vol 62, no 3, pp 379–401.

Fischer, M. (2012) 'Organizational turbulence, trouble and trauma: Theorizing the collapse of a mental health setting', *Organization Studies*, vol 33, no 9, pp 1153–73.

Fook, J. (2012) *Social work: A critical approach to practice* (2nd edn), London: Sage.

Fotaki, M. and Hyde, P. (2014) 'Organisational blind spots: Splitting, blame and idealization in the National Health Service', *Human Relations*, 14 June, doi:10.1177/0018726714530012

Froggett, L., Manley, J. and Roy, A. (2015) 'The visual matrix method: Imagery and affect in a group-based research setting', *Forum: Qualitative Research*, vol 16, no 3 (www.qualitative-research.net/index.php/fqs/article/view/2308).

Gabriel, Y. (2012) 'Organizations in a state of darkness: Towards a theory of organizational miasma', *Organization Studies*, vol 33, no 9, pp 1137–52.

Goodwin, M.H. (2006) *The hidden life of girls: Games of stance, status and exclusion*, Malden, MA: Blackwell.

Hammed, S. (2004) 'Affective economies', *Social Text*, vol 22, no 2, pp 117–39.

Hardt, M. (1999) 'Affective labour', *Boundary 2*, vol 26, no 2, pp 89–100.

Healy, K. (2000) *Social work practices*, London: Sage.

Jacques, E. (1956) *Measurement of responsibility: A study of work, payment, and individual capacity*, London: Tavistock.

Jordan, B. (2011) 'Making sense of the "Big Society": Social work and the moral order', *Journal of Social Work*, vol 12, no 6, pp 630–46.

Kemper, T. (2000) 'Social models in the explanation of emotions', in M. Lewis and J. Haviland-Jones (eds) *The handbook of emotions* (2nd edn), New York: Guilford Press, pp 91–115.

Klein, M. (1952) 'Some theoretical conclusions regarding the emotional life of the infant', in *Envy and gratitude and other works 1946–1963*, Hogarth Press and the Institute of Psycho-Analysis (published 1975).

Menzies Lyth, I. (1960) 'A case in the functioning of social systems as a defence against anxiety: A report on a study of the nursing service of a general hospital', *Human Relations*, vol 13, pp 95–121.

Morrison, T. (1997) 'Emotionally competent child protection organisations: Fallacy, fiction or necessity?', in J. Bates, R. Pugh and N. Thompson (eds) *Protecting children: Challengers and changes*, Aldershot: Arena, pp 193–211.

Morrison, T. (2007) 'Emotional intelligence, emotion and social work: Context, characteristics, complications and contribution', *British Journal of Social Work*, vol 37, no 2, pp 245–63.

Reddy, W. (2001) *The navigation of feelings: A framework for the history of emotions*, Cambridge: Cambridge University Press.

Ruch, G. and Murray, C. (2011) 'Anxiety, defences and the primary task in integrated children's services: Enhancing inter-professional practice', *Journal of Social Work Practice*, vol 25, no 4.

Tomkins S. (1963) *Affect, imagery, consciousness, Vol 2: The negative affects*, New York: Springer.

Walton, R.E. (1987) *Managing conflict* (2nd edn), Menlo Park, CA: Addison Wesley.

Watson, T.J. (1997) 'The labour of division: The manager as "self" and "other"', *The Sociological Review*, pp 139–52.

Watson, T.J. (2001) *In search of management: Culture, chaos and control in managerial work*, Andover: Thomson Learning.

Warner, J. (2015) *Emotional politics in child protection*, Bristol: Policy Press.

Wetherell, M. (2012) *Affect and emotion: A new social science understanding*, London: Sage.

Whittaker, A. (2011) 'Social defences and organisational culture in a local authority child protection setting: Challenges for the Munro Review?', *Journal of Social Work Practice*, vol 25, no 4.

5

Once a risk always a risk – So what exactly are we assessing?

Introduction

This case study considers an adult male in his early thirties who had sexually abused his sibling as a child. Care proceedings were initiated due to the potential risk to his newborn daughter. An assessment had been carried out that highlighted some risks to the child in terms of the potential for neglect, but that there were no issues with regard to sexual abuse. However, the Family Placement team manager concerned didn't accept the assessment and attempted to undermine the outcome, to the extent that he attempted to misrepresent the case entirely to the child's guardian during a meeting to look at the potential for reunification.

In this chapter, we examine how the perception of others can lead to a presumption of ongoing risk, despite indicators to the contrary. We also think about our own value base and the extent to which this alters the way in which we view those with whom we work. The difficulty of proving a 'negative' was key in this case. As has often been shown in the media, it is easy with hindsight to show where things have gone wrong, but it is very difficult to prove how children have not been harmed as a result of direct social work action. How, then, does one evidence an absence of risk? And how do we reconcile the entrenched views of others while drawing from a social work value base that emphasises there may be a chance positive change has occurred?

Case study

James (aged 34) appeared to have finally got his life together. Married to Marie (aged 28), they had just moved into their first home after years of living in a one-bedroomed council flat. James had been working as a fabricator for a steel works for the last three years and, with Marie's wages from a part-time secretarial job, they had managed to save a deposit for a small house in disrepair. It wasn't much, but it was theirs. They were planning on settling in, fixing the place up and then starting a family. However, within a few weeks Marie became pregnant and Louise was born a year to the day after they had moved into their new home.

Marie loved children and, although it came as a shock, the couple were delighted. She was particularly pleased that her nephew Matthew would have someone to play with. The six-year-old was a frequent visitor to the family home, and James enjoyed spending time with him, so much so that it had been arranged that James would collect him from holiday club during the six-week summer holidays. Marie's sister worked full time and so, as James tended to finish early, he would collect Matthew and care for him for a couple of hours until Marie finished work.

Social workers became aware of this arrangement when James was recognised by the mother of one of the other children at the holiday club. As someone who used to live next door to James as a child, she had recalled some gossip about the family from other neighbours. The referrer had been unsure about what to do and so spoke to her own mother who had remembered the family well, and they were both sufficiently concerned to report the matter to us.

The history of the family was complex. James was the eldest of four siblings and lived with his brothers, Andrew and Raymond, along with their sister Polly, in an over-crowded privately rented house. Their mother, Stephanie was a single parent who had had several live-in boyfriends. It was unclear who had fathered the children. As a result, the children had other 'half-siblings' of various ages in the area who would come and stay periodically when they had had fallen out with their families, only to move out again after a few weeks. This led to an atmosphere of chaos in which the right to a bed of his own couldn't be taken for granted, and James would frequently find himself either squeezing into a bed with whoever happened to be there, or sleeping in the bath covered by a jacket or a towel.

When Raymond was nine, he told a lunchtime supervisor at school that his eight-year-old sister Polly had disclosed that James had been "touching her front bottom", and that she didn't like it. James was 11 at the time. A joint investigation under Section 47 of the Children Act 1989 between the police and social care was initiated; however, both James and Polly denied that anything had happened. Stephanie refuted that anything inappropriate could have happened, as "my children are never left alone." She stated that the children would not have had the opportunity to do anything of which she would not have been aware.

As there was no evidence of any specific child protection concerns, the investigation didn't proceed further. The family was offered ongoing support from the local children's centre as Stephanie was struggling to care for the children alone; however, shortly after, a boyfriend moved into the family home and the intervention ceased. Stephanie's boyfriend worked full time. The family's fortunes appeared to have changed for the better, and the need for support was greatly lessened. The case was subsequently closed.

Sexual abuse, risk and actuarial assessments

Harmful sexual behaviour includes using sexually explicit words and phrases, inappropriate touching, using sexual violence or threats or having full penetrative sex with other children or adults. Children and young people who develop harmful sexual behaviour are believed to harm themselves and others. Sexual behaviour between children is also considered harmful if one of the children is much older – particularly if there is more than two years' difference in age, or if one of the children is pre-pubescent and the other is not (Davies, 2012).

It is important to highlight that disclosing any kind of sexual abuse, whether it occurs between children or a child and an adult, is difficult. There are many reasons why a young child might choose to deny having made a disclosure, and Salter (1995, p 243) has discussed the burden placed on children to keep the secret:

> The child is viewed as having betrayed the family by telling "strangers," and such children are frequently pressured to recant…. Denial is not a door that victims exit; it is a line that victims walk back and forth many times before moving forward.

In other words, a retracted disclosure is much more complex than simply saying that the child has lied. There may be much more going on. The fact that a child recants doesn't mean that abuse has never happened; it often means that pressure has been applied to the child and the child has acquiesced.

If a child has been a perpetrator of sexual abuse, assessing whether they pose a risk to other children and adults when they grow older requires social workers to undertake a comprehensive assessment. Interest in the concept of risk in the context of social work research, theory, education and practice has grown rapidly over the past 10 to 15 years, encompassing an increasingly wide range of questions and areas of enquiry (Warner and Sharland, 2010). On the micro level, this has included empirical work on the processes of risk assessment with specific service user groups; on the meso level, the development of organisational and cross-organisational strategies of risk management; and on the macro level, an analysis of how practice is conducted in a risk society. Trying to balance risks with rights or with needs often leads social workers into debates about how risk itself should be defined and how these definitions should then be operationalised.

Criminal justice is the field that is possibly the most influenced by the media and the views of the wider public in relation to the dangerousness of offenders and the vulnerability of their future victims (Webb, 2006; Barry, 2007). The criminal justice system is also believed to house the most risk assessment tools, mainly actuarial rather than clinical, which has resulted in a preoccupation with how risk factors can be measured. This has often been argued to come at the expense of what exactly is being measured, to what end, and whether other forms of intervention may not prove more effective in reducing longer-term offending (Stanley, 2011). Supervising social workers have been criticised for using actuarial tools to make defensible decisions that often relate to matters of how the perceived perpetrator can be contained rather than search for a resolution (see Barry, 2007). Organisational culture undoubtedly plays a factor in influencing the way a risk is perceived and managed within that agency, and the following case study explores how this kind of situation can occur.

Reflection points

1. When I think of the enormity of the situation, of how it must feel for children to disclose sexual abuse, it seems only reasonable that they later recant their allegations. Pause for a moment and imagine what it would be like if you found yourself in a similar situation at that age.
2. Even if you were brave enough to disclose abuse, what would you do if you were then threatened by the offender? Or your family became angry with you? Or the perpetrator was arrested and taken from the family home? Then your neighbours and your friends at school find out about it and your whole world comes down around you?
3. What if all your siblings also pressurised you to say that you were attention-seeking and it didn't happen?
4. And what if your abuser made you feel it was your fault that it happened in the first place? That you were equally to blame, if not more so. You would be the one getting into trouble – because of what you did.
5. All you would need to do to get your life back, and make it all go away, is say it didn't happen. What would you do?

The case was reopened two years later when Raymond, now aged 11, was admitted to hospital having taken an overdose of Paracetamol. There was considerable concern that such a young child might wish to harm himself, and following a great deal of sensitive work carried out by the allocated social worker, Raymond finally disclosed that he and James had been having sexual contact on and off for the last two years, but felt that he would never now be believed. It transpired that the sexual relationship between them had developed on a gradual basis. From the evidence, I was able to gather it appeared that the boys had turned to each other for a level of human comfort, and it had actually been Raymond who had instigated the sexual contact on the first few occasions but had then wanted it to stop. However, James had then threatened to tell their mother and Raymond was afraid of getting into trouble.

Despite Raymond's view that to a degree it had commenced 'consensually', it did appear that there was then a level of coercion. Raymond was clear, however, that at no time had James been aggressive towards him; in fact, he had been careful to ensure that Raymond was not physically harmed. But there was one notable factor that emerged during discussions, and that was how James would always insist on Raymond never looking at him and that he should always look at the wall when the abuse was happening. A further Section 47 investigation was undertaken, and both children provided a formal statement to the police. Although evidential medicals were completed these were inconclusive, although in interview James admitted that Raymond's account was accurate.

Reflection point

1. What struck me more than anything about this case was the fact that Raymond had originally disclosed on behalf of his sister, even though he was also, in fact, the victim. Having gone through the difficulty of raising the issue and dealing with the aftermath of his family's reaction to it, it would seem extraordinary that Raymond would not try to help himself and prevent the abuse from continuing. So, I couldn't help wondering, why did Raymond not tell anyone?

When I revisited this question with him as an adult, Raymond told me that he had had two thoughts. His first thought had been to "test the water"; he wanted to gauge the reaction from adults to see how they responded to what he had said. He said that if the family had accepted his story about his sister, then he had intended telling them what was really happening to him. However, he was also scared that people would think he was gay. This is indicative of gender analysis research carried out by Alaggia (2005) with regard to the disclosure of child sexual abuse. It found that for males the themes that inhibited disclosure were fear of being seen as homosexual, feelings of isolation due to the belief that boys are rarely victims and fear of becoming an abuser. Raymond had also thought that by telling others about his sister's abuse, James would be sent to prison and he would no longer abuse Raymond. He also thought that if the family split up because of the allegation, then it would be seen as his sister's fault.

However, Raymond told me that what actually happened was that it "all just took off like a runaway train, police, social workers. No one even asked if it was happening to me. My mum knew I was lying, but she didn't see why. I was in so much trouble with everyone. I was scared. I knew they would never believe me now. So I just said I lied to get James in trouble. Then Max [Stephanie's new partner] moved in and we got back to what was our 'normal'."

The sexual abuse against Raymond became more frequent following this episode, and the fact that the family now saw him as a troublemaker and a liar meant that James felt safe to abuse him, even when other people were in the house. Research carried out by the Children's Protection Society (2003) suggested sexual abuse of one sibling by another is significantly more common than that by a parent. In addition, Hatch and Northam (2005) found that in sibling abuse 'grooming' of the victim into compliance is more easily achieved due to their close proximity and ease of access.

Aged 13, James was then above the age of criminal responsibility. At the time, children aged between 10 and 14 could be tried for criminal behaviour in the UK under the Children and Young Persons Act 1963, provided the prosecution could prove they were aware of the nature of their act and that it was seriously wrong. The case was referred to the Crime Prosecution Service (CPS) for a decision about whether or not to take the case to Court. Remarkably, although James had admitted what he had done and there was clear evidence to suggest that he was culpable, the CPS felt that it was not in the public interest to prosecute. Significant weight was placed on the fact that James was very young and although he was the perpetrator, the law had to consider his best interests and welfare, as well as those of the victim, including considering the likely effect that a conviction might have on him in the future.

Therefore, the judge had to consider the 1989 United Nations Convention on the Rights of the Child and in this instance, the ruling went in James' favour. The seriousness of the allegation and the forensic evidence was outweighed by the fact that James had readily admitted his guilt. Instead, it was agreed that an out-of-court disposal was appropriate, and James was placed in a secure unit on welfare grounds, alongside a Care Order that granted the local authority shared parental responsibility with Stephanie. This meant that he could receive treatment for his offending behaviour and also ensure the safety of his siblings, as there were grave doubts regarding Stephanie's ability to protect. James spent the next two years in 'secure', and was then placed with a specialist foster carer until the age of 16. The foster carer Zoe wanted James to remain with her longer but due to funding cuts, there were no available resources for this to happen. James moved into his own bedsit. However, the relationship between James and Zoe continued, and Zoe became a godmother to Louise. James later told me that he wished Zoe could have been the mother he'd never had.

The assessment

The situation I was now faced with was a couple with a newborn and doubts regarding not only whether James still posed a sexual risk, but also if his wife understood those potential risks sufficiently to act appropriately in order to protect their daughter. As my organisation didn't wish to separate Marie from Louise, it was agreed that James would stay with a friend while the assessment was carried out. In the meantime, James' contact with Louise would be supervised.

Reflection points

1. What is your assessment of the risks posed?

The assessment of risk with regard to historical sexual abuse is always likely to be complex, particularly when the perpetrator was a child at the time the offences were committed. I was aware that it takes time to complete. I wanted, and needed, to be methodical and gather the historical information in order to place those offences in their appropriate context; I needed time to get to know those involved in the assessment. I wanted to develop a good rapport with all of them, even though I would have to ask some difficult questions. More importantly, perhaps, I needed to draw on expert knowledge and skills in order to make sense of the information I had and analyse it in a way that took account of all of the possible variables. This would mean for example, considering the risk a person may pose and to whom, and thinking about what circumstances might increase the likelihood of further abuse happening, but also taking into consideration the kinds of protective factors that are already present that might reduce that perceived risk.

2. Do you feel that you have the skills to deal with this kind of case? Why?

In terms of developing my specialist role, I had spent many years honing my knowledge and skills through extensive postgraduate training, and I did feel I was suitably qualified for the task. Although this was a complex case, it wasn't the most difficult case I had worked on in my practice. I did, however, feel worried and apprehensive. I wanted to make sure that I 'got it right' in that I would make the right decisions for all involved: Marie, Louise and James. However, I was also concerned about those who we had not got it right for in the past: Polly, Raymond and also James.

3. How do you make a decision when others' views conflict with your own?

Munro (2008) found evidence of social workers rejecting information from both children and junior staff such as day nursery helpers and junior nurses when the information didn't conform to their preconceptions. I had to therefore make sure that my own biases didn't affect the assessment process, and I felt this was an aspect I could only consider properly in supervision. I would need to get an objective perspective on my subjective thoughts and feelings.

As part of the assessment I spent a great deal of time over the period of two months with James and Marie in discussion and completing actuarial testing of James. Actuarial tools are used to support the decision-making process in complex cases, which I always found useful; however, I was mindful that Kirkman and Melrose (2014) criticised the way in which they have been used by social workers they evaluated. They observed that practitioners either rely on decision-making tools too heavily or not enough. I wanted to make sure that I used an intuitive actuarial tool that would enable me to use my professional judgement that was informed by a decision-making process.

I therefore spent my time with James asking him about the behaviours of concern, including the offences against his brother, Raymond. I wanted to understand his views on his own childhood and why he felt the abuse started. I also needed to know whether he accepted responsibility for his behaviour and what his attitude was now towards Raymond. We talked about the therapeutic programme he had completed while in the secure unit, and I was able to discuss his case with some of the members of his original therapy team, those who treated him, as well as access his case notes. It appeared that James had been deeply troubled as a boy and had suffered not only neglect from Stephanie, but also physical abuse from her partners. It also appeared that James was not a 'fixated' child abuser, one who has a primary sexual attraction to children; rather, he had been assessed as a 'situational abuser'.

According to Groth (1999), when we describe someone as a 'situational abuser', their primary sexual attraction is to adult females and not children. Their sexual contact with children has most likely developed as a response to abuse and is used as a coping strategy for external stressors in order to help them feel better about themselves. Therefore, being removed from perceived stressors and being given the opportunity to develop more appropriate coping strategies should have reduced James' need to act out his stress sexually. While this may be seen as a fairly male–orientated, heteronormative view of child abuse, I feel that nevertheless it was useful in this case.

In addition, I gathered that his time in the secure unit had been the most stable period of his whole childhood. He had been able to take full advantage of the opportunities for recovery and could develop appropriate relationships for the first time in his life. He felt it was this opportunity that then allowed him to build an appropriate relationship with his foster carer, Zoe, and also Marie. James told me that without Jack and Claire (therapists) he would have had no idea what appropriate relationships looked like; all he had known was pain and sadness. James felt that it was through therapy that he grown to understand what he had done to Raymond, and that it had been his way of dealing with the extreme emotional difficulties in other aspects of his life.

Research carried out by Cortoni and Marshall (2001) found that intimacy deficits and loneliness create negative emotional states; a corresponding need is required to relieve such states. Sexual activity therefore provides therefore a powerfully pleasurable experience that can temporarily relieve such negative emotional states. In some people, sex may easily come to serve as a coping mechanism to deal with loneliness and intimacy problems. The benefit of such a coping strategy is, however, short-lived and not satisfactory, as it doesn't address the original stressor.

While James was in the secure unit, Stephanie didn't visit him, and at the time of my assessment, he had no idea where she was. He had resumed a relationship with Raymond and Polly, and while his brother was still angry with him for what had happened, they were all able to spend time together at family gatherings, and he and Raymond went fishing together most weekends. Although Raymond hadn't entirely put it behind him, his view was that James was as much a victim of their childhood as he was. For example, he told me: "I don't like what happened to us, to us as a family, but he's my brother and I think he is truly sorry. He has to live with it as much as me. That must play on his mind more than it does mine."

In addition to the clinical interviews that I carried out, as part of the assessment of James I also employed the use of actuarial assessment tools that measured the static (unchangeable) factors associated with future offending. For example, relevant to James' case would be that sexual reoffending is more common among those who have prior sexual offences, one or more boy victims, victims who are not family members, and who have shown a sexual preference for children

(Hanson and Bussière, 1996a, b; Hanson, 1997). However, from what I gathered, there was no evidence that James had abused anyone other than his brother or had shown any interest in children per se, particularly those outside the family.

While no form of assessment can accurately predict the future, research has shown that a combination of these two forms of assessment can allow for a more robust decision-making regarding risk. Clinical expertise (appropriate academic, clinical and legal training, knowledge of the risk literature), coupled with some form of statistical prediction, allows the greatest accuracy of prediction at the present time (Hart, 1995). Thus, there is general agreement among risk assessment professionals that an increased number of factors considered by both clinical and actuarial methods can lead to more accurate risk assessments (Bjorkly, 1993; Clark et al, 1993; Shaffer et al, 1994; Grubin, 1999). Therefore, by combining the predictive power of both clinical and actuarial methods, a more accurate determination of risk can be made in sentencing as well as in release risk management and planning.

Given all of the information gathered from my assessment, I was of the view that James would be able to return home to live with Marie and Louise, but that given their troubled histories, that family support would have a role to play in helping James and Marie adapt to family life.

Acceptance of the outcome

My assessment was completed and signed off by a senior manager. It was then filed at Court as part of the local authority's evidence. Given that I was not involved in the case other than to complete the professional assessment of James, I was regarded as an expert witness and so had no other contact with the family with regard to the Care Proceedings. My only other outstanding task in this case was to make myself available to the Court during the hearing in case I was called to give evidence, and to be cross-examined by the legal representatives for James and Marie or the children's guardian. The role of the children's guardian is that of an independent representative of the child who is there to ensure the rights or interests of that child are placed before the Court for consideration.

I had been confident in the recommendations I had made and the report I had subsequently submitted. I was pleased to hear that the judge also felt that it was one of the best risk assessments she had ever read. This would have strongly indicated to the other parties that they should accept all my findings. This was good news for me and for James and his family. James' representative was, of course, very happy to accept the assessment, as it was precisely what they had wanted to hear as it strengthened their case to have James returned to the family home. The guardian, Bernard, was also satisfied with my findings and made a comment in his report that the risk factors had been carefully analysed and that he, too, was satisfied that James no longer posed a risk to children. However, despite having had the report scrutinised by senior social care managers, a judge, a clinical psychologist, three barristers and an experienced children's guardian, there was someone who was not happy with the outcome.

During the course of the Care Proceedings a newly appointed agency team manager, called Robert, took over the team in which the allocated social worker for this case was based, and as such took over management of the case. As part of a process of bringing himself up to date with the cases within the team, he had read my assessment and asked to discuss it with Jenny, the senior manager who had signed off the report.

I didn't find out about this immediately, and it was only when Jenny and I had supervision that it was mentioned. Jenny told me that Robert was unhappy with the assessment as he didn't agree that someone who had been a risk as a young person could now be considered as 'unlikely to reoffend'. His view was that anyone who had committed a sexual offence should never be allowed into a home with children and, as a result, he felt the plan should change.

Reflection 'in' action

I was quite taken aback when I heard this. First, because I felt that every avenue had been explored with the family and that I was as sure as I reasonably could be that James no longer posed a significant risk; second, because Robert had been the only professional who felt differently; and third, because I felt that such judgements were incompatible with social work values and ethical principles, for example, the human rights value (see BASW, 2017), which outlines how social workers should identify and adhere to practising ethically by making sure that the strengths of all individuals are considered.

I have always considered the concept of 'challenging practice' an important aspect of my own development and accountability, and I believed that this should have played a key role in my supervisions. Therefore, I had consciously used supervision sessions to get an objective view on my practice that would assist me to identify any assumptions I may have made or any particular behaviours or bias I had exhibited that could have questioned my practice.

I took a step back from how I felt and asked Jenny what her view was of Robert's statement. Jenny said that she had been surprised but that she understood because "it's sexual abuse". I asked her what she meant, and she told me that many workers struggle to understand sexual abuse, and that they will always see offenders as being a risk. This annoyed me so I challenged this by saying that while Robert was entitled to a personal view, it shouldn't cloud his professional judgement.

I have to admit that I was particularly concerned about the potential of there being disruption with regard to the Care Proceedings, which were going well and were likely to conclude within the next six weeks with a recommendation from all parties that James should return to live within the family home. I was concerned that if Robert, a team manager, was voicing views while the case was in progress, they could panic the guardian by leading him to believe that the local authority was not in control of the situation. I was worried such comments would cast doubt on all of the hard work carried out by the allocated social worker, the family, and not to mention my own frustration at being professionally undermined.

I was annoyed but I agreed with Jenny that I would make time to speak to Robert about his views. I am pleased that I did. It was only during our discussion that I learned that, while he was an experienced manager, he had not had any formal training with regard to carrying out risk assessments with sex offenders. He said that he had "studiously avoided them whenever possible. I don't like sex offenders." This annoyed me once more, but I calmly discussed his view of the assessment, giving him the opportunity to voice his concerns.

Robert told me that he could not understand how I could take the view that James was at 'very low risk' of reoffending. I took a breath and explained my findings that generated from numerous meetings with all the family alongside the results of the actuarial testing I had carried out on James. I also discussed how Marie had been assessed by a clinical psychologist who had seen her as part of the proceedings, and had had access to my report, and that collectively we were as sure as we could be that there would be no concerns.

However, despite me stating my case, it is important to consider if Robert did have a legitimate concern, and in order to do this it is important to explore whether young people do go on to reoffend in cases of childhood sexual abuse. The findings suggest that children with sexual behaviour problems, as a group, pose a low long-term risk for future child sexual abuse perpetration and other sex-related crimes. A 10-year long-term follow-up study by Carpentier et al (2006) of children under the age of 13 with sexual problems found reoffending rates of 2–10 per cent at 10-year follow-up depending on the type of treatment received. In addition, similar rates for teenage offenders have consistently been found in the US by several research studies including Alexander (1999) and Caldwell (2007), within the range of 5–15 per cent, the 5 per cent accounting for those who had completed some sort of treatment programme.

Reflection 'in' action

It could still be argued that even these very low rates are unacceptably high, and that Robert's view that we should err on the side of caution is entirely appropriate. My experience has taught me that such justifications are overly simplistic and often misguided and so are unhelpful in terms of advising the Court. In addition, I felt that it was poor practice that, as a local authority, we would offer an individual an assessment that promised to be conducted without bias, only to decide that because a team manager didn't like sex offenders, we would not uphold our duty.

I am aware that some reading this may now recognise that actually Robert and I were both in a similar position, where our professional values were perhaps conflicting with our personal ones. While Robert was allowing his personal views to cloud his professional judgement, I felt that my decision-making was being undermined. Being seen as credible is a social work characteristic trait that is performed when we are in interaction with others (Leigh, 2017). Philip

Manning (2000, p 284) once suggested that credibility was 'the quality of being believable', and that this quality was 'integral to both trust and deception'. In this instance, I felt my professional integrity was being questioned, and this situation was suggesting I could not be trusted. It made me feel very angry and upset.

I felt that we needed to reach an agreement, and the only way to do this would be to address the conflict that had emerged between us. This was particularly difficult as Robert appeared to disagree with most of my conclusions, and as Hocker and Wilmot (1995) noted, conflict transpires when there is the perception of incompatible goals and interference from the other party in achieving one's goals. I felt frustrated and unsure of how to progress.

I decided to speak to Jenny again, and she agreed to speak to Robert. I was expecting her to say something along the lines of, "the local authority has a plan which has been carefully thought through and tested and the Court is satisfied with the arrangements". I have to admit that I also secretly hoped Robert would be reminded that if he did not agree with the plan or how the local authority conducted its business, he was under no obligation to stay! However, I wasn't hopeful. I was really disappointed to learn that what actually happened was that Jenny had said "Nobody likes working with sex offenders, but we've got no choice. It's too late now anyway, so let's go with what we've got." I was less than pleased when I heard this. However, I didn't have the time to argue, and got on with other work and awaited the final hearing. Robert and I had agreed to disagree and to leave the Court to deliberate.

Just a few weeks before the final hearing I was asked to attend a brief planning meeting with our legal team and with Bernard, the children's guardian, to look in detail at the proposed plan for James to return home, should the Court agree, which now seemed likely. During the meeting, the allocated social worker was asked to outline the case. Although the social worker was extremely competent, Robert continually interrupted with comments of his own, which were distracting and didn't add anything of value to the discussion. I was then asked to talk through my assessment and the rationale behind my conclusions and recommendations. After doing this, Bernard said that he felt that everything that could have been done on this case had been done, and that he was satisfied the appropriate plans were now in place to conclude the case and allow James to move back into the family home and care for their daughter. He said he was curious, however, purely from a professional point of view, as to why it was that James always insisted on Raymond facing the wall when he was abusing him. He wondered if had anything to do with James feeling bad about the abuse.

Before I had the chance to answer Robert jumped in, "It's all to do with power. He just wanted to dominate him and telling him what to do was just part of it. There are probably lots of other things he did to sexually bully him but we will never know the true extent of what that child went through." He followed this statement up with, "That's what these people are like. They can never be trusted." Robert therefore felt that James had told Raymond to look at the wall in order to make him more frightened and to show him that he could do whatever he liked. "It's just about power. These people can't stop. It's a compulsion." Everyone in the room was taken aback by this outburst, and in an effort to salvage the situation, I suggested it might be helpful to take a short break, after which I would be happy to share my thoughts on the case. Both Bernard and each of the legal representatives said they felt that this would be helpful.

As soon as we took a break, I took Robert into a side office and asked what he was doing. He refused to discuss the comments and rather abruptly announced that he was leaving to go to another meeting. "You can all do what you like; you've made your minds up anyway." I was annoyed and disappointed that Robert had left me to try and salvage the situation alone. I walked back into the room and took a deep breath. I explained that from my research I had found that at some level the vast majority of abusers knew that what they were doing was harmful and, in turn, develop distorted views about appropriate behaviour in order to justify their actions.

I returned to Robert's point by explaining that there are situations where individuals have sexually abused children and find it difficult to accept that they have abused children. I went on to explain that this action was partly due to an avoidance of cognitive dissonance (see Festinger, 1957), that is, an avoidance of holding contradictory beliefs. So, for example, a person may think, "People who sexually abuse children are bad; I am not a bad person", therefore "I cannot be a sexual abuser." A cognitive dissonance would occur if a person held two opposing opinions simultaneously: "I cannot be a sexual abuser" and "I have sexually abused". Such challenges to an individual's attitudes and beliefs are immensely powerful, and can lead to the adoption of numerous defence mechanisms in order for the individual to preserve their cognitive integrity.

However, in order to assess for the presence of such cognitive dissonance, I framed my discussions with James around the concepts of guilt and shame. Guilt and shame are terms that are often used interchangeably, although they have very different meanings. Shame is an egocentric, self-involved, self-focused experience. The individual immersed in a moment of shame is far more concerned with the implications of their transgression for themselves than for others (Tangney and Dearing, 2002). Therefore, instead of believing that they 'did wrong', they come to the conclusion that they 'are' wrong (that is, 'I am a bad person'). Unfortunately this doesn't assist the person in being able to stop the behaviour that generated the emotion in the first place. Guilt, on the other hand, is associated with empathy for those who have been harmed by the individual's actions, thus facilitating reparative action. Empathy is crucial to the development of trusting relationships (Rogers, 1961), and promotes altruistic behaviour (Eisenberg, 2000), and suppresses aggression (Saami, 1999). The relevance of such emotions in assessment is that if shame inhibits the experience of empathy and guilt facilitates it, it would be very important to understand James' emotions as he disclosed his behaviours towards his family.

I then referred Bernard back to his question regarding the reason for James insisting that Raymond look at the wall during the abuse. I explained that my belief was that this was a defence mechanism, which protected James from having to deal with two opposing beliefs: one being a source of protection ('I'm not really hurting him'), the other being faced, through the evidence of Raymond's distress, with the reality of the harm he was inflicting. It appeared that James, through the process of therapy and now a greater level of maturity, was able to recognise that although he was not a 'bad person', he had done a very bad thing. Alongside the evidence I had garnered from other agencies and from the other areas of the assessment I was therefore able to conclude that James posed a reduced risk to children.

I was pleased to hear that those present agreed with my findings and the outcome of the assessment. They signed off the plan for James to return to his family. As we left the meeting, the allocated social worker and I looked at each other and breathed an audible sigh of relief. Despite Robert airing his views in an inappropriate manner, we had managed to reassure the professionals that thorough assessments had been carried out. All being well, James would be return home and we would offer the family the right support to get their lives back on track.

Reflection 'on' action

In my time, when I have asked people, members of the public and professionals alike, whether individuals who have sexually abused others as a child will always pose a risk to others, they have normally said 'yes'. And sadly, the conversation has ended there. In my experience, this simplification of the problem prevents two things from happening – first, having to contemplate what we mean by 'risk', and second, how we then go on to consider whether there is a possibility for change to occur.

So what is risk? Risk is a judgement that recognises we don't know what to do in a particular context (Webb, 2006). My practice has taught me that when we talk about risk management, the most effective of approaches is to say 'no'. In this case, by not allowing James to have contact with children would have removed the risk. However, this decision negates the possibility of individuals being able to have future positive and meaningful relationships, not just with children, but also with adults. It also makes it much more likely that individuals will become isolated and disconnected from society and, in turn, that disconnect will increase the risk of future offending behaviour (Tangney, 1992).

I believe that the only way to deal with thinking about the risk individuals may pose is to listen to them. When I have spent time listening to them, I have often learned how that person has reached a stage where they recognise that what they did wasn't right, that it hurt someone else. However, they have often said that as long as people have seen them as 'other', they have struggled to make a change. For example, Tangney (1991) found that guilt-prone individuals might experience greater difficulty if they feel responsible for the other person's distress. Rather than repair, it could create a vicious circle for sex offenders, where negative affect such as guilt is an antecedent to sexual offending, and where the knowledge that one is responsible for their victim's distress exacerbates feelings of personal distress and guilt.

I still feel humbled by the trust people have put in me when sharing their narrative of what they have done during their darkest hours, which are often accompanied by stories of deep-rooted fear, shame and guilt. This is not to say that I condone their behaviour; absolutely not. The damage that sex offenders do to their victims and their families can be catastrophic and can have life-long consequences. However, by hearing them, we at least have a chance of preventing further damage to lives, their own included.

Summary

Social work is an activity that is inevitably bound by and preoccupied with managing risk. The Department of Education has tried to develop sophisticated technologies and systems that attempt to manage risk so that professionals can find it easier to make decisions (Webb, 2006). This preoccupation with risk has often been driven by a rhetoric that risk can be controlled and that society should be made safe (Giddens, 1991; Beck, 1992). We live in a risk society, and individuals often find they are being monitored by institutions whose aim it is to determine what is safe and what is not (Beck, 1992). The problem is that the concept of risk changes depending on values, views, contexts and new anxieties.

It is important to acknowledge that we live in a blame culture, a culture where people increasingly point the finger at others, a culture that makes it difficult for social workers to work with risk (Leigh, 2017). This is reiterated by the fact that in the UK, the number of complaints made to Children's Social Care (CSC) agencies has increased by 500 per cent in the last five years (Webb, 2017). Although actuarial tools are commonplace in social work practice, many argue for these to be used in conjunction with other skills, thus as a way to support current practice rather than to replace it (Webb, 2006; Kirkman and Melrose; 2014; Wilkins, 2015). Reflection, both in action and on action, is, therefore, an integral part of social work practice when attempting to work with or manage risk.

Further reading
Webb, S. (2006) *Social work in a risk society: Social and political perspectives*, London: Palgrave Macmillan
    This path-breaking text constructs a new way of thinking about social work based on contemporary social theory. Working in a counter-tradition that is suspicious of a number of governing ideas and practices in social work, it draws on themes from Beck, Giddens and Rose to explore the impact of risk society and neoliberalism on social work.

Calder, M. (2007) *Working with young children who sexually abuse: Taking the field forward*, Lyme Regis: Russell House Publishing

This volume builds on research and theory; assessment; intervention; treatment; engagement; and management and outcomes. It draws on an even wider range of professional disciplines, continues to offer a range of perspectives, and crucially extends the availability of options for workers. Using typologies to individualise the assessment, treatment and supervision of young people who sexually abuse, this book provides a theoretical model of rehabilitation, reducing risks and promoting strengths with adolescent sexual offenders as well as emerging personality disorders in sexually harmful young people. The relationship between deviant arousal and sexual recidivism in adolescent sex offenders is also explored.

References

Alaggia, R. (2005) 'Disclosing the trauma of child sexual abuse: A gender analysis', *Journal of Loss and Trauma*, vol 10, no 5, pp 453–70.

Alexander, M.A. (1999) 'Sexual offenders treatment efficacy revisited', *Sexual Abuse: A Journal of Research and Treatment*, vol 11, no 2, pp 101–16.

Barry, M. (2007) *Effective approaches to risk assessment in social work: An international literature review*, Scottish Executive (www.gov.scot/resource/doc/194419/0052192.pdf).

BASW (British Association of Social Workers) (2017) *The code of ethics for social workers: Values and principles* (http://cdn.basw.co.uk/upload/basw_112315-7.pdf).

Beck, U. (1992) *Risk society: Towards a new modernity*, London: Sage.

Bjorkly, S. (1993) 'Scale for the prediction of aggression and dangerousness in psychotic patients, an introduction', *Psychological Reports*, vol 73, pp 1363–77.

Brizer, D. (1989) 'Introduction: Overview of current approaches to the prediction of violence', in D. Brizer and M. Crowner (eds) *Current approaches to the prediction of violence*, Washington, DC: American Psychiatric Press, Inc, pp xi–xxx.

Calder, M. (2007) *Working with young children who sexually abuse: Taking the field forward*, Lyme Regis: Russell House Publishing.

Caldwell, M.F. (2007) 'Sexual offense adjudication and sexual recidivism among juvenile offenders', *Sexual Abuse: A Journal of Research and Treatment*, vol 19, pp 107–13.

Carpentier, M., Silovsky, J., Chaffin, M. and La Greca, A.M. (2006) 'Randomized trial of treatment for children with sexual behavior problems: Ten-year follow-up', *Journal of Consulting and Clinical Psychology*, vol 74, no 3, pp 482–8.

Children's Protection Society (2003) *Working together for children*, Heidelberg West, VIC: Children's Protection Society Inc.

Clark, D., Fisher, M. and McDougall, C. (1993) 'A new methodology for assessing the level of risk in incarcerated offenders', *British Journal of Criminology*, vol 33, no 3, pp 436–48.

Cortoni, F. and Marshall, W. (2001) 'Sex as a coping strategy and its relationship to juvenile sexual history and intimacy in sexual offenders', *Sexual Abuse: A Journal of Research and Treatment*, vol 13, no 1, pp 27–43.

Davies, C. (2012) "It's not all chic to be denied your civil rights". Performing sexual and gendered citizenship in Holly Hughes'. *Preaching to the Perverted, Sexualities*, vol 15 , no 3, pp 277-96.

Eisenberg, N. (2000) 'Motion, regulation, and moral development', *Annual Review of Psychology*, vol 51, pp 665–97.

Festinger, L. (1957) *The theory of cognitive dissonance*, Stanford, CA: Stanford University Press.

Giddens, A. (1991) *The consequences of modernity*, Cambridge: Polity Press.

Grubin, D. (1999) 'Actuarial and clinical assessment of risk in sex offenders', *Journal of Interpersonal Violence*, vol 14, no 3, pp 331–43.

Hanson, R.K. (1997) *The development of a brief actuarial risk scale for sexual offence recidivism*, Ottawa: Public Works and Government Services Canada.

Hanson, R.K. and Bussière, M.T. (1996a) *Predictors of sexual offender recidivism: A meta-analysis*, Ottawa: Public Works and Government Services Canada.

Hanson, R.K. and Bussière, M.T. (1996b) 'Sex offender risk predictors: A summary of the research results', *Forum on Corrections Research*, vol 8, no 2, pp 10–12.

Hart, S. (1995) 'The ability to predict violence and dangerousness', Technical session at the Canadian Congress on Criminal Justice, Winnipeg, Manitoba, October.

Hatch, J.M. and Northam, E. (2005) 'Adolescents who sexually abuse their siblings: A study of family factors and victim selection', PhD thesis, Melbourne: School of Behavioural Science, University of Melbourne.

Hocker, J.L. and Wilmot, W.W. (1995) *Interpersonal conflict* (4th edn), Dubuque, IA: W.C. Brown.

Kirkman, E. and Melrose, K. (2014) *Clinical judgement and decision-making in children's social care: An analysis of the 'front door' system*, London: Department for Education (www.gov.uk/government/uploads/system/uploads/attachment_data/file/305516/RR337_-_Clinical_Judgement_and_Decision-Making_in_Childrens_Social_Work.pdf).

Leigh, J. (2017) 'Credible performances: Affect and professional identity', in S. Webb (ed) *Professional identity in social work*, London: Routledge.

Manning, P. (2000) *Erving Goffman and modern sociology*, Cambridge: Polity Press.

Munro, E. (2008) 'Lessons from research on decision-making', in D. Lindsey and A. Shlonsky (eds) *Child welfare research: Advances for practice and policy*, Oxford and New York: Oxford University Press, pp 194–200.

Rogers, C. (1961) *On becoming a person*, Boston. MA: Houghton Mifflin.

Saami, C. (1999) *The development of emotional competence*, New York: Guilford Press.

Salter, A.C. (ed) (1995) *Transforming trauma: A guide to understanding and treating adult survivors of child sexual abuse*, Thousand Oaks, CA: Sage.

Shaffer, Jr, C., Waters, W. and Adams, Jr, S. (1994) 'Dangerousness: Assessing the risk of violent behaviour', *Journal of Consulting and Clinical Psychology*, vol 62, no 5, pp 1064–8.

Stanley, N. (2011) *Children experiencing domestic violence: A research review*, Research in Practice, Dartington, Totnes, Devon.

Tangney. J.P. (1991) 'Moral affect: the good, the bad, and the ugly', *Journal of Personal Social Psychology*, 61, pp 598–607.

Tangney J.P. (1992) 'Situational determinants of shame and guilt in young adulthood', *Personality and Social Psychology Bulletin*, 18, pp 199–206.

Tangney, J. and Dearing, R. (2002) *Shame and guilt*, New York: Guilford Press.

Warner, J. and Sharland, E. (2010) 'Risk and social work', Editorial, *British Journal of Social Work*, vol 40, no 4, pp 1035–45.

Webb, S. (2006) *Social work in a risk society: Social and political perspectives*, London: Sage.

Webb, S. (2017) *Professional identity in social work*, London: Routledge.

Wilkins, D. (2015) 'Balancing risk and protective factors: How do social workers and social work managers analyse referrals that may indicate children are at risk of significant harm', *British Journal of Social Work*, vol 45, no 1, pp 395–411.

6

Dealing with attachment and trust issues

Introduction

This chapter discusses the experience of unwittingly placing a child in an unsafe environment, and questions how far professional relationships can be taken for granted. Broader theories are examined with regard to attachment, abuse and the child's expectations of how they might expect to be cared for. While this is not a chapter dedicated to an in-depth critique of attachment theory, I make reference to it where it pertains to the case in question. There are many useful texts in respect to this for those who wish to explore this theory further, and they are referred to at the end of the chapter.

Social workers place a great deal of faith in their multiagency colleagues, and none more so than foster carers. Having removed the child from the care of neglectful or abusive parents, the local authority has a legal, and certainly a moral, duty to ensure that the alternative carers are able to meet the needs of that particular child, however complex – what might be termed 'better than good enough'. The term 'good enough parenting' was coined by Winnicott (1965), recognising that it is unrealistic to expect parents to be perfect, and to do so undermines the vast majority of parents who are, in most respects, 'good enough' in meeting the needs of their child.

What social care asks of carers is no small task. Thinking about this from a foster carer's perspective, it could be seen as a challenging prospect, to take a child they don't know into their family and to care for them as if they are their own child, 24 hours a day, 7 days a week. Then, in addition, to be expected to work through the potential challenges of tears, tantrums, defiance and sometimes aggression in order to gradually build up a child's self-esteem, emotional intelligence and confidence. Some children arrive into foster care without the basic life skills, such as using a knife and fork, using the toilet appropriately, changing their clothes or bathing. It is a job that not many of us would envy, and I can recall many occasions when I have finally left a child in their new placement and driven away feeling relieved that I no longer had to worry about caring for the child, but recognising that it was now the foster carer who had been left with this huge responsibility.

However, although I say this, this is not entirely true, because even once the child is placed, the overall responsibility remains at all times with the social worker, and it is vital that a positive and trusting relationship is built up with the foster carer as quickly as possible. They are my eyes and ears and no one else, other than their parents, will know this child as well as their carers – the information and insight they bring to the situation is invaluable.

The issue of managing situations in which children are neglected or abused by such trusted carers is one fraught with emotion. Severe abuse in foster care does happen, but fortunately, it is very rare. Research by Biehal et al (2014) found that there were an estimated 450–550 confirmed cases of abuse or neglect in foster care per year, which equates to less than one substantiated allegation per 100 children in foster care.

One such case occurred when I was a newly qualified worker, and it was, in fact, the first time I had been involved in Care Proceedings and removed a child from the care of a parent. Looking back now, I had no idea just how vulnerable I was. As a newly qualified worker, I relied on other people who were more experienced to appropriately guide me through complex issues. The support at the time in terms of smaller caseloads and active mentoring was less obvious, and supervision was focused primarily on opening and closing cases. Taking the opportunity for critical reflection was not embedded into the practice of the agency, and so the challenge in terms of making sense of what I was seeing was missing. This often meant that both I, and the children I was looking out, for were left disillusioned.

Attachment theory

Attachment has been described as a deep and enduring emotional bond that connects one person to another across time and space (Bowlby, 1969; Ainsworth, 1973). Attachment is symbolised by specific behaviours in children, such as seeking to be close to a particular person when upset or threatened. It can be one-sided, and it doesn't have to be reciprocal. Therefore, a child may have an attachment to a person but this may not be returned (Bowlby, 1969).

Neglect and abuse at a young age can disrupt critical developmental processes that lay the foundation for healthy emotional regulation, and leave many individuals unable to tolerate, modulate and communicate painful emotions (Ruisard, 2016). Attachment behaviour in adults towards children involves responding sensitively and appropriately to the child's needs. Attachment theory provides social workers with an explanation of how a parent–child relationship can emerge, and how it then influences subsequent development.

Exploring relationships through the lens of attachment theory, one can see that there is a solid framework that supports the healing nature of human connection that is inherent in the therapeutic relationship (Ruisard, 2016). The founder of classic attachment theory, John Bowlby (1953) studied the biological attachment process between child and caregiver, and found that an instinctual bond between the two ensured the physical survival of the infant. He theorised that attachment to a primary caregiver contributes to a child's creation of intimate emotional bonds that are necessary for effective personality functioning and mental health.

Bowlby (1953) therefore proposed that attachment can be understood within a context where the caregiver provides safety and security for their infant.

A positive attachment is thus believed to improve the child's survival and subsequent development. Socially indiscriminate attachment behaviour has been repeatedly observed among children who have been raised in care (Lyons–Ruth et al, 2009). This kind of attachment can lead to indiscriminate friendliness, when children approach and interact with strangers in the same way they would their primary caregiver. In such cases, children are not scared or cautious of strangers; instead, they are overly friendly towards them. This is called indiscriminate because it is the kind of behaviour children usually save for their primary caregiver.

Offering clients an opportunity to establish new relationships not only encourages healthy attachment patterns to develop, but can also repair the damage done in early parent–child interactions by modelling effective emotional regulation techniques and setting in motion a fresh way of relating to others (Ruisard, 2016). It is within this relationship that young people can experience implicit emotional regulation from an attuned attachment figure they didn't experience during their early childhood years and, in turn, internalise these new experiences in adulthood. The following case study draws from this knowledge on attachment to explore Michael's behaviour.

Case study

Context

Nine-year-old Michael came to the notice of social care when a concerned member of the public overheard his mother asking him if he'd like to live with a local butcher (who she knew only through going into the shop). She had suggested that Michael would be useful around the house and could look after the butcher's other children when he was in the shop. Michael and his mother had already had social care contact when he had sustained a serious burn to his hand six years earlier. He had climbed on to a work surface near an unattended chip pan and had spilt the hot fat on to his skin. An assessment had been completed but no further action had been taken.

The member of the public who made this new referral was extremely concerned about this situation, and I was duly dispatched by my manager to assess what was going on.

The council estate where the families I worked with lived had a reputation for being a tough place to grow up. It was characterised by high levels of economic and social deprivation. Crime was rife and Michael grew up surrounded by violence and drug-dealing. Many of the children with whom I worked were street-wise and lived, as described by a colleague, 'free-range', meaning that there was little parental guidance or supervision. These children were difficult to reach and wary of any form of professional intervention. Michael, in contrast, appeared to crave adult attention.

It was clear that Michael had developed acute survival skills. For the most part he was left to his own devices and usually cooked for himself or foraged in the food cupboards and came and went as he pleased. He presented as quiet and shy, extremely well-mannered and cooperative on a one-to-one basis; however, he couldn't maintain this for long, and was presenting with increasing behavioural issues at school. For example, he had got into a fight with another child whose mother had died when his reaction to this news was to laugh uncontrollably. He was deeply sensitive and would react to any perceived slight, however small, by becoming inconsolable, and this again led to fights. He was known to steal from other children and lie whenever he felt it was necessary. He appeared to have problems in thinking about his own needs and continually deferred to his mother, by talking about 'we' when asked about his views. Equally, he would frequently ask me about things that I liked and immediately agree that he liked the same things too. Michael showed indiscriminate affection, and within minutes of meeting each other, I was his 'best friend' and he wanted to live in my house. Boris et al (2005) found that such indiscriminate attachments are common in children who have been maltreated, perhaps in an effort to find ways to get their needs met.

Michael had a diagnosis of attention deficit hyperactivity disorder (ADHD), and his medication was very poorly managed by his mother, so from my perspective, it was difficult to see what was related to symptoms of ADHD and what was related to neglect issues. However, I was extremely concerned that there was more going on. Although Michael had demonstrable hyperactivity and impulsivity found in ADHD, his symptoms appeared much more akin to reactive attachment disorder (RAD). From consultation with other colleagues and my own research, I had found that diagnoses were rarely straightforward, and that children with complex behaviours frequently had other co-morbid conditions. Minnis et al (2009) have argued that in clinical routines RAD is often misdiagnosed as ADHD. Taking this into consideration, I felt it was vital to get further information, and arranged for a formal psychological assessment. It was confirmed that, in addition to ADHD, Michael did have significant attachment difficulties that were likely to have resulted from an inconsistent and neglectful relationship with his mother, and that any future care arrangements would need to take account of this.

In the meantime, I had completed my social care assessment of Michael, his mother and the extended family and, as part of the commencement of Care Proceedings, a decision had been made by the Court that Michael should be removed from her care on an Interim Care Order under Section 38 of the Children Act 1989. This was due to further evidence of neglect, as it transpired that he was being increasingly left alone for long periods of time while his mother visited friends or worked. Given his age and the level of his impulsivity, it was felt that he was at risk of harm when alone in the house. No other relatives came forward to care for Michael, and so I was in the position of looking at a suitable short-term foster placement to care for him during the remainder of the proceedings, pending a final decision by the Court.

I did have a concern when looking for a suitable placement, however, and this was because I knew that children who have attachment difficulties are particularly vulnerable within the care system, and are likely to experience disrupted foster placements. This worried me as it could be an aspect that would only serve to add to Michael's difficulties. I knew that what Michael needed to start the recovery process was security and stability in his life. He needed to be placed with highly skilled foster carers who could understand and work with Michael's difficulties.

I had reflected on what he would need in terms of an alternative family, and having consulted with the Child and Adolescent Mental Health team and listened carefully to Michael's own thoughts, I came to the conclusion that he would thrive in an environment in which he was the youngest child, with plenty of opportunity for the main carer to have individual time for him, and to begin to establish an appropriate parent–child relationship. I had specified to the Family Placement team that he should be placed with a couple with older children, and that the main carer should be at home full time. Following further consultation, it was agreed that Michael should be placed with local authority foster carers, Mark and Sarah, and their two daughters, Abby (14) and Kirsty (17).

The factory in the town where the foster carers lived and worked had closed several years previously, and since then, they had struggled to find alternative work. In fact, there were a number of families in the area who had applied for and been accepted as foster carers. Michael's carers, their respective parents and their adult siblings had all had children placed with them by different local authorities. The eldest daughter of the family cited an intention to likewise become a carer as soon as she was old enough. The couple came highly recommended by their supporting social worker as being extremely motivated to support Michael during the remainder of the Care Proceedings, and to prepare him for a long-term placement or rehabilitation home.

My first impression of Mark and Sarah was that they seemed a little disinterested, and Mark, in particular, appeared quite dour. Perhaps on reflection another interpretation might have been that he was a little unfriendly and unwelcoming. Due to the urgency of the placement there was little opportunity for Michael to meet the family prior to moving in, but I had met with them and their support worker, seen his room, and was able to tell him about them during the journey. He had been very excited to get in my car and I had had to remind him to say 'goodbye' to his mother. Again, this highlighted the issue of indiscriminate attachments for me. I was a relative stranger and I was taking him off in my car to live with a new family, yet he was completely unfazed. I could imagine myself at that age being more than a little frightened at the prospect. As we left, his mother grabbed the bag of his medication from my hand, and wrote on outside of the bag in pink lipstick her new mobile telephone number. This was, she said, so that she could be doubly sure that the carers had it. I reassured her that of course her contact details would be passed on and that I would be sure to give them the bag.

Mark was out when we arrived, but Sarah welcomed us in and Abby quickly took Michael upstairs to unpack his things and look around the rest of the house while I updated the foster carer on how he was doing. Again, perhaps on reflection the fact that Mark wasn't there to meet Michael who would be living with them for possibly several months could have been significant in terms of his feelings regarding the placement, but it didn't particularly cross my mind at the time. I realise, in hindsight, this was perhaps naive of me.

Initially the placement went well. Michael was found a place at a specialist school four miles away, and he soon got used to the routine of being collected by minibus every morning.

As the allocated social worker, I, too, got into a routine. The Children Act 1989, and the resulting local authority policy and procedures, with its emphasis on child protection, meant that once a child was in care, your eye could easily be 'taken off the ball'. They were no longer 'at risk', and so the visiting pattern could be reduced on the basis that their day-to-day care was being safeguarded by their carers. This meant that I went from visiting Michael two or three times a week to making statutory visits on a six-weekly basis. Although I was making the right amount of visits, I realise now that what was missing was guidance and information in relation to what I should have been looking for when I was doing the visit.

This was at a time when the Integrated Children's System had not yet been introduced. It wouldn't be for some time that the *Framework for the assessment of children in need and their families* (DH et al, 2000) would be part of my working life. My instructions from my manager were to visit regularly and to fill in a fairly brief paper document with regard to Michael's health and wellbeing. The form that these statutory visits generally took were to chat to Michael with his carers, talk to them alone (while Michael tidied his room) to primarily update them regarding proceedings, and to find out from their point of view how the placement and contact was going. I would then spend time with Michael either in his room or we would go out for tea together. I didn't know how else to go about these visits and received little guidance other than being aware that they were a 'formality'. However, statutory visits to children in foster care are vitally important, particularly seeing the child alone. Sections 17 and 47 of the Children Act 1989 (amended by Section 53 of the Children Act 2004) outlines the legal duty to ascertain the wishes and feelings of children, particularly those in local authority care. Statutory visits were not just a legal requirement, however; it was also important that I spent time with Michael alone, not just to gain his views about how he was doing, but to understand him better. I had to think about finding a permanent placement for him, and so it was important that I had a real sense of who he was and what his needs were. Research with foster children shows they want to be heard and have their views taken into account, including the way decisions are taken in their day-to-day lives (Golding et al, 2006; Ofsted, 2009).

One thing I had learned from more experienced workers was the benefit of seeing the child away from the placement, more crucially, talking in the car. Ferguson (2011) describes this as an extremely important space in which children feel more able to talk about their troubles, and where some excellent direct work can be undertaken. I have often reflected on what it is about being in the car that assists. I feel that it is a combination of being away from placement. I also believe that while you are concentrating on the process of driving and the child is looking out of the window, there are fewer opportunities to look at each other, and so perhaps this allows children to feel less inhibited. I have worked with countless children who could not talk to me anywhere else but the car.

The first statutory visit was also attended by the foster carers' support worker. We talked about Michael's health and his ADHD medication. The fosters carers hadn't yet registered him with their local GP as he had brought a month's supply of Ritalin from home; however, I highlighted that this was important, and they agreed to take Michael along the next day after school. Other than that there appeared to be no issues. Michael had settled in well and was playing out – mostly in the garden – and one or two boys from the street had been playing football with him. He was pleased to be making new friends and was keen to spend more time with them. We also talked about his upcoming birthday. Michael wanted a "bright red bike" and a watch, and the foster carers said they would speak to his mother next time she phoned.

When we were alone Michael said he was happy and that the family were nice. He missed his mother but saw her every week and she telephoned him most weekends, but he said he was fine. I reminded him that if he had any issues about where he was living or about how contact with his mother was going then he should tell me and we would try to sort it out together. After, he mentioned wanting a "bright red bike" and a watch, and I reassured him that his mother had got him one and that he would see her that week.

Although I was not overly concerned at that time, there were two things that happened on the third statutory visit that on reflection should have alerted me that things were not quite as they seemed on the surface and that should have started the alarm bells ringing. The first thing that happened was that I noticed that the family members were 'sharing' Michael's belongings. Abby was seen to be wearing his jumper, the explanation being that he didn't like wearing it; and Sarah, the foster carer. was wearing his watch. I knew it was his watch because his mother had bought it for his birthday just a couple of weeks previously. When I asked about this, she said that he was always leaving it lying around and so she was looking after it for him. At the time these explanations seemed reasonable, but having reflected on it since, my starting point was based on a mistaken assumption – that this was Michael's alternative 'family' and an extension of this thinking was that these were his foster 'parents' and his foster 'siblings'. Therefore, in that context the swapping/borrowing of clothes or looking after children's belongings would appear to be all part of normal family behaviour.

This presented as a complex issue for all concerned. On the one hand, it is vital that foster carers' professional knowledge and skills are recognised and that their views need to form part of the overall understanding of the lives of these very vulnerable children. In addition, as previously stated, we expect carers to welcome children into their homes, families and hearts, and to treat them as 'their own'. The carers' own children will be very aware of the circumstances of the children placed with them, and research shows that having a succession of children living with you to whom you are not related can have a negative effect (Sinclair et al, 2005). In addition, it is highly likely that Mark and Sarah's children will have observed the lack of boundaries regarding the rights of Michael to his property and copied that behaviour.

Reflection points

1. Should social workers work on the basis that a 'family' relationship is important?
2. Do you think we should we expect a 'sibling' relationship to develop if we are expecting the foster carers to begin to 're-parent' the child and make them feel part of the family?
3. How far are the foster carers viewed as part of the professional multi-agency team by social workers and by the children for whom they care?

Children come into care for a variety of reasons, including neglect arising from a level of family dysfunction. I preferred the notion of a family placement rather than a residential unit, because it provides children with an opportunity to experience what a functional family should look like. In addition to having good physical care, children also need time, love and the attention from a caring attachment figure with whom they can develop a secure base on which their future relationships are built.

The relationships between foster 'siblings' is complex, but healthy relationships can be of benefit to children who have not experienced siblings with whom they do not need to compete with for attention.

The second thing that happened was that Mark mentioned in passing that Michael had run out of his ADHD medication and needed a new prescription. He had an appointment with the GP the next day. I was a little concerned that this had not been pre-empted as it was important that Michael took his medication regularly. We had discussed the carers talking to the GP about Michael's behaviour at school, and whether this needed reviewing. However, again, through my lack of experience, I was taken in by their assurances that everything was in hand.

In his book *The story of Baby P: Setting the record straight*, Ray Jones (2014) explores this very issue – the reassurances the mother gave to the allocated social worker for Peter Connelly that he was being cared for appropriately. Jones describes how the social worker's observations were of a single mother who had some difficulties with parenting Peter and his siblings, but who was committed to improving their care. The social worker was seeing Peter on a regular basis, but failed to realise that three other individuals had moved in to the property, one of whom had been abusing Peter for nine months before his death. While clearly the case on which I was engaged bore no resemblance to 'Baby P' in terms of the level of seriousness, it is important to consider the fact that social workers rely heavily on the information they are provided with during a home visit.

It wasn't until two weeks after the last visit that I received a concerned telephone call from the headteacher at Michael's school that things began to fall into place. Michael was said to be having fairly significant problems at school with some of the other pupils. There had been a couple of occasions when he had been fighting on the minibus and he had come into conflict in the classroom when he had struggled to keep 'on task' and disrupted the other pupils. Consequently, he had begun to fall behind. The school was managing this on the basis that this signified the end of the 'honeymoon' period, and that following a further period of adjustment, Michael would once again begin to settle down again. However, the headteacher did question the wisdom of removing the support provided by his prescription of medication to control his impulsivity, as they had found that if he took it at lunchtime he was very much calmer in the afternoon. I was surprised by this, and told the headteacher that it was my understanding that he had continued with his medication as this was in line with medical advice. We agreed that I would find out what was going on and let him know.

I spoke to my line manager and we agreed that I would go over to the foster carers later that day to discuss what the situation was, and to share the concerns cited by the school. I arrived just after 4pm. Michael had just returned home from school on the minibus. We sat down together with the foster carers and talked about what was happening in school and what he thought the problem might be. Michael said that other children and the teachers were picking on him and that it wasn't his fault. "I try to do my school work but my head gets whizzy and I have to get up. Then I get told off. My tablets used to make me feel sleepy but I liked that better than being whizzy all the time", he said. At this point, I noticed Michael look at Sarah. I wasn't sure what this meant, and so I asked Michael if he would mind going off to play while I talked to Mark and Sarah.

However, as he was leaving the room, I noticed a large red mark that covered most of his knee, and I asked him what it was. Michael said that it was from when he was playing out the week before. I asked him how he had done it and he said he couldn't remember, but he thought he had fallen over. I asked him to show me properly as it looked quite red and 'angry'. Although I'm not medically trained, it did look as if it wasn't healing well. It appeared to be a little infected. I asked him if it hurt and he said it was a bit sore but that it didn't matter.

When Michael went upstairs, I told Mark and Sarah that there were two issues we needed to discuss. The first was Michael's medication and his prescriptions, and the second was the circumstances of the injury to his knee. With regard to Michael's medication, Sarah said that he was just being silly as he always had his medication every morning, and that the school had a supply for him during lunchtime. I asked her when she had last renewed his prescription, and she told me that she had collected his monthly supply the previous week. I asked her if I could have a look to see what the dosage was and whether anything had changed, as it seemed that there had been increasing issues with his behaviour, certainly at school. Sarah, however, was somewhat reluctant to get his tablets, and it seemed that she had trouble laying her hands on them. After a few minutes, she came back with a creased and dirty-looking chemist bag, one that I instantly recognised. There, on the outside, was the telephone number of Michael's mother written in pink lipstick. I looked inside at the tablets. There were six missing – three days' supply – but the issue date on them was prior to Michael coming into care. They were the same tablets I had brought with me from his home.

I asked Sarah where his new prescription was. She told me that it was in the bag. I pointed to the lipstick on the outside and she told me that they just reused the bag so they didn't lose the number. I challenged this by saying that the tablets were clearly old ones given the issue date on the boxes. Mark then told me that they also reused the boxes. Although these could have been reasonable explanations I was, at this stage, very concerned. It appeared that the foster carers were deliberately lying to me and I wondered what else was going on.

I moved on to the issue with regard to the injury to Michael's knee and began by asking them how it had happened. Sarah said that Michael had gone out to play on some waste ground and had taken some lighter fuel and matches from the kitchen to make a bonfire. Michael had managed to start a small fire but the grass was wet and so he sprayed lighter fuel on it in order to make it burn quicker. The fuel had 'blown back' and he had burnt his knee. I asked the carers if he had had medical attention and they told me that they had run it under cold water and rubbed antiseptic cream on it.

This concerned me greatly given the size of the burn and the fact that they had not sought medical attention. I knew that the foster carers' regulations for this particular local authority required that medical opinion be sought for any burn larger than a 50 pence piece. This was considerably larger than that, and the use of antiseptic cream was contraindicated for any form of burn as it may actually increase the risk of infection, as appeared to have been the case.

Reflection points

1. What do you think your starting point would be in terms of addressing these issues with the foster carer?
2. If you were not medically trained, how would you know a burn from another form of injury?
3. How would you know if it was a serious burn?

As a newly qualified worker it can be hard to tackle issues that even a more experienced worker would need to think about. A good starting point would be to take down the information, inform a team manager, liaise with the Fostering Support worker and suggest a joint visit at the earliest opportunity. It is very important to seek medical advice as soon as possible.

I wanted to speak to my manager regarding the issue of the medication, but felt that what was of more immediate concern was Michael's burn. I asked the foster carer to take Michael to the GP that day, to which she agreed; however, given all of my other concerns, I was worried that she might not, and so I asked that she telephone the GP while I was there. Mark said he was going outside to work on his car. Michael was upstairs and the other children were outside, so the room was very quiet while Sarah made the telephone call. Apparently aware of this, Sarah went out into the kitchen and I followed her. The conversation that I could clearly overhear went as follows:

"Oh hello love, this is Mrs Bradbury."
"Hello Mrs Bradbury, how can I help?"
"Oh it's about our Michael. Well he's gone and burned himself and I was wondering if Dr Connor could have a quick look this afternoon – or tomorrow?"
"Certainly Mrs Bradbury, What's Michael's full name?"

Sarah then put her hand over the mouth piece and said to me, "It's alright, they are seeing him today, so I'll ring you tomorrow", and opened the back door to gesture me to leave. However, I didn't move. I stood my ground and waited. Sarah said again, rather pointedly to me, "So I'll ring you tomorrow, shall I?" I could hear the receptionist getting a little agitated on the other end of the telephone line, so I suggested to Sarah that she should continue with the telephone call and that I would stay, "Just in case there are any problems." She seemed quite displeased with this and moved to the dining room. I followed her once again. Unable to dismiss me, Sarah appeared as if she had no other choice than to admit that there was an issue, or continue the telephone call.

"So, Mrs Bradbury, what did you say Michael's details are? Is it Bradbury?" "Er, yes that's right." I put my hand on Sarah's arm and said, "Aren't you forgetting, it's Ashford?" "Oh yes, sorry love, it's Ashford, Michael James Ashford." "I'm sorry Mrs Bradbury, I can't seem to find him on the system. Let me check again, how are you spelling his name?" Sarah spelt his name again and looked at me and tutted, indicating that the receptionist was not being very efficient. Almost immediately, the receptionist came back and said, "I'm sorry Mrs Bradbury, there is no one of that name registered here. Are you sure you have the right surgery?" "Yes, that's right, Dr Connor. Oh yes, five today is fine." "No, Mrs Bradbury, you misheard me. There is no one of that name registered with this surgery." "Oh smashing, thanks love, I'll pop him down in a bit." "Mrs Bradbury...." Sarah hung up and said, "Right, that's that sorted then, five today and he is seeing Dr Connor."

It was clear to me that Sarah and Mark hadn't even provided the basic care required of them to Michael. If he wasn't registered with a GP, he had no medication and no access to medical intervention when injured. To say I was angry didn't even begin to describe my feelings. I also felt stupid, naive and completely deskilled. I excused myself and went outside to first telephone my manager and then the Fostering Support worker.

The allegation of abuse and neglect is probably the most serious complaint that can be made against a foster carer, and Section 47 of the Children Act 1989 requires that social care respond to such allegations in the same robust manner as a similar allegation made against a birth family member:

> … if the Local Authority has reasonable cause to believe that a child who lives, or is found in their area, is suffering or likely to suffer, significant harm … the authority shall make, or cause to be made, such enquires as they consider necessary to enable them to decide whether they should take any form of action to safeguard and promote the child's welfare.

A strategy discussion was held by my manager with both the head of the Fostering Service and the police, and it was agreed that in the first instance Michael would be moved to a new placement pending the outcome of an investigation. The foster carers would be referred to the local authority designated officer (LADO) who would bring all parties together to investigate the circumstances in which Michael had been neglected, and so reach a decision regarding their continued registration. I was mindful that Michael was on an Interim Care Order and as such, we shared parental responsibility with his mother. Therefore, my manager said that he would telephone her to tell her what was happening.

While the fostering team were trying to arrange an emergency placement for Michael and the support worker was on the way to see Sarah and Mark, I took Michael to the hospital to get his burn looked at. The hospital was concerned when I explained what had happened, and while we were there, they did a full statutory medical. They pronounced him well but a little under-nourished. The burn was dressed, and I then took Michael out for tea while we waited for the fostering team to let me know where he was going. It was the conversation we had over tea that made me realise just how bad things had been.

Michael told me how Sarah and Mark (and their children) would often help themselves to his things. For example, his auntie had given his mother some chocolate for him, and the family had said it was bad for his teeth so they ate it while watching a film. Abby often borrowed his new clothes, bought at the start of placement by social care, and Sarah wouldn't let him have his birthday watch. His mother had noticed he never wore it at contact and told him off for wasting her money. This had made Michael feel sad, but he had felt unable to tell her. Perhaps the most concerning thing for me, other than the lack of care regarding his burn, was that when the family all went out for the day, he had to stay in his room and wasn't allowed to come out until they got back. They had given him a bucket for a toilet. He wasn't locked in, but they put tape on the corner of the door so they would know if he had left his room.

It troubled me greatly that Michael had never complained about his placement or how things were for him. I asked him if he was afraid to tell me. He said that, "No, it was just ordinary." I asked him what he meant. He said "just like home, it was just like home." It seemed that Michael had arrived in placement with no clear views on what his life could be like. He was used to being alone and having little in the way of possessions. He was used to having little say on how his life could be. It had simply been replicated in his placement. This made me feel terrible. I realised that if I had asked Michael the right questions and seen him more regularly, I would have learned about his situation much earlier.

I told Michael that what he had endured was not acceptable and that it was important that we put it right. I explained that I was going to find another place for him to live away from Sarah and Mark. I told him that he was too special to have to stay at home when people went out to have fun without him, and that it was important that he be looked after properly when he was hurt.

Michael asked me if boys were special. I told him that all boys and girls were special and that they needed to be looked after. He told me that he thought only girls could be special because he had never been special to anyone. I told him that he was special to me and that I would make sure that he had somewhere lovely to live, but that if he was ever in a similar situation where people were not being nice to him, he had to tell me straightaway and I would try to put it right. However, although he readily agreed, I wasn't convinced. Michael was apparently so used to having an unhappy life that I was concerned as to what his future would look like if he was continually given the message that he was not worthy of even being happy.

It took the commitment of two remarkable long-term foster carers with considerable time, love and care for Michael to begin to forge trusting relationships with those around him, and when I last saw him he was clearly developing into an emotionally intelligent, sensitive and caring young man with a steady girlfriend and a group of loyal friends. Research completed by Schofield and Simmonds (2011) and Woolgar (2013) found that consistent high-quality nurturing care and other positive experiences can help repair earlier damage. What this demonstrates is that the continuing plasticity of the brain, which allows therapeutic work to be completed, can help a child to become, over time, less impulsive and more engaged in relationships. However, I recognise that this isn't always the case. It could have turned out entirely differently, and for many young people, even within (and in some cases because of) the care system, things don't change for them, and so the cycle begins as they themselves embark on parenthood and struggle to meet their children's needs.

Reflection points

1. Think about how the story unfolded. At what point do you think alarm bells would have sounded for you?
2. Do you think that the way in which the case was managed could have been done differently? What would you have done?
3. Other than statutory checks, do you think we can ever know what happens in foster placements?

Reflection 'on' action

Reflecting on this case now, I still cringe at the errors I made. I had spent a great deal of time doing direct work with Michael when he was at home, to try and understand what his life was like. However, once he went into care, I hadn't really asked what his days were like. I believed he was safe, I took this for granted, and as a result, I'd let him down.

The fact that I had noticed certain oddities means that I was aware things were not as they seemed. I should have immediately challenged the family for wearing his belongings and insisted it didn't happen again. I should also have referred the family to the Fostering Support worker as this could have been prevented, been seen as a possible training issue or certainly been a point for discussion. The fact that Michael's possessions weren't exclusively his own reinforced his general feeling of being insignificant. He didn't feel he was worthy enough to even have his own belongings.

In addition, as soon as I knew Michael's prescription had run out, I should have insisted that it was dealt with immediately and telephoned the GP surgery myself rather than trusted the foster carers to do this. The new GP was part of the multiagency group supporting Michael, and so I should have endeavoured to form a collaborative relationship with them. *Working together to safeguard children* (Home Office and DfEE, 2015) highlights the importance of agencies working together in this way, and states that children's wellbeing, and safeguarding them from significant harm, depends crucially on effective information–sharing, collaboration and understanding between agencies and professionals. Constructive relationships between workers need to therefore be supported by a strong lead from elected or appointed authority members, and the commitment of chief officers.

Although I had had an initial meeting with both the foster carers and the school headteacher about Michael, where we discussed how we were going to manage his transition and use of medication in school time, I didn't follow this up by having regular contact with the school to discuss how things were going. There are so many things I could have done differently that would have meant using the time we spent together or me working on the case much more productively. I consider that Michael (and myself) had a lucky escape. It was a distressing experience, but I realise it could have been much worse. The key things I took from this whole experience were that I needed to ask questions and then ask more questions. If the answers didn't make sense, I needed to keep digging until they did.

Mark and Sarah were de-registered and no longer allowed to care for children for the local authority again. When I went to collect Michael's things, they wanted to keep Michael's 'bright red bike' – "We've bought it, it's ours" – but I insisted, and Mark threw it at my car. He told me to take it and to never come back. I was more than happy to oblige.

Summary

This case study demonstrates the importance of shadowing newly qualified social workers (NQSWs). What we have now is the Assessed and Supported Year in Employment (ASYE). This is designed to help NQSWs develop their skills, knowledge and capability, and strengthen their professional confidence. It is a framework that provides them with access to regular and focused support during their first year of employment in social work.

It is also linked to the Professional Capabilities Framework (PCF), which was originally developed by the College of Social Work, and outlines exactly what skills, knowledge and capabilities NQSWs are expected to attain during their ASYE. This means that NQSWs are mentored and supported to understand what is required when working with children in care.

It is also important to recognise that NQSWs need ongoing training and support if they are to consider and address thresholds of poor care and actual abuse. Some of the people social workers work with may have had poor experiences of engaging with services or be anxious about becoming involved with a social worker. It is crucial to remain objective and sensitive to those experiences, and be reminded that social workers may have to make unwelcome decisions. Maintaining relationships and open forums for effective communication to take place in times of conflict is one of the biggest challenges of social work, as practitioners have to balance needs and risks with rights and choices.

Although I have drawn predominantly from attachment theory in this case study, it is important to recognise that this perspective does have its limitations. One of the main critics of Bowlby's attachment theory is Harris (1998). She argued that people make assumptions that kind, honest and respectful parents will produce kind, honest and respectful children. Likewise, parents who are rude and disrespectful will have children who behave in the same way. However, Harris (1998) believed that parents do not shape their child's personality or character. A child's peers will have more influence than their parents. Children will learn things from their peers because they want to be liked and fit in.

Harris (1998) also argued that children will not use everything that they have learned from their parents. Children learn how to behave, for the most part, from other people in their social group. This is also noticeable with adults; they behave more like the people in their social groups than they do their parents (Lee, 2003). This is applicable to Michael, who, although he had a disrupted childhood and a subsequent difficult foster placement, did go on to develop good relationships with future foster carers and friends.

Further reading

Howe, D. (2011) *Attachment across the life course: A brief introduction*, London: Palgrave Macmillan

This succinct and highly readable book offers the perfect introduction to a fascinating and fast-growing field. It explains the key concepts in attachment theory, and describes how the main attachment types play out both in childhood and later life. It identifies some of the intriguing questions being explored by research, such as: what part do individuals' attachment histories play in adult relationships? What scope is there for attachment styles established in infancy to change later in life?

Dunk-West, P. (2013) *How to be a social worker: A critical guide for students*, London: Palgrave Macmillan

Through the course of studying social work and beyond it can be difficult to take a step back and reflect on what it is to be a social worker, such are the demands of the process of qualification and the role itself. Using this as a starting point, *How to be a social worker* critically examines the knowledge base of social work – from human growth and development to social work research – and explores how your own values, principles and experience combine to shape your social work identity and practice alongside this.

SCIE (Social Care Institute for Excellence) Resources for newly qualified social workers, www.scie.org.uk/publications/nqswtool/

This online tool provides a wealth of information from building relationships, writing assessments and planning intervention.

References

Ainsworth, M.D.S. (1973) 'The development of infant-mother attachment', in B. Cardwell and H. Ricciuti (eds) *Review of child development research* (vol 3), Chicago, IL: University of Chicago Press, pp 1–94.

Biehal, N., Cusworth, L., Wade, J. and Clarke, S. (2014) *Keeping children safe*, London: NSPCC.

Boris, N.W., Zeanah, C.H. and Work Group on Quality Issues (2005) 'Practice parameter for the assessment and treatment of children and adolescents with reactive attachment disorder of infancy and early childhood', *Journal of American Academy of Child and Adolescent Psychiatry*, vol 44, no 11, pp 1206–19.

Bowlby, J. (1953) *Child care and the growth of love*, London: Penguin Books.

Bowlby, J. (1969) *Attachment and loss. Volume 1: Attachment*, New York: Basic Books.

DH (Department of Health), DfEE (Department for Education and Employment) and Home Office (2000) *Framework for the assessment of children in need and their families*, London: The Stationery Office (http://webarchive.nationalarchives. gov.uk/20130105133840/http://www.dh.gov.uk/prod_consum_dh/groups/ dh_digitalassets/@dh/@en/documents/digitalasset/dh_4014430.pdf).

Ferguson, H. (2011) *Child protection practice*, Houndmills, Basingstoke and New York: Palgrave Macmillan.

Golding, K.S., Dent, H.R., Nissim, R. and Stott, L. (2006) 'Being heard: Listening to the voices of young people and their families', in K.S. Golding, H.R. Dent, R. Nissim and L. Stott (eds) *Thinking psychologically about children who are looked after and adopted*, Chichester: Wiley & Sons Ltd, pp 1–33.

Harris, J.R. (1998) *The nurture assumption: Why children turn out the way they do*, New York: Free Press.

Home Office and DfEE (Department for Education and Employment) (1999) *Working together to safeguard children*, London: The Stationery Office.

Jones, R. (2014) *The story of Baby P: Setting the record straight*, Bristol: Policy Press.

Lyons-Ruth, K., Bureau, J., Riley, C. and Atlas-Corbett, A. (2009) 'Socially indiscriminate attachment behavior in the Strange Situation: Convergent and discriminant validity in relation to caregiving risk, later behavior problems, and attachment insecurity', *Development and Psychopathology*, vol 21, no 2, pp 355–72.

Minnis, H., Green, J., O'Connor, T.G., Liew, A., Glaser, D., Taylor, E. et al (2009) 'An exploratory study of the association between reactive attachment disorder and attachment narratives in early school-age children', *Journal of Child Psychology and Psychiatry*, vol 50, pp 931–42.

Ofsted (2009) *Children's care monitor 2009*, London: Ofsted.

Ruisard, J. (2016) 'Transformation through attachment: The power of relationship in clinical social work', *Clinical Social Work Journal*, vol 44, no 3, pp 279–92.

Schofield, G. and Simmonds, J. (2011) 'Contact for infants subject to care proceedings', *Family Law*, vol 41, pp 617–22.

Sinclair, I., Wilson, K. and Gibbs, I. (2005) *Foster placements: Why they succeed and why they fail*, London: Jessica Kingsley Publications.

Winnicott, D.W. (1965) *The maturation process and the facilitating environment*, New York: International Universities Press.

Woolgar, M. (2013) 'The practical implications of the emerging findings in the neurobiology of maltreatment for looked after and adopted children: Recognising the diversity of outcomes', *Adoption and Fostering*, vol 37, no 3, pp 237–52.

7

Working constructively with uncooperative clients

Introduction

This chapter looks at a case study of an assessment session with a father who was the subject of a Fact Finding Hearing with regard to two serious non-accidental injuries to a pre-mobile child. Although the Court believed the father was guilty of the injuries, he had always maintained his innocence. This assessment session was to look specifically at the occurrence of one of the injuries that was slightly less contentious in that he did admit to bumping the child's head but not to causing a skull fracture.

The chapter starts with an overview of the case and the rationale for the assessment. It then moves on to look at how complex assessments should be approached in order to increase the chances of good client engagement, and provides techniques for dealing with denial and how good rapport building will ensure that the information gathered is of the highest quality, leading to robust assessment outcomes.

Within the early discussion is my reflection on why previous cases were difficult and the way in which I have developed skills of not only resilience but also practice wisdom, which have enabled me to become a confident and competent practitioner. Theories and current research with regard to client engagement and body language are considered, and the power of bringing interview techniques to investigational assessment is examined throughout.

Theory of mind and using space in practice

Within this chapter, I draw from the parents' attributions of child behaviour, drawing on the role played by theory of mind (see Premack and Woodruff, 1978) in the care of the child. Theory of mind is a theory insofar as the mind is the only thing being directly observed. The belief that others have a mind leads to why this concept is termed a 'theory of mind' because each human can only understand the existence of their own mind through reflection, as no one has direct access to the mind of another. Drawing from the theory of mind allows a person to attribute thoughts, desires and intentions to others, to predict or explain their actions, and to theorise their intentions.

Research on theory of mind, has grown rapidly in the 35 years since Premack and Woodruff's paper. An alternative account is offered in operant psychology, and develops the idea that interactions between practitioner and client should involve a functional account of both perspective taking and empathy. Empathy and perspective taking comprises of a complex set of relational abilities based on learning to differentiate and react verbally to ever more complex relations between self, others, place and time.

Attention to the use of space and environment in practice is the hallmark of good social work. Clients' environment includes both the social and physical worlds, but social workers often neglect to consider the physical surroundings when carrying out assessments (Gutheil, 1992). Environment strongly affects people's daily activities, social interaction and general wellbeing (Cantor, 1979). Many factors that contribute to the way in which a person will behave often stem from physical properties and material objects such as lighting, furniture arrangement and the people who are present (Gutheil, 1992). This case study draws from and applies all of the above concepts.

Case study

Context

Three-month-old Stanley attended Accident and Emergency (A&E) with his parents. They said that he had been found to have bruising and swelling to the back of his head. He was X-rayed and found to have suffered a skull fracture. Further skeletal surveys also found a healing fracture of his pelvis. It was believed that this injury had occurred approximately five weeks previously. Initially, the parents couldn't provide an explanation for either injury. However, such an injury in a non-ambulant child was of grave concern to medical staff, who found it difficult to conceive. An investigation under Section 47 of the Children Act 1989 was launched. A Fact Finding Hearing was held, and findings were made that both injuries were non-accidental and had been inflicted by the father (Simon) who had sole care of the child at the time, although he denied any knowledge of the injuries. The police had referred the case to the Crown Prosecution Service (CPS), and Simon had subsequently been found guilty of grievous bodily harm. He had served 18 months of a three-year sentence. He continued to deny the offence.

The assessment that relates to this case study was to make recommendations to the Family Court regarding contact and residence. This was the third of eight assessment sessions, and the aim was to explore the father's understanding of the circumstances in which the injuries had occurred. It may appear to the reader that for us to have reached a third meeting without discussing in depth the detail and context of the offences or allegations would create an unnecessary delay. However, by slowing the assessment down and allowing time to develop a rapport with the parents, we (my organisation and myself) were of the belief that the offence disclosure may have elicited a far more fruitful discussion than otherwise. For example, in some cases, a client may discuss the offence in a general way (for example, "I've served my time, I've said I'm sorry so there is nothing more to be said"), and will then leave, believing that the assessment has been completed after their version of events has been heard. This can cause some difficulty for future engagement, as they may believe that revisiting their account of what happened is unnecessary.

As I was acting as an expert witness in this case, I was mindful of the fact that Simon wasn't a voluntary client. The possibility of his returning home rested on the Court's decision, which would be influenced by my assessment report and recommendations. Therefore, in order to assist the Court, I needed to support Simon to be frank about Stanley's injuries, and ensure that he understood why they had happened. Therefore, I wanted to take my time in building Simon's confidence and allowing him to feel that he would be treated fairly, as all relevant information would be presented to the Court.

I was also very much aware of the importance of developing a rapport with Simon. As part of this, I recognised that I would have to suspend my disbelief of the account he had given, at least temporarily, in order to build a relationship with him. As will be seen in the following interview transcript, I held back in the early stages from challenging too much as I was worried that this may have made him defensive and had a negative effective on building rapport together. However, I was concerned that I may miss the moment and be too late when trying to challenge him. At this point in my career I was frequently anxious that by not addressing things immediately I was in danger of either not remembering to come back to important issues, or of being distracted and forgetting where I was up to, if I did spend time exploring some of the other concerns.

Before commencing the assessment session, I realised that I needed to be prepared by making sure I understood the issues in relation to the case, and also in terms of how I needed to carry out the assessment. Simon was often referred to as 'an unassessed risk', and as it seemed likely that he had been violent towards his son, I couldn't be sure he was not a danger to adults. I had to consider my own safety within the session at all times, and ensure that other colleagues knew where I was and whom I was with.

However, I recognised that rapport is a key component of any good assessment, and while it cannot be guaranteed, I believe it should always be strived for. By being well prepared for the session and presenting as calm and relaxed, I was able to put Simon at ease. I had considered the dynamics of the room and how this might be best set out to ensure that Simon would wish to engage with me. Although this may appear to be a minor consideration, it is nonetheless important in terms of not only ensuring safety (should I have needed to leave the room quickly) but also in terms of building rapport.

Haase et al (1970) carried out a study that explored how counsellors used space during client sessions. They found that when there was no table between the client and the counsellor, the counsellor felt more empathic. In addition, I realised that when I carried out a complex assessment I used to find it helpful to observe the client's entire body language. This would lead me to look for signs of agitation or discomfort when I broached a particular area of discussion. If I noticed a change in body movement, I would revisit this same subject later in the conversation to see if a similar reaction was displayed.

As well as being mindful of space, I was always concerned about making clients feel comfortable. Schroeder et al (2014) have shown that people shake hands before negotiations as a signal of their willingness to cooperate. Based on the results of their research, they concluded that when compared to negotiators who don't shake hands, those who do so are more open in the way they share information and are less likely to lie. While clearly there are cultural differences in expectations regarding handshakes, particularly between men and women, this wasn't relevant in my meeting with Simon who shook my hand on our first greeting.

When I welcomed Simon into the interviewing room, I asked him if he wanted a drink. I was aware that cups of tea work well when social workers try to build rapport with clients. I made sure that I made a mental note of Simon's drink preference at the first session so that later I could begin subsequent sessions with, "Hi Simon, come in. How are you? I've just put the kettle on – it is milk and two sugars, isn't it?" Although this was a short exchange, I felt that it set the scene well for a more relaxed meeting, and I do believe that because I had memorised how he liked his tea, it was important to him on some level that I had taken the trouble to remember this.

My role as the assessor in this case was to explore the historical information available from the Court and other professionals by carrying out an assessment of Simon and his understanding of why the injuries had been caused, how far he was able to accept responsibility for his actions and to determine whether there were any remaining cognitive distortions that may mean he continued to pose a risk to children, more specifically, his son. Therefore, unlike my social worker role where I would often work with parents to help them change an aspect of their lives that prevented them from parenting effectively, this role focused on engagement and disclosure. In the next part, I attempt to analyse how I carried this out with the use of subtle yet effective interviewing techniques. These techniques draw, in spirit, on Motivational Interviewing principles; however, these have not been applied consistently or sufficiently; rather, they have been used as a loose guide to enable dialogue and reflection.

Record of dialogue and reflection in action

Me: 'So, Simon, as we discussed last week, I want to focus today on the events surrounding Stanley being injured and which led to his hospital admission. Do you feel okay to talk about it?'

It could be argued that 'pre-warning' of subject areas for future discussion can give defensive clients, who do not wish to engage, time to 'get their story straight'. However, in this situation I wanted to be transparent about the format, context and timing of the assessment sessions. I felt it was important to engage with Simon and be honest about my intentions and that I wanted him to reciprocate and encourage him to engage with me.

Simon: 'Yeah I think so, but I'm not sure what good it will do. I've already talked to the therapist about all this. Can't you just get her report or something? You people should just talk to each other. I shouldn't have to keep going over things all the time.'

I considered that perhaps Simon would say this, but I also realised that I may have done so in the same situation. By putting myself in his shoes I was able to roll with the resistance and think about how I could identify the benefits of cooperation and so move the discussion on.

Me: 'You're right and I will be doing that, but I'd like to hear from you about what happened. I know that during the Fact Finding you gave different versions of what happened and you haven't had the chance since to set the record straight, so I thought this could be your opportunity. The judge needs to understand how and why Stanley was hurt because only then can he make recommendations about whether you can go home and live with your family.'

I had read the Court bundle and was familiar with the facts of the case, but it was important for me to hear Simon's story. This not only gave me an opportunity to pick up on things that were important to him, but also enabled me to explore the inconsistencies or changes in accounts given.

Simon: 'Well, yeah, I suppose so. It's just. Well I'm not sure I can remember. It's so long ago now.'

Me: 'Well, yes, I can understand you feeling that, but what you may find as we start to go through it is that things will start to come back and you might remember much more than you think.'

Although I was certain at the time that Simon did remember what had happened, I felt that if I challenged him at this point it could have made him defensive and he would have perhaps refused to engage. Instead, I wanted to make it clear, in a non-threatening way, that he could change his view or account without losing face.

Me: 'So, Simon, I am going to go through with you now the day that Stanley hurt his head. Now if you feel that you don't understand something I have asked, then tell me as we go and I will try to help you by asking it in a different way.'

I wanted to make sure that Simon understood everything that I was going to say as at a later date he may have tried to retract what he had told me on the basis that 'I didn't understand what she was asking.'

Simon: 'Yeah, okay. So what do you want to know? It's all in the doctor's report anyway.'

I felt that if I returned to this deflection it would continue throughout our session, so I chose not to respond and moved on.

Me: 'Well, let's start off with that morning. Now you told the Court that you had been working all night at the studio. So, do you want to talk me through that morning? How was Stanley that day?'

Simon was a graphic designer for a large advertising company. He had previously cited stress due to overwork on a large project for a very important international client. He had gone to work at around 10am the previous day and had worked right through the night.

Simon: 'Well, I got home about half eight, I'd been working all night and I was just knackered. I just wanted to go to bed to be honest. When I got in, I could already hear him and Claire said he'd been screaming since just after I'd gone to work the night before and he'd hardly slept since then. She said that he would drop off for a bit but as soon as she tried to put him down he'd just kick off again.'

Me: 'Okay, right.'

This confirmed what Simon had said following the Court hearing about Claire not being present at the time of Stanley's head injury, and I was satisfied that this was the case.

Simon: 'Yeah, well I just said "Come here little man, come to your dad", and I took him off her and started, like, walking around, bouncing him in my arms, trying to settle him down but he was just bright red in the face with screaming.'

Me: [Silence, but nods]

Simon: 'Well, I got his bottle and tried to get him to take it just so Claire could have 5 minutes. She popped down to her mum's just to have a bit of time out and I had Stan…. So I tried to put him in his cot because the health visitor had told Claire that it wasn't good just to cuddle him to sleep all the time and he should be able to settle himself.'

Me: 'Okay….'

I wanted to make sure that I remained neutral throughout the interview. I didn't want Simon to feel I was interrogating him. What I wanted from Simon was much more in terms of a carefully considered, multilayered discussion of his life and the reasons why he had arrived at this point. In order to do this, I was aware that I needed him to talk much more than I did, and so I employed a device I thought would allow this to happen in a fairly natural way, known as 'controlled non-directive probing' (Kahn and Cannell, 1957), or 'nods and gurgles', as Richardson et al (1965) refer to it. This process involves taking turns to talk. My turn involved acknowledging that I had heard what Simon had said by the use of a nod or an 'okay' without actually adding to the conversation. These short comments ensure that the conversation continues to flow without me using Simon's 'talking time'.

Simon: 'He was crying and kicking off so I picked him back up again and I was walking round and bouncing him up and down because he likes that normally but it wasn't working and that's when I think I might have bumped his head a bit.'

Me: 'Okay....'

I was tempted to step in here and ask Simon more about bumping Stanley's head, but I wanted to give him a little more room to complete his account. I therefore parked this important piece of information for later, and allowed Simon's story to unfold in his own time. I wanted to get a broad view of what had occurred before delving in to the specifics. I knew I could easily have got carried away and tried to pursue this revelation, but I wouldn't have picked the story back up again, and the moment would have been lost. I was also aware that that if I did, there may have been other, seemingly insignificant, pieces of important information missed. Instead, I decided to acknowledge I had heard what he had said without getting into further discussion.

Simon: 'So he was still crying and I went downstairs and I said to Claire that we could put him in the car and see if he would fall asleep then, because he always likes to sleep in the car. So she went and got his snowsuit and his hat and she was getting him dressed and she said "Simon, he's got a lump in his head", so I said "What do you mean, a lump?", so she showed me and there was this lump on the back of his head right enough, and then when Claire touched it he was holding his breath and went blue and then he went all floppy.'

I was unsure if this was denial on Simon's part or if he was pretending to be innocent. However, I also was aware that even if he had banged Stanley's head he may have had no idea that the blow had been severe enough to have caused that level of injury. It appeared from his description that he had been as surprised as Claire to find the lump on his son's head.

Me: 'He was holding his breath, he went blue, and then he went floppy?'

Simon: 'Yeah, he was just as blue as my jumper. Well Claire was screaming and she said "Quick, do something, ring an ambulance." So I rang me mum and I said "Mum, it's Stanley", and I told her and she said "Me and your dad will meet you at the hospital but you have to get him there right now." So that's what we did.'

What I found interesting was that Simon's first thought had been to telephone his family. This may have simply been a reaction to a stressful situation, but I knew that I needed to find out more about his apparent reluctance to call for immediate medical help. I also wondered whether, even if on one level he had not thought he had caused the injury, he had wanted, if possible, to avoid scrutiny. I made a note of this so that I could return to this point in a later session. I realised that it would also be important to explore the relationships within the extended family in order to try and understand why he wanted to contact his mother first.

Me: 'And that's how you came to take him into hospital. Okay, well that's very helpful. Thank you Simon. I think now we should take a 10-minute break to allow you to stretch your legs and for me to have a think. Why don't I make us both a cup of tea?'

I believe that it is important to include breaks within assessment sessions, but these must be carefully timed and controlled by the assessor, if possible. Some clients may need to take breaks during their assessment session due to them having a limited attention span or due to the distressing nature of the issues being discussed. I was also aware that because I was concentrating so hard I, too, needed to take a break; it is possible when involved in lengthy or complex discussions to suffer from the effects of fatigue.

From previous experience, I had learned that the best way to manage these situations was to plan for when natural breaks could occur. If I had planned to look at themes, for example, early peer relationships, education, previous offending history etc, I could input breaks in between the themes. It may also be that 'themes within themes' develop, as was the case here. In this situation, Simon and I had come to a natural pause within the discussion, and this felt like a good place to take a break to allow not only my client to have a cigarette, but also to allow myself to collect my thoughts and consider what I needed to cover next. I realised that after I had heard Simon's general description of the day in which Stanley received his head injury, I needed to slow things down and revisit the events in greater detail. Following the break I reminded Simon that he had told me the events leading up to Stanley being taken to hospital, but that I wanted to go back to when he had first arrived at home that morning. I wanted now to explore further how he had felt after he had come home from a long day at work to find his wife tired and tearful and his son distressed.

Simon: 'Oh, it was awful I could hear him when I pulled up in the car. He was just, like, screaming the house down. I was mentally all over the place; I was knackered. I just wanted to sleep. Then I get in and I see Claire's face and she was just like "I've had enough." He could be really hard work. He used to go ballistic when you changed his nappy. It would take ages for him to settle again... He was a nightmare. Even me mum said he was a difficult baby, but this was the worst he's ever been.'

However, what Simon's mother didn't know was that Stanley had a broken pelvis that had not been treated. This may have been why Stanley had been 'a nightmare' when he was having his nappy changed.
I was curious to understand why it was that Stanley was particularly distressed that day. Perhaps this would shed some light on what the dynamic had been like within the home and between Simon and Claire prior to the injury occurring. I knew I had to return to this point so I made a note to explore their relationship further in a separate session.

Me: 'Had anything been different before you had gone to work?'

Simon: 'Well, he was just being whiney. He just wouldn't shut up, you know? He was just crying and there was nothing I could do to shut him up.'

Me: 'How was that making you feel?'

Simon: Well, he was takin' the piss. You know. He was takin' the piss. What was I supposed to do right? I'm his dad, he should listen to me. If he'd just.... If he'd just do what he was told.'

Me: [Nods]

As Simon began to speak I started watching his body language carefully and I became increasingly aware that he was speaking more quickly and at times appeared almost desperate. He became increasingly restless and was moving around in his seat and shifted his eye contact continually. I felt that as he was talking he was almost revisiting the moment and the increasing tension within the room was palpable.

Simon: 'I just told him.... I just said look shut up now, that's enough. You're being naughty now.'

Me: 'Do you think he understood what you were saying?'

Simon: 'Well, he soon shut up anyway.'

Me: 'Why did he shut up, Simon?'

As Simon was telling me this he was gripping the arms of the chair and had his feet planted firmly and squarely on the floor. He appeared physically rigid and gave little in the way of eye contact, and fluctuated between glancing at me and then staring down at the floor.

Simon: 'Well, I did what any other dad would do. You have to show them. I know what you're thinking. I didn't hit him. I just shouted at him. And he went really quiet.... You have to show them....'

Me: 'Okay....'

Simon: 'He was just, like, looking at me, staring. I think I might have frightened him a bit. Then Claire came in and said "What's going on?" And she took Stan and then it was like a switch had been turned on and he started screaming again. I just said to Claire, "I've had enough of this" and I went to work.'

Me: 'It sounds like you were really angry with Stanley. Do you think that he understood that?'

Simon: 'Yeah, well he knew I was angry with him. That's why he shut up. I didn't mean to frighten him, but he knew he was just being naughty.'

I was very concerned with what I was hearing. Simon appeared to have little understanding of child development, and seemed to have unrealistic expectation of what Stanley could understand and fulfil. There is a known association between parents' affective states (particularly emotional upset and anger) and their attributions for children's behaviour. Barnes and Azar (1990) found a significant positive relation between the degree to which participants attributed negative intent to child misbehaviour and unrealistic expectations for children's abilities.

While listening to his account I was considering the theory of mind. Coined by Premack and Woodruff, theory of mind is the ability to attribute mental states – beliefs, intents, desires, pretending, knowledge, etc – to oneself and others and to understand that others have beliefs, desires, intentions and perspectives that are different from one's own. A central component includes an understanding of intentionality. One common mistake young children make is basing their judgements of others' intentions (as good or bad) on the outcomes of their actions (for example, bad outcomes are the product of bad intentions) when, in fact, intent and outcome don't always match in real life (Feinfield et al, 1999).

Abusive parents often believe that babies should not be "given in to" or allowed to "get away with anything." They believe that their children must periodically be shown "who is boss" and made to respect authority so they will not become disobedient (Steele, 1975).

Me: 'How do you know he knew he was being naughty? What was it that told you that?'

Simon: 'Well, he soon shut up when I shouted at him, didn't he?'

Me: 'Do you think that it may have been because you made a loud noise at him? He may have been frightened into being quiet because of the noise.'

Simon: 'No, he knew all right.'

Me: 'Do you think that babies as young as Stanley understand what adults are saying to them?'

Simon: 'Well, no, not everything, no. But they get what you mean.'

Me: 'How do you think they learn to do that? How would he have known, for example, that you would think his crying was being naughty?'

Simon: 'Well, I shouted at him. That would have told him.'

Me: 'Had you shouted at him before for other things?'

Simon: 'Well, not like that, no. But he was really bad that day.'

Me: 'So you think that because he had been shouted at before, he would understand that it meant you didn't like his behaviour. He was being naughty?'

Simon: 'Well, yeah, I suppose. I dunno. Look, I don't know where all this is going. I know what you're saying, this is my fault.'

Me: 'Do you think it is?'

Simon: 'Maybe, well yeah, yeah, it is I suppose…. I guess that's why we are here….'

This felt like a fairly significant breakthrough. It was the first time in the entire case that we had heard like Simon acknowledging being angry with Stanley, and he was clearly beginning to look at the irrationality of his behaviour towards his son.
My experience had taught me that there is a point in sessions when clients begin to respond less to specific questions and instead start to tell a more reflective narrative, which is the telling of their own story rather than a story they think professionals want to hear. I thought that this was a sign that Simon could be about to tell me his story of what happened. I was pleased because not only was it a useful way of moving forwards, but it also demonstrated that Simon was starting to trust me. I felt that this also showed that he was willing to engage with me and give me a real insight into his thoughts and feelings.

Simon: 'I never meant to frighten him though. I just got frustrated. I was out of my depth, if I'm honest. I didn't know anything about babies. What would I know? I've had me nieces and nephews around and that but that's been at my mums. I've not had to look after one. Not properly.'

Me: 'Do you think looking back you were looking after Stanley properly?'

Simon: 'No, I wasn't. I let him down.'

Me: 'So you took him from Claire and you got his bottle and took him upstairs. What were you thinking about at the time?'

Simon: 'Well, I just thought, like, give him his bottle, settle him down and then see if he will go down in his cot. But he wouldn't take his bottle, he was kicking and screaming and pushing it away. I was getting really frustrated. Then I leaned forward to put him down and his head just bumped on the cot side. That was all. You could hardly hear it.'

Me: 'So you came upstairs to settle Stan down and give him his bottle and he was crying and not wanting to take it and you were getting frustrated. [Simon agrees] You decided to put Stan in the cot and you think that as you did so you bumped Stan's head on the cot? [Simon agrees] When you say you felt frustrated, what did that look like? So, if I had been there, what might I have seen?'

Simon: 'Well, I was just rushing about; I was getting a bit, well, a bit angry if I'm honest. I was just that tired.'

Me: 'What was it do you think that you found frustrating?'

Simon: 'Well, he was, just, he wouldn't do what I told him, he just wouldn't help me and he was pushing me away. He was making me angry with him.'

Me: 'Tell me more about feeling angry.'

Simon: 'He was just making me angry, he kept kicking at me and arching his back. It was like he was trying to get away.'

Me: 'And that was frustrating you and making you angry?'

Simon: 'Yeah, it was just a nightmare.'

Although I was tempted to question Simon about bumping Stan's head on the cot side, I held back for a moment to instead spend time exploring his emotions while they were fresh in his mind, particularly his description of himself as getting frustrated. I thought it would be helpful to slow things down at this point and try to get him to describe his feelings in greater detail, as I felt it was important to understand what 'frustrated' meant in his world. My view of what frustrated might look like may have been very different from his, and I couldn't assume I was clear about his use of 'frustrated' over the many other adjectives he may have chosen. What was of interest is that when I did explore the meaning of this word, it changed to 'a bit angry', which describes another emotion altogether. However, this tactic appeared to prompt Simon to disclose some more information as he then described how Stanley's rejection of him appeared to have made him angry. Simon seemed to have unrealistic expectations of how a baby could meet his needs on some level. I noticed, for example, how he said "He wouldn't help me." I was curious and I wanted to find out how far Simon felt that Stanley was being wilfully difficult as opposed to be simply a baby who was very distressed.

Me: 'So, during this time upstairs, when you were trying to get Stanley to take his bottle and you were getting frustrated and angry with him, did you say anything to him?'

Simon: 'What like? He doesn't really understand what you say.'

This was a complete contrast to what Simon had been saying earlier about Stanley understanding when he was 'being naughty', and I was confused as to why this had changed. However, with a little more questioning it became clearer.

Me: 'Well, it's just that earlier, when you took him upstairs, you picked him up off Claire's lap and talked to him then. You called him "little man".'

Simon: 'I don't think he really knows what we are saying. I just say things like that because Claire likes it.' [Simon laughs]

Me: 'Simon, do you remember that earlier we were talking about Stanley being "naughty" and how he understood when he had done the wrong thing because he responded when you shouted at him?'

Simon: 'Yeah.'

Me: 'Well, I'm a bit confused. You told me that Stanley was being naughty and you needed to tell him off, but you are also saying that you don't think he really understands what you are saying to him.'

Simon: 'Well, yeah, like when he's being naughty, oh he knows all right. He does it to wind me up, he pushes it, you know? Like I was saying, he takes the piss. He tries to make me look stupid. But I'm not right. He needs to learn that.'

Me: 'So you think Stan does have enough understanding to know when he is deliberately making you angry – when he's "taking the piss"?'

Simon: 'Well, yeah, but all that other stuff – that "Mumsie talk." What's the point? I just was saying all that stuff 'cos Claire likes it. I think it's stupid really to do all that. He's just a baby, they don't know jack....'

Me: 'Do you talk to Stanley when you are on your own?'

Simon: 'No, why would you? No, I just let him get on with it. You might as well talk to that wall.' [Simon smiles]

This clearly showed a real split in Simon's thinking in terms of Stanley's level of development. On the one hand, he regarded him as being a child with advanced abilities in terms of having a complex theory of mind with regard to intentionality; on the other, he felt that actually Stanley had very little understanding of anything that was being said to him and that to think he did was ridiculous. Again, this heightened my concern in terms of Simon being a safe carer for Stanley, and that if Claire didn't understand the way he was thinking and feeling, her ability to protect Stanley would be compromised.

Me: 'Okay, so let's go back to your account of what happened. You were saying that when you were trying to give Stanley his bottle, he was crying and not wanting to take it and you were getting frustrated. You were putting him down and you "bumped" Stan's head on the cot?'

Simon: 'Yeah, that's right, that's what happened. It was just a bump.'

Me: 'How did you know you had "bumped" it?'

Simon: 'Well I heard it, it was just like a bash, like, a proper bash.'

I was interested in this contrast because what Simon had said earlier was that the 'bump' could hardly be heard.

Me: 'So it was more as if he'd hit his head rather than bumped it, would you say?'

Simon: 'Well, yeah, it was, to be honest. It was more like he'd hit it. But I didn't mean it, I hadn't like cracked his head on purpose or anything.'

Me: 'Well, no, I don't think we are saying that, but I was just wondering if you maybe hit it harder than you had first thought, now you are looking back on it?'

Simon: 'Well, yeah, I think I must have. It's all there, like, in the doctor's report. So, yeah, I must have.'

Me: 'Do you think, Simon, that perhaps when he was crying downstairs and then went floppy in Claire's arms, you already knew then that you had seriously hurt him when you hit his head?'

At this point I knew I had to provide Simon with some space, and so I used my own silence to provide Simon with some thinking time.

Simon: [Silence, but he looks down at his hands and shuffles back on his seat] 'This is just a mess....'

Me: [Silence]

Simon: 'Yeah, I did....'

Me: [Silence]

Simon: 'I heard his head bash on the cot and he screamed and I thought ... well that's not good, but I just gave it a rub and that. The lump had already come up and I thought, oh no, Claire's going to kill me. So I got a bit scared, I thought she's going to go ballistic.'

Me: 'So when were you going to tell her what happened?'

Simon: 'Well, when I took him down I was going to say, but then he was screaming and that and she took him and I just didn't say. And then when she saw the bump and he went all blue I was just scared, I thought he was going to die and then the hospital, and the police and we're being interviewed and that, and I just wanted it to all go away.'

Me: [Silence]

Simon: 'Will you help me tell her I'm sorry?'

Reflection 'on' action

As a newly qualified worker, I often placed myself in situations that were considered risky so that I could work with people. I think that sometimes my need to get clients to work with me seemed to be a prize, the goal of my intervention. However, on occasion I had become entangled in their denial and often felt I was being drawn in. Sometimes I think I was even on the periphery of collusion. Some of this was about my own personal and professional naivety, but I also believe now that it was often born out of fear. Partly the fear was related to me being anxious to be seen by my new colleagues as a competent worker, someone who could 'hack it'. However, on reflection I think it was also born out of the naive belief that if I was nice to my clients, they would want to be different with me. They would want to work with me, and if they did, then I could reach them in a way that no one else had been able to.

Looking back, I think I was also driven by a fear of conflict with others. By nature, I am a quiet, reflective soul, and had been quite frightened by the raised angry voices of some of my clients, particularly men. I dealt with this by placating wherever possible and avoiding confrontation where I could. When I look back now at my early practice and how little guidance I received in dealing with these feelings, it concerns me greatly. Perhaps this is something I needed to think about in more detail and work out over time. In contrast, however, over the years, I have increasingly observed other workers adopt what I refer to as 'modern social work practice'. By this I mean I have noticed a covert, aggressive attitude emerge between social worker and parent, and it has worried me. I have often heard this approach being described as 'robust', 'challenging' or 'evidence-based'. However, I think this approach has actually just disguised a form of aggression as it borders on a punitive rather than productive approach.

Instead of mirroring this technique, I have tried over the years to develop a style that is compassionate and that works hard to establish a collaborative relationship, one that is based on ensuring my communication has clarity and structure, and I think I achieved this with Simon. I have also tried to create an evidence-informed practice, which is based on what I believe to be sound professional judgement. That is not to say that I, in any way, condone the behaviour of some of my clients, but I do try to understand what lies beneath such behaviour for them. I try to achieve this by challenging their beliefs and behaviours, not in a brutal, confrontational or argumentative way, but by using an approach that is designed to encourage disclosure rather than inhibit it.

I believe that observing the way someone behaves is important during assessments such as these; however, I am also aware that I could make assumptions, so I always feel it is important to check out my observations by checking with the client their thoughts on what I had seen. For example, I might say, "I have noticed that whenever we talk about your childhood, you start to scratch your neck and pick at your hands. Why do you think that is?"

Sometimes I have found that the client has not noticed this behaviour before, and this would then lead us to explore it in more detail together. Over the years, my experience has taught me that it is important to talk to people about their action in the moment of the behaviour because returning to that point later in the conversation may leave the client anxious. This is because they are unlikely to remember the specifics of what was said or why the movement was made.

Again, these small pieces add to the overall jigsaw of the rapport that I am trying to create. In addition, the offer of a drink provides other assessment opportunities, and despite appearing at first sight to be an unusual assessment tool, it can be used to good effect with uncooperative or avoidant clients. For example, if a client is presenting as unresponsive or avoidant to questioning of the assessor, perhaps sitting with a closed body posture such as folded arms, the dynamic of the room can be changed, first by suggesting a short break, and then by offering a cup of tea.

I also realised the importance of body positions when working with Simon. Rossberg-Gempton and Poole (1993) found that open postures were often associated with increased positive emotions, whereas closed postures elicited negative emotions. I had learned from this research that if I placed Simon's drink just slightly out of reach, when he reached for it he was forced to alter his body posture. This, in turn, appeared to alter his emotional state. Therefore, if he was initially refusing to discuss a matter, he would change by talking and opening up. I would also try to mirror Simon's body language and try to make use of unconscious processes to build rapport with him. Maxwell and Cook (1985) found that postural congruence between individuals can improve a relationship between two people, and by mirroring Simon's body language while drinking my tea, I felt I was naturally creating a warm conducive atmosphere of rapport without him being aware of it.

Summary

I began this chapter by describing the case as presented to me by the Court with regard to very serious injuries to a very young child, and went on to discuss the complexities inherent in revisiting a historical event and trying to make sense of the situation as it stands now.

Although Simon was a complex character, he did not present as being a particularly difficult case to manage in that he was compliant and motivated to engage in the assessment. This, however, was conditional on the fact that he also wanted to go home. Throughout the assessment, I was aware of the fact that as assessing social workers, we wield a lot of power, and the client is aware that we can give a negative report to Court if they don't comply. This knowledge is a burdening presence within any assessment session. As a result, I needed to work hard to build a trusting and respectful relationship with Simon, and this was at the forefront of my mind, particularly in the earlier sessions.

The fact that Simon was able to talk more honestly about his part in the head injury was at least a start, but the issue of the pelvis fracture was still yet to be addressed. I was aware of this, but I had decided that it would be better to address this in the next session. I did not make any assumptions that we would necessarily pick up where we left off. Simon would have had time to reflect on our discussion and may have arrived at the next session wishing to retract some, or all, of what he had said. While this is not unusual, it does highlight the need to keep working at relationships in complex assessment, and the need for social workers to use every means at their disposal in order to ensure a good outcome for the children we work for.

In conclusion, although Simon had admitted causing an injury and his remorse was taken into consideration, the fact that he had confessed to seriously injuring his child meant that there were sufficient ongoing safeguarding concerns. It was recommended that he should not return to the family home. Even though Stanley had made a full recovery and was progressing extremely well, it was agreed that Simon would not be allowed to have unsupervised contact until Stanley was old enough to self-protect. When Claire heard this news, she filed for divorce and refused to have any further contact with Simon. An agreement was reached with the family that Simon's parents would manage the contact with Simon by having Stanley at their home on a weekly basis.

Further reading

Doherty, M. (2008) *Theory of mind: How children understand others' thoughts and feelings*, International Texts in Developmental Psychology, Kindle Amazon

The understanding of belief is central to this text, which explains in simple terms what representational theory of mind is all about, and shows how researchers have demonstrated this understanding in children. The book considers what leads to this understanding, including the role of pretend play, understanding of attention and eye direction, and other precursors to representational understanding of mind. The general relevance of theory of mind is demonstrated through coverage of the development of other mental state concepts, and the relationship between understanding mental representation and other representational media.

Holman, M. (2015) *Motivational Interviewing in social work practice*, Applications of Motivational Interviewing, New York: Guilford Press
Motivational interviewing (MI) offers powerful tools for helping social work clients draw on their strengths to make desired changes in their lives. This reader-friendly book introduces practitioners and students to MI, and demonstrates how to integrate this evidence-based method into direct practice. Extensive sample dialogues illustrate MI skills in action with individuals and groups. The book also presents best practice for MI training, teaching and agency-wide integration.

References

Barnes, K.T. and Azar, S.T. (1990) 'Maternal expectations and attributions in discipline situation: A test of a cognitive model or parenting', Paper presented at the annual meeting of the American Psychological Association, Boston, MA.

Cantor, M.H. (1979) 'Neighbors and friends: An overlooked resource in the informal support system', *Research on Aging*, vol 1, pp 434–63.

Feinfield, K.A., Lee, P.P., Flavell, E.R., Green, F.L. and Flavell, J.H. (1999) 'Young children's understanding of intention', *Cognitive Development*, vol 14, pp 463–86.

Gutheil, I. (1992) 'Considering the physical environment: An essential component of good practice', *Social Work*, vol 37, pp 361–6.

Haase, R., DiMattia, D. and Berdie, R.F. (1970) 'Proxemic behaviour: Counselor, administrator, and client preference for seating arrangement in dyadic interaction', *Journal of Counselling Psychology*, vol 17, no 4, pp 319–25.

Kahn, R.L. and Cannell, C.F. (1957) *The dynamics of interviewing: Theory, technique and cases*, New York: Wiley.

Maxwell, G. and Cook, M. (1985) 'Postural congruence and judgments of liking and perceived similarity', *New Zealand Journal of Psychology*, vol 14, no 1, pp 20–6.

Premack, D. and Woodruff, G. (1978) 'Does the chimpanzee have a theory of mind?', *Behavioral and Brain Science*, vol 4, pp 515–26.

Richardson, S.A., Dohrenwend, B.S. and Klein, D. (1965) *Interviewing: Its forms and functions*, New York: Basic Books.

Rossberg-Gempton, I. and Poole, G.D. (1993) 'The effect of open and closed postures on pleasant and unpleasant emotions', *The Arts in Psychotherapy*, vol 20, no 1, pp 75–82.

Schroeder, J., Risen, J., Gino, F. and Norton, M.I. (2014) *Handshaking promotes cooperative dealmaking*, Harvard Business School Working Paper No 14-117, May.

Steele, B.F. (1975) 'Working with abusive parents from a psychiatric point of view', Bulletin, DHEW Publication No (OHD) 76-30070, Washington, DC: US Government Printing Office.

8

Dealing with manipulative parents and unhealthy attachments

Introduction

This case examines an apparently intractable private law case in which two children (aged 5 and 11) had been caught up in a battle for custody. The father was manipulative of the children and his relationship with them appeared to be one of viewing his son as his peer and his daughter as a tool with which to control the behaviour of his ex-wife.

Of all cases, perhaps the ones I found most difficult were those in private law proceedings. In private law cases, the issues tended to relate to applications in respect of the child's residence and with whom they would be having contact following the divorce or separation of the parents. The difficulty that arose was that, as a social worker, I felt placed in a complex position. Normally within Care Proceedings one would expect to have a solicitor or barrister to represent the local authority, and a guardian to represent the child. However, within private law cases, only the parents (and perhaps other parties such as grandparents) are represented, and it is the duty of the social worker to take the lead in negotiation.

More complex situations arise when one or both parents decide not to have legal advice and instead represent themselves. I am then often faced with not only dealing with my own position but also having to be the 'voice of reason' with respect to at least one (if not two) people who have no prior experience of the legal system but have firm views regarding what they feel is the best course of action. This often happened when the parents had reached an impasse and were unable to take the matter further. In this kind of situation, the judge who hears the case will look to the social worker to take a lead in ensuring that the matter will be resolved to the benefit of the child. However, the situation is complicated further when one or both parents has concerning personality traits that make it difficult for the social worker to work with them, particularly when this then appears to have a detrimental effect on the children.

Theoretical perspectives

Within this chapter I draw on research with regard to the effect of acrimonious divorce on children and the effects that emotional abuse may have on the internal working model, as proposed by Bowlby (1979). In addition, theory with regard to domestic abuse is discussed.

Acrimony and divorce

In families in which domestic abuse has been an issue, it is likely that immediately following separation, children will be exposed to especially high levels of conflict between parents. If post-separation conflict does occur between parents, it is less likely to involve compromise, and some of the key issues will be in relation to child-related matters (Buchanan and Heiges, 2001). This would include issues with regard to contact and residence. In addition, El-Sheikh and Harger (2001) found that children most vulnerable to marital conflict perceived high levels of threat in their parents' behaviour and tended to blame themselves for the conflict. Parents involved in a high-conflict relationship are often distracted from their roles as parents by the amount of energy and time they expend warring with each other. They are less emotionally available to the children and less effective as parents (Emery and Coiro, 1995). In cases in which divorce fails to resolve the conflict between the parents in which there is protracted litigation, the children may become caught up in the middle, with no clear avenue of escape.

Internal working model theory

The internal working model (IWM) developed from Bowlby's work on attachment (Bowlby, 1979). The IWM is defined as a process of thinking about the world based on previous experiences. It helps the child to consider the most appropriate responses and actions. So, for example, as children interact with their caregivers, they begin to internalise those experiences and form 'schemas' or representations of the world, in the same way expectations with regard to relationships develop. In cases where the IWM becomes maladapted, social workers will see children who perhaps view the world as a threatening and dangerous place. They may view their parents as powerless, unable to protect them from that danger or perhaps, paradoxically, be the cause of it.

Domestic violence in families

Humphreys (2006) found that children exposed to domestic violence are more likely to have behavioural and emotional problems. Children are also at risk of being caught up in the violence being perpetrated, either through being injured while being held by their mother during an attack, or in the case of older children being injured while trying to protect their mother. There are, of course, some cases where children have been directly abused by the perpetrator. In cases where children have died, violence towards their mother has frequently featured in the family's dynamics (Sidebotham et al, 2016).

Case study

Context

This case relates to Craig and Eve, the children of Terry and Samantha. Terry and Samantha had recently separated under acrimonious circumstances when Samantha had commenced a relationship with someone else. Samantha and her partner were, at the time of this assessment, living together.

Although there was a shared care arrangement in place, concerns had been raised in relation to Terry's influence on the children. Terry used his parents to try to control Samantha by asking them to question the children when they had contact visits. It appeared that Terry would then use this information against Samantha whenever possible. The children were often heard to refer to their mother as an 'adulterer' and a 'slut', and while Craig was not entirely averse to this in the presence of his father, when he was with his mother he would become inconsolable and tell her he didn't mean it.

While Craig was not entirely averse to this in the presence of his father, when he was with his mother he would become inconsolable and tell her he didn't mean it. Craig would also become aggressive towards his mother and had assaulted her more than once. Anna Freud (1936) suggested that children placed in stressful situations often protect themselves by impersonating the aggressor, assuming his [sic] attributes or imitating his aggression. The child, therefore, transforms themself from the person threatened into the person who makes the threat. Although Craig understood the meaning of the words used, Eve did not, and was confused when Samantha became cross with her for saying them. It appeared as if the children were being manipulated so that Terry could assert pressure on Samantha.

Terry and Samantha each insisted that the children should live with them, and had not been able to agree on arrangements for contact and residence, and so the matter had gone to Court for an application for a Contact and Residence Order under Section 8 of the Children Act 1989. Child Arrangements Orders were introduced by the Children and Families Act 2014 to replace Contact and Residence Orders. The Section 7 welfare report arose from this application and was meant to provide the Court with all the available evidence and information about the children's situation. It was supposed to advise the Court of their wishes and feelings. It also included what the court welfare officer (CWO) considered to be the best outcome for them.

However, on looking at this case, it appeared to me that the CWO had been somewhat intimidated by Terry who had been quite aggressive and challenging towards him. The CWO knew that Terry's primary interest was Craig, and in my view, he had submitted a report that had recommended that the simplest solution was for Craig to reside with Terry, and for Eve to reside with Samantha.

However, given the concerns regarding the ongoing emotional abuse of Craig, in terms of his father's damaging influence, the judge in the matter expressed some concern. Therefore, an application had been made for a further Section 37 report (Children Act 1989) to be compiled by the local authority in order to address some of the issues of concern and to look at whether Care Proceedings may need to be instigated. Section 37 of the Children Act 1989 allows the Court to direct the local authority to conduct an investigation into a child's circumstances and report its findings, if, during any private law proceedings, a question arises about the welfare of the child, and it seems to the Court that it might be appropriate for a Care Order or Supervision Order to be made.

This was the situation that I was faced with when I first attended Court. I had read all of the Court papers that had been filed – the 'Court Bundle' – and felt that the situation needed re-examining given the changes to the children's circumstances. I was concerned that this case had been going on for quite some time and that the children had apparently been privy to many arguments, not only between the parents, but also between extended family members. The attitude of Terry towards the Court process had been dismissive (he had been warned by the judge on two occasions that he was in danger of being found in contempt due to his disrespectful behaviour). Although the CWO had reported the children's wishes and feelings, I was concerned that Craig had been quoted as repeating almost word for word the views expressed by his father, and I was curious as to what was going on in this context. What were the children's wishes and feelings? How was I going to engage this family and assist the Court in understanding what the children's needs were?

I knew I needed more time, and so, when I attended Court that morning, I requested that the judge grant me a three-week adjournment to allow me to meet with the family. I needed to assess not only what might be the most appropriate living and contact arrangements, but also to look at the issues with regard to the possible emotional abuse of the children caused by the acrimonious situation between the parents. I knew that time was of the essence, and so I arranged to visit Terry that afternoon in order to gain his views. The paternal grandparents agreed to take the children to the cinema.

On arriving at the family home, I found the door open. When I rang the bell, I heard Terry shout for me to come in. He was in the living room. I was struck immediately by how untidy everything was, with unwashed dishes on every surface, and pizza boxes and empty drinks cans and clothes strewn around the floor and furniture. There was a large television and a games console showed a game was in progress. I also noted the half-eaten chicken leg on the arm of a chair. It reminded me of visiting a house shared by young students. Terry was sitting in a chair in front of the television and he asked me to wait a minute as he was just at a difficult part of the game. He never took his eyes of the screen and continued playing for a few more minutes.

Reflection points

1. Faced with this situation what might you have done?
2. He had been expecting me to call round. Why do you think he behaved as he did?
3. Should I have interrupted what he was doing and insisted that he stop playing his game and listen to what I had to say?
4. I could have just left. Why do you think I felt it benefited me to stay?
5. What would be the advantages and disadvantages of such action?

I was tempted to tell Terry that I could see he had other priorities and that perhaps he could ring me when he was not too busy to discuss the care of his children and then leave. However, I wanted to observe why he was behaving in the way that he was and why he felt this was appropriate behaviour. I have found that sometimes allowing situations to play out can be informative and helpful for learning more about families rather than worrying about my own pride.

Although I was well used to challenging behaviour on home visits, I felt that perhaps Terry had a particular strategy in mind. I wondered if this was more than simple rudeness rather than an attempt to assert a level of control, putting me in my place, 'I'll deal with you in my own time and you will wait until I am good and ready.' At one time it would have made me feel somewhat 'wrong-footed' and awkward, unsure of what to do next, but I have learned over the years that people have a range of strategies for dealing with stressful situations, and that attempting to take back or at least equalise power may be one of them. Rather than respond to Terry's 'challenge', I simply waited him out and moved the items of clothing and a pizza box from the sofa to make room for me to sit down.

After a few minutes, Terry saved the game and then turned to me, "Oh, I'd almost forgotten you were there, sit down then." It would have been easy to respond to this, as it was clearly highly unlikely he would have forgotten about me, but I chose to ignore his comment and suggested to Terry that we go through where the case was up to so that I could understand what had happened from his perspective. I began by checking some of the basic details of his personal circumstances and then moved on to ask Terry about Samantha's written statements, the ones that suggested he was trying to turn Craig against her and was neglectful of Eve.

'You can't believe everything you read you know. She doesn't know what day of the week it is. Can't look after them kids you know. I can tell you plenty about her. You ask the neighbours, they know it all. Of course, I don't need to tell you anything; I bet you've seen it all before. Oh yes, I can tell you aren't the type of person to be taken in by someone like her. I bet you have already made your mind up about the kind of person she is. Yes, no one is going to pull the wool over your eyes.'

He continued this flattery by talking about how I had presented at Court, and even went on to use the words 'ultimate professional'.

Reflection points
1. How would you have felt if this was directed at you?
2. What do you think was going through his mind at the time?
3. How would you have dealt with the situation?

In my experience, this kind of behaviour can be interpreted as a form of manipulation. People like to be liked, they like to hear people say they are doing a good job and to have validation from clients, especially in complex child protection situations, can be particularly appealing. However, for those workers who lack confidence, this can be the short road to disaster. Cialdini and Goldstein (2004) present flattery as a tactic used by individuals to persuade others to perform activities or actions they would not otherwise conduct. Therefore, when you are flattered, you are more likely to feel a desire to favour people and be nicer to them. Such lack of objectivity by the worker can be dangerous.

There were two ways in which I could have dealt with it. First, by invalidating the flattery and removing any potential power: 'Thanks for that, but what we were discussing was....' However, given the reports throughout the case files that recorded Terry's attempts at manipulating professionals, I felt that it needed to be dealt with once and for all. The method I have found most effective in the past is simply to place the situation 'on the table', that is, 'You are trying to win me over and I spotted it.' By making the person feel uncomfortable, one usually finds that the tactic stops. I did this by saying to Terry, "My experience tells me that you are trying to win me over through flattery, and that makes me suspicious about the situation with your children. Do you think that's an accurate observation?" Terry's face flushed, he appeared lost for words and it took a moment or two for him to recover his composure. "No, no, it's not that love, I was just saying like...." Once that was dealt with, I chose to simply move on.

We then discussed his views with regard to residence. It was clear that from his perspective that Samantha had caused irreparable damage to the children by leaving. He felt they would be further damaged by having any form of contact with her or with her family. He believed it was in the children's best interests to "forget they even have a mother". Although I could understand his anger and distress at his wife leaving him, I felt that Terry was not thinking about the children's needs in terms of the importance of their relationship with their mother, which, up until the divorce, had been extremely close. I suggested to Terry that the children's relationship *with* their parents was a separate issue from the relationship *between* the parents, and that perhaps there was a way to maintain one without needing to continue the other. However, Terry was adamant that the children didn't need any form of relationship with Samantha, who he called "The adulterer", or her family, and that he would do whatever he needed to ensure that that did not happen. "Yeah, the kids might get hurt in the process but that's her fault, not mine. I hope she can live with what happens."

This comment seemed to me to be consistent with the traits of a narcissistic personality. His behaviour towards the children was primarily focused on his own needs and his primary goal was to 'win', whatever the cost. He appeared to feign genuine empathy and made me feel that he was entitled to special treatment. Samantha, in particular, had mentioned in one of her statements that he treated her, and others around him, like staff, and that everything was on his terms, in his own time. This resonated with me in terms of the way in which he made me wait for him to finish his game.

When I asked Terry what he thought the children's view of their mother was, he told me that they hated her and never wanted to see her again. "They only want me and my family. No one else. They want to live with me." As Terry spent quite some time saying the same thing in different ways, I felt that at this point I had gone as far as I could, and so I told Terry that I would continue my enquires and would get back to him.

I reflected later about the effect of acrimonious divorces on the parties concerned. Although it appeared from the Court evidence that Terry may always have struggled in relationships, I wondered what happened to people psychologically during the process. It certainly appeared that both Samantha and Terry individually had the perception that, rightly or wrongly, the Court system was not recognising their needs or interests. I felt that this was likely to increase feelings of animosity towards each other and would not benefit the children. It seemed to me that these parents saw themselves through a lens of being 'winners' or 'losers', not only in the eyes of the law, but also in how they were perceived by the children. However, whatever the outcome of the case, both Terry and Samantha would need to continue to bring up the children, and so needed to learn to deal with their relationships on this new footing. The children needed them to find some middle ground if they were not to be damaged by their parents' behaviour, and that meant that each would need to offer some concessions.

As I was leaving Terry's house, a neighbour came out into the front garden and began sharpening a pencil into the grill outside her door while paying close attention to me as I said goodbye. This was not an especially unusual occurrence, if neighbours become aware of social care involvement; they can become interested in the reason why. Sharpening a pencil into the grill, however, seemed a particularly spurious reason for being in the garden. It is more often likely to be a case of emergency weeding that is required. I was just about to get into my car when she ran across the road to me and asked if I was "The Social".

Reflection point

1. This is always a tricky situation to manage. On the one hand, it is very important to respect the confidentiality of the family concerned; on the other, quite often neighbours are an important source of information with regard to children's safety. Given what you now know about this family. what would you do?

   It would have been easy to have denied all knowledge and got into my car and drive away; however, I was wary of doing that in case the neighbour had important safeguarding information. I therefore decided it was better to stay and hear what she had to stay without disclosing any confidential information.

Health and Care Professions Council (HCPC) requirements are very clear that, as a registrant, I have a professional and legal duty to 'respect and protect the confidentiality of service users at all times' (HCPC 2008). However, in certain circumstances, such confidentiality may be broken in order to prevent serious harm to others and so be in the public interest.

I felt that given the concerns Samantha had expressed regarding Terry's care of the children that I needed to be sure that I was not missing any vital pieces of information that may assist me in my duty to safeguard. However, I was somewhat wary. I had no way of knowing what the relationship was between the family and this person and indeed, at that point, I had no idea what it was she wanted. She may have wished to report on another matter entirely. I needed to be cautious.

Therefore, without actually disclosing my identity, I asked the neighbour what she wanted. She simply thrust a piece of paper in my hand and went back to her house. I didn't respond but got into my car and drove off. When I got around the corner, I looked at the paper and saw that it contained a name and telephone number. I rang the number from my mobile phone and while not divulging the nature of my involvement, I had, what turned out to be, a very long conversation with the neighbour in which she cited numerous concerns regarding the family.

The neighbour (Agnes) was particularly worried about Eve who appeared to be quite isolated within the household. "I often see her sitting on her own on the front step with her dolls while Terry and Craig are in the back garden. Sometimes it can be quite late in the evening. She seems so sad, bless her.... That lad [Craig] is out of control, well him *and* his dad. The noise they make, and the daft things they do." The neighbour told me that Terry and Craig had been engaging in dangerous behaviour with fireworks and had been tying large rockets onto stuffed toys and then letting them off. She had seen Eve very upset when one of her Barbie dolls suffered a similar fate. "You'd think he'd know better, a grown-man behaving like that."

Agnes went on to tell me that Terry had been encouraging Craig to hit his sister, telling her she needed to 'toughen up'. He had even gone so far as to buy them boxing gloves.

This information made me feel distressed and worried for Eve. If what Agnes had said was true, then it seemed that Eve was suffering abuse not only from her father but also from her brother. As a mother myself, I thought about how my own child might have fared and the effect such parenting might have had on him, and I felt angry that Eve was being placed in this situation. It reminded me that no matter how highly trained and experienced professionals may be, we are not immune to the effect of cases on our own emotions.

In research into the feelings of social workers who are parents, Zubrzycki (1999) described how, after returning to work from maternity leave, she found herself at times more emotionally affected by issues, and yet more professionally attuned to the needs of parents. I could understand this sentiment entirely. I felt that my own situation not only allowed me to empathise with Eve, but I could also understood how worried Samantha was and why she felt it was urgent that she needed to protect her children. In addition, I was concerned for Craig in terms of what messages Terry was giving him regarding safe boundaries.

There is a considerable amount of research that demonstrates that children are most likely to have better psychological and social outcomes through authoritative parenting, which combines behavioural regulation with high levels of support (Lamborn et al, 1991; Steinberg, 2001). The evidence provided through the statements of not only the parents and the children but also now the neighbour made me wonder how Craig functioned socially if, on the one hand, his father was providing little in the way of boundaries, and, on the other, his mother tried hard to model an authoritative parenting style. I also wondered why it was that Terry was unable to model safe boundaries, why it was that he appeared to be acting as a peer and not as a parent. What need was this behaviour meeting in Terry? I wondered, too, about how Terry maintained boundaries in other areas of the family's life.

The following day I arranged to meet with Samantha while the children were at school. The contrast between the two visits was truly significant. The home of Samantha and her new partner Mike was warm and homely throughout. She presented well and was clearly an intelligent, articulate woman who had time to consider carefully all of the issues with regard to her children and the end of her marriage to Terry. At times, she became tearful, but she was able to give a quietly dignified explanation of the situation to date.

Samantha told me that she and Terry met when they were around 18. He was one of her first boyfriends. Terry had been jealous of any attention Samantha received, and would become quite volatile in his behaviour. He would, she said, dress this up as being protective, but as he became increasingly verbal and physically abusive towards her, he became more possessive, telling her that she was his now. She said he had said to her, "The relationship is over when I say it is and not before. And then I will destroy you."

On one occasion, Terry had hit Samantha in the face, giving her a black eye and a split lip. She had tried to end the relationship several times but he would come to her parents' home and demand to see her. In the end, she capitulated, as she was afraid of what he might do. Her parents were against the marriage as they had seen her injuries and were extremely worried about her. Shortly before the marriage both of her parents had moved away and so, feeling she had few other options at the time, she agreed to marry Terry.

In terms of the children, Samantha said that while she had been delighted at becoming pregnant, Terry, in contrast, was less than pleased. She believed that he was resentful of the attention being paid to her rather than him, and would insist on her walking several yards behind him when they went out. He would say derogatory things to her about her weight and that she should be ashamed of herself for looking as she did. This was reinforced by his father, Edward, who would ring her up and recommend that she stay at home for the remainder of her pregnancy, as "it's not nice for people to see you waddling around like that." Samantha felt quite pressured by this attitude in two such strong members of the family, and having few other people to talk to, she again capitulated.

On the day of Craig's birth, Terry didn't come to the hospital as he was playing golf with a friend. His mother came briefly, and while she was kind, she needed to leave in order to do Edward's evening meal for when he got home. However, when it was known that Craig was a healthy baby boy, Samantha told me that "everything changed". Within an hour of the birth, both Terry and Edward were at the hospital and she was effectively ignored, while they discussed which members of their family he looked like and their plans for his future. Samantha said that she felt as if she had been incidental to the whole process, and that Craig was clearly going to 'belong' to the paternal family. In the weeks that followed, Terry enjoyed showing Craig off to people when they visited and excluded Samantha wherever possible. Samantha told me she felt as if she were the family nanny rather than a mother, restricted to feeding and changing while Terry "had all of the fun".

Samantha thought carefully about having another baby, but she desperately wanted a little girl. "I think I wanted something out of this marriage for me. I felt as if Craig wasn't mine." When Eve was born the attitude of the paternal family towards her could not have been more marked. When Terry and his father discovered that she was a girl, they both immediately left the hospital and Samantha didn't see Terry again until she brought the baby home the next day. "I felt so ashamed, the staff in the hospital thought I was a single mum." Terry would insist that Eve was put alone in the bedroom when she cried, on the basis that it disturbed Terry's evening and that it was for her own good so that she wasn't spoilt.

Reflection points

1. If Eve was still a baby and it was happening now, what would you have felt if you had heard this?
2. What would you have done?
3. What do you think the implications of having had such an early experience would be for a child?
4. Do you think there is a potential for harm?
5. Can you say what that harm might be and why?

As discussed, early bonding and attachment are important for child development. If Eve felt that no one would come to her aid or meet her needs, I was worried she may have disengaged emotionally.

On hearing this story, I felt sad, not just for Eve, but also for Samantha. There are many debates about the efficacy of allowing babies to cry themselves to sleep and with regard to leaving a child alone in their room; however, the fundamental issue for me was that Samantha had not wished for this to happen. She had, instead, felt unable to challenge Terry's beliefs. Seeking the support of a health visitor would have been a good basis to assist both parents in finding a balance in terms of their different approaches to parenting.

It seemed that as the children moved out of 'babyhood', Craig continued to be treated differently to his sister. He was allowed special privileges such as choosing his own bedtimes, what he wore, ate and did during the day, and appeared over time to have developed a strong sense of entitlement: things should always be done to benefit him. The only person he deferred to was his father, Terry, who referred to him on occasion as "My Prince".

As Craig got older, he and Terry chose family holidays based on their own interests, and Craig chose the make and model of the family car. Both he and Terry had the same haircuts and dressed the same whenever possible. At the same time, Samantha told me, he was also close to his mother and looked to her for emotional support, for example, running to her when he hurt himself; however, this was never done in the presence of his father. Samantha said that when she was alone with the children she tried hard to instil appropriate behaviour and values and was successful to a degree, until Terry came home and Craig would revert to matching his father's behaviour.

Anna Freud (1936) used the term 'identify with the aggressor', in which she described how by impersonating the aggressor, assuming his [sic] attributes or imitating his aggression, the child could transform themself from the person threatened into the person who makes the threat. In addition, Hetherington et al (1967) found that in high-conflict families, where the father was dominant, boys had a tendency to imitate a dominant father and this would often override the effects of variations in conflict and warmth, such as having a mother who expressed warmth towards them. I felt that there was a strong likelihood that Craig was using this identification as a form of 'survival' strategy in order to protect himself.

Eve, in contrast, was shy and appeared as overwhelmed as her mother by the behaviour of her father and brother, whose dangerous stunts were inspired by an American television programme. These would involve setting fire to her dolls. On one occasion, when Samantha was not at home, they even tried to convince Eve to jump off the first floor balcony with an umbrella to see if it would break her fall. Eve only told her mother after the marriage had ended. It emerged that this idea had been Terry's suggestion.

I was shocked when I heard about this reckless behaviour. If it was true, and at this point I didn't know for sure, I was very concerned, not only because of the risk I felt was posed to Eve's welfare, but also because it seemed she was being used as a source of entertainment. As my reservations towards Terry increased so did my sympathy towards Samantha. I tried to maintain an objective and professional stance, but I was concerned that my own feelings may have been interfering with the assessment.

Reflection points

1. Do you think I let my own feelings interfere with the assessment?
2. Do you think Craig was a willing participant in the dangerous stunts?
3. What might have been going through Eve's head when the idea to jump was proposed?

It is always difficult as a parent, and also as a social worker, not to imagine one's own child in that situation and to prevent personal feelings affecting decision-making. The urge to agree with the person who seemed the most reasonable parent was strong; however, I recognised that I needed to remember that it was not my child who was part of this assessment. Adopting the role of 'child rescuer' would not have been of benefit to the children in the long term. I needed to be sure that I was listening to all involved and taking their views into consideration as well as thinking about how their actions were affecting the children. It could have been that Samantha was trying to manipulate me in the same way that Terry had tried. I needed to remain aware and make sure that I was critically reflecting on my own thoughts and feelings throughout. As a young boy, Craig was likely to be enjoying time with his father and unaware of the risks. Eve may have felt confused and unsure of what to say or do.

I met with my supervisor to discuss what was happening, and we agreed that I needed to make sure that the decisions I made were the right ones for both Eve and Craig, not because I didn't like Terry.

I realised during my supervision that I had been quite persuaded by Samantha's story, but if I was to maintain a clear focus on the purpose of the assessment, I had to talk to Eve to gain her version of the events. When I asked Eve about the stories that her mother had told me, she confirmed that her mother was telling the truth. This had happened. I was not imagining it. Eve then told me that after this incident, she had tried whenever possible to avoid being with Terry and Craig. She would spend most of her time in her room.

It made me realise that Terry's favouritism towards Craig and his subsequent rejection of Eve, combined with Samantha's desperate attempts to give the children some consistency, might have affected the development of their internal working models (see Bowlby, 1979). This meant that for Craig, he would have had a propensity to over-step boundaries and to think that social conventions and rules didn't apply to him due to him being allowed to do as he pleased. Samantha told me that if Craig didn't get his own way he would sometimes resort to violent tantrums.

Eve, on the other hand, appeared to demonstrate a deep sadness and hopelessness. It seemed that while she looked only to her mother to meet her needs, she was aware that this wouldn't always be possible. She was therefore at risk of developing an internal working model that led her to believe she was 'unworthy', or that she didn't deserve to have her needs met (see Cassidy, 1990). This led me to believe that both of the children's capacity to establish and maintain meaningful peer and intimate attachments would be compromised in future.

I could understand why Samantha thought the situation at home was untenable. Samantha told me that it had reached the point at which she felt that if she didn't act soon, she would lose the children. She could already see that Craig was being increasingly used by Terry and she was concerned about how this would affect him as he developed into a young man. Samantha was also worried about the effect that both Craig and Terry were having on Eve, who she felt was becoming increasingly withdrawn. To make matters worse, Terry had started to be more violent towards her. She told me, "I thought he would kill me and I didn't want the children to see it."

Samantha's decision to leave home that night had almost been spontaneous, but she said she didn't leave without intending to return for the children. Samantha said that she felt that a negotiated end to their marriage would have been in the children's interests, but Terry regarded them *all* as his possessions. Samantha felt that Terry's primary interest was to use the children as a weapon with which he could control and manipulate her.

On the day that Samantha left Terry, she had intended leaving with both of the children, but Craig had been taken out for the day by the paternal grandfather. She left with Eve and went to the home of her new partner. She told me that she sent a text message to Terry to say she had left home for good, but that she would return to collect Craig, her property and the dog. When she did return, Terry was out. He had left Craig alone in the house. She described the state of the property as "wrecked". "All my clothes had been cut up and photos destroyed, ornaments smashed, food smeared in my shoes. The eyes had been cut out of Eve's photographs and my glasses scratched and broken up."

Having heard this story, I could see how things had been gradually spiralling out of control and I was surprised that both the children and Samantha had not been physically injured in this household. It seemed evident that the children had not only been witness to abuse, but in the case of Craig, also potentially been encouraged to take part in it. I felt angry for these children that they had not been protected. Although I understood, of course, that Samantha's ability to do this had been severely compromised by the threats of harm from Terry, I couldn't help but empathise with the sense of fear and hopelessness that the children, Eve in particular, must have felt. I thought about the theories in relation to domestic violence, and I tried hard to imagine what it must have been like for Samantha to go through such an experience. Would she be able to recover sufficiently to support these children in the future?

Samantha's reasons for finally leaving fitted well with research completed by Gelles (1976) and Short et al (2000). Both have described how victims are more likely to seek help or end an abusive relationship when their children's risk of becoming emotionally or physically harmed by the family violence increases. In addition, studies have found that when the victim has increased access to avenues of support, they are more likely to leave a violent relationship (Gelles, 1976; Strube and Barbour, 1984; Short et al, 2000). This new avenue, or support, appeared to have arrived in the form of Samantha's new relationship. Her new partner offered her a glimpse of what life could be like for both her and the children, and she developed the courage to finally make the changes needed to protect her family from further abuses.

I also reflected deeply on Terry. I was so angry with him. What was it that could lead an individual to behave in such a way towards people he said he cared about? Could he not see the damage he was causing? In order to deal with these feelings, I needed to understand things from Terry's perspective. Even if I couldn't agree with him, I had to gain some insight in order to consider the best way forward. I needed to find out more about where his ideas on what constituted family relationships had come from.

From what I had gathered in my discussions with the family and with the CWO, it seemed that a key influence on Terry was his father, Edward, to whom he looked for advice in all areas of his life and with whom the children spent quite a bit of time. I therefore felt it would be useful to gain an understanding of his perspective by visiting them. With Terry's permission, I telephoned Edward and arranged to visit the next morning.

This proved to be an interesting visit as Edward demonstrated examples of behaviour that mirrored some of the boundary issues I had seen in Terry. Edward also made connotations that appeared 'over-friendly' towards women.

For example, when I arrived at their home, Edward opened the door and, as I introduced myself, he held out his hand as if to shake mine but then kissed the back of my hand and immediately asked me if I would like to use the toilet. I was taken aback at first. I felt his behaviour was rather familiar and it left me feeling quite uncomfortable. I politely, but firmly, declined his offer of using the toilet and tried to work out what was going on.

Edward's welcome seemed to contrast completely with the dismissive attitude of Terry who had ignored me at the start of my first visit. Both strategies appeared to work in different ways – both made me feel 'wrong-footed' or unsure of myself. I felt I was being tested and that I needed to think quickly if I was to come across well professionally, and so I suggested we sit down and have a chat. I noticed that Terry's mother, Denise, didn't leave the kitchen, and when I tried to engage with her, she told me that she didn't know anything about the family and that I should speak to her husband.

This struck me as strange given that Denise would have been familiar with Terry and his family. It made me question why she was distancing herself from the matter. I wondered if the attempts of controlling others, exhibited by Terry, were also a factor that played out in the relationship between Edward and Denise. Was Denise 'allowed' to give her views? Had she been told to stay in the kitchen by Edward? Or had she decided that she didn't want to be involved?

Throughout my discussion with Edward, he tried to convince me that Samantha was a flawed character, saying things like "she may be a little simple in the head, I think she drinks, you know, well women like that, they do. A woman like that, well, who knows what she may do." When I asked him to clarify what he meant, Edward told me that part of the problem in his son's marriage was that he allowed Samantha to have too much to say. "Women and children need to have strong characters in their lives, especially boys. Boys today, they're soft." He didn't offer any evidence to support his claims, and this seemed to be used as an opportunity to malign Samantha.

Rather than let him continue in this vein, I stopped him to ask about Terry. Edward said: "She's broken him, he loved her, yes, but, well, women like that … they will go against better judgements and won't listen to reason. Well, we never liked her, me and the wife. Too wilful." I asked Edward what he meant. He told me, "Well, there has to be someone who runs things, gets things done. Be the leader, so to speak. I'm surprised your husband allows you to do the job you do. Doesn't he have any pride? Wouldn't you be happier with a little office job, dear?"

I felt butterflies in my stomach as the adrenaline kicked in. This conversation was making me feel annoyed, just like I had felt when I had been with Terry. Edward's questions were challenging my beliefs, my values and my identity. I had been qualified for many years and had worked hard to reach the position of social worker. I was proud of my professional knowledge and expertise, but these comments felt as if Edward was attacking me, or poking me to see if he could get a reaction.

Part of me wanted to respond quite vociferously to this challenge, to tell him what I thought and how I felt. However, the other part of me realised that I needed to stay calm. I needed to exert some self-control. Although more overt than many of the misogynistic comments I have been either subject or witness to, I was still shocked and felt uncomfortable. I was aware that I already knew a lot about this family and I had grown to understand the value placed on males within the family. It would have been easy for me to have dismissed Edward's comments as simply old-fashioned or to have argued that he was trying to undermine me. But I started to feel calmer when I realised that actually it didn't really matter what Edward thought of me or of my life choices. This wasn't about me; it was about Craig and Eve. My visit to Edward and Denise was so that I could gain information to assist the children. I didn't need to impress Edward or build a relationship with him as part of an ongoing assessment. It was a one-off visit.

The more I thought about it in this way, the more I realised that Edward had actually peaked my interest. I wanted to learn more about these views and where they came from. I wanted to explore the comment about my husband allowing me to do things that appeared to be somewhat shameful. I decided therefore to not immediately respond to the challenge. I didn't want to inhibit Edward from talking, and chose therefore to respond by asking him to tell me more about his view that Samantha was "too wilful". What had she done and why was this behaviour not what he had expected?

Edward told me that Samantha had always acted against Terry. "She always wanted her own way. She was never satisfied. She had a nice home, a good husband. Most young girls would be happy with that, but no, she always seemed to be moping around. Always wanted the last word. Things I could tell you." I told Edward that I was here to listen, and if there was anything he knew that would help his grandchildren, this would be a good opportunity to tell me. But he didn't seem to want to disclose what he had to tell me; instead, he replied, "What's done is done."

I was confused. It seemed like Edward wanted me to be suspicious of Samantha, but when probed didn't feel able to explain why. I asked Edward, "When you say there needs to be someone who runs things, what was it you meant, exactly? From your comment regarding whether or not I should be allowed to go out to work, you seem to be implying that men should be in charge of their wives?" Edward seemed to lose his composure a little and looked flustered. I didn't wait and so went on: "Was Terry the person who was in charge? I understand Samantha was hospitalised on three occasions due to the violence she experienced from him. What are your views on how that happened?" Edward looked down and didn't reply. I sensed that he felt uncomfortable so I suggested we move on to other areas of discussion. He appeared a little relieved.

During the remainder of the visit, I tried hard to move the topic on to both of the children. About Eve he said, "She needs to be put in a home, some sort of institution. You can just tell. It's to be expected I suppose, coming from a mother like that." I tried to ascertain what Edward meant by his comments, but he told me that it was his belief that Eve "should have been drowned at birth". When I heard this, I was speechless. Over the years I have heard similar attitudes from various people, but I was always of the view that these comments were meant in a figurative, rather than a literal, sense. This time, however, I felt Edward meant it. He said it in such a fierce and intense way it left me deeply concerned about Eve's emotional and physical welfare.

About Craig, Edward told me that he was a fine boy who needed a father, not a nursemaid. "He needs to learn to be a man. How is he going to learn that from her? If she gets him, I'm through with him. I'll cut him out of my will. He will no longer part of my family, so you had better tell him to do the right thing." I asked Edward what the 'right thing' was, and he told me "He knows." This was quite chilling and carried a level of threat towards Craig. I decided that I had gone as far as I could with this discussion and I concluded the meeting.

Reflection points
1. What are your thoughts and feelings while reading this account?
2. Do you agree with my approach?
3. What would you have done differently?
4. What would you do next?

Thinking about this encounter later, I was struck by the uncomfortable feelings I was left with when I drove home. It made me wonder how Eve and Craig had felt when they went to visit their grandparents. Such extremes of attitude combined with the vehemence with which Samantha was openly discussed left me concerned about the influence this was having on the children's emotional development. I was also worried about the 'threats' directed at Craig with regard to what was expected of him. The children were in a situation that was heavily influenced by the feelings, emotions and views of the parents and grandparents.

On the one hand, they spent half of their time with a father who had appeared to place them at risk, often overlooking their emotional welfare; on the other was Samantha who tried to provide some balance in their lives. Such inconsistency can lead to a situation in which coalitions, or perverse triangles (see Haley, 1976), can develop. This is when an alliance can form between two family members of different generations against another. According to Haley (1976), this can have adverse consequences for family relationship functioning and children's adjustment in a number of ways.

First, an alliance between one parent and a child undermines the formation of an alliance between both parents, and so interferes with consistent parental authority. Second, alliances across generations place the child in the position of an expectation that they will side with their ally over the other parent. This undoubtedly creates anxiety for them. Finally, over-involvement by a parent impedes children's social development with their siblings and peers. It has even been suggested that coercive interaction styles learned in the context of sibling conflict extend to aggression with peers (Bank et al, 2004; Criss and Shaw, 2005).

Applying these theoretical perspectives to this case helped me to consider whether Samantha and Eve had been forced into the position of creating another alliance, one that would protect them from the dominant family discourse that appeared to favour men above women.

Reflection 'on' action

Throughout my assessment I often wondered whether Terry and Edward meant to harm their children. It became clear by the end that they both held similar views, and these views certainly affected the way they interacted with their children.

Although my own feelings were challenged during this case, I found that regular supervision helped me to regulate my views. I also believe that reflecting on each encounter, especially going over my behaviour, my thoughts and feelings, enabled me to focus on the needs of the children, and not my wishes. In my experience, it is always important when assessing parents in terms of contact and residence to consider the 'meaning' of the child for the adults.

Research completed by Reder and Duncan (1999) described certain children to be at risk of harm because they carry a psychological significance for their caretakers. In other words, in some cases children appear to need an implicit script or specific design for their life that must be submerged into their personal identity and characteristics. This can then start to dominate the parent–child relationship as children are expected to fulfil a particular role in their parent's life. In this case, it certainly appeared as if Craig was indeed regarded by Terry and Edward as the next heir in the family hierarchy. Eve, in contrast, appeared to have been overlooked by both Terry and the paternal side of the family.

Summary

Entering the assessment in Contact and Residence Order cases as an outsider means getting to grips with internal dynamics and realising that there is so much that the social worker doesn't know, hasn't seen and is unaware of. So how do social workers begin to unpick such complex dynamics? In cases of acrimonious divorce, it is important to establish, as far as possible, whether domestic abuse is or may be present. While controlling or even coercive behaviour is not uncommon, it doesn't necessarily follow that it is present in all contested child custody cases. If violence was evidenced, how might this impact on the safety and wellbeing of the children? What might be in their best interests?

In this case, I also needed to think about how far the ability of both parents was compromised by the way in which the family functioned. I needed to carefully gather information about what was actually going on for this family, and think about the fact that their lives and relationships, for the foreseeable future, were going to be regulated through the judicial system. Therefore, I needed to treat this case on an individual level and consider the implications, specific nature and context of what was happening. By doing this, I was able put aside my own personal assumptions, biases and beliefs in favour of an approach that brought some clarity to the situation.

The fact that I felt uncomfortable around Terry was irrelevant when it came to ensuring that the welfare of the children were protected; it was an aspect of the assessment I needed to be aware of, reflect on and manage. The key issue for me, as with all such cases, was to ensure that the Court was made aware of all the issues that I was aware of in relation to the family. This included explicating how the family functioned and including the voices of the children.

Despite my efforts, however, Terry refused to work with me during the final stages of the case. The only contact he would have with me was via threatening and abusive letters. These often outlined what would happen to me if I didn't revise my recommendations. Although these letters were difficult to read at the time, I realised that Terry was frustrated with the whole process, and later learned that he believed (as expressed in person within Court) that by not seeing me I would not be able to write a report or make recommendations without his input. Terry learned that trying to bully a judge by shouting at her in the final hearing would not be accepted. He was removed from Court, charged with contempt and received a suspended sentence.

The Court must start from the position that no order shall be made unless the court considers that doing so would be better for the child than making no order at all (Section 1(5), Children Act 1989). However, in this case, such orders were necessary due to the ongoing concerns in relation to Terry and his relationship with the children. Ultimately, the case had concluded with a Residence Order giving care of the children to Samantha and a Contact Order for supervised contact with respect to Terry. However, Terry had already stated his intention to abduct the children as he felt he should be able to see the children whenever he liked, and, as a result, refused any form of supervision. Therefore, in recognition of the likelihood that Terry would disrupt the children's placement with their mother, the Court also granted a Care Order to the local authority, which would be in place until they were 18. This would allow the local authority to support Samantha in parenting the children. The offer of supervised contact was withdrawn.

I supported Samantha and the children to feel safe in their new home, found school places for the children, and worked alongside the police to ensure that restraining orders were in place. At last contact, the children were doing well. Samantha and her new partner were married and were planning to emigrate to start afresh. Both Craig and Eve were now close, and Craig had become protective of his sister. Samantha's view was that, between us, we had saved not only their childhoods, but also potentially their lives.

Further reading

Laing, L., Humphreys, C. and Cavanagh, K. (2013) *Social work and domestic violence: Developing critical and reflective practice*, London: Sage Publications Ltd

Domestic violence affects all areas of social work. This book shows how social workers can intervene in everyday practice with victims, their families and perpetrators of domestic abuse. It provides students with knowledge of theory, research and policy to put directly in practice across a variety of legal and service user contexts.

Stanley, N. (2015) *Domestic violence and protecting children*, London: Jessica Kingsley Publishers

This book looks at new prevention initiatives and how interventions for children exposed to domestic violence have been developed. It shows how services for abusive fathers have evolved, and provides a discussion and critique of a number of new initiatives in the field of inter-agency risk assessment. With international perspectives and examples drawn from social care, healthcare and the voluntary sector, this book brings together established ideas with recent thinking to provide an authoritative summary of current domestic violence and child protection practice.

Howe, D. (1995) *Attachment theory for social work practice*, Basingstoke: Palgrave Macmillan.

The quality of early social relationships has a deep bearing on our psychological and social development; adversity in childhood can lead to adult relationships that may be difficult and distressing. This book addresses the needs of social workers in understanding and assessing the nature and origins of such disturbed social relationships. Taking a comprehensive and wide-ranging look at the theories emerging in and around attachment theory, it provides a sophisticated but accessible base from which social workers can make sensitive assessments and develop humane practices.

References

Bank, L., Burraston, B. and Snyder, J. (2004) 'Sibling conflict and ineffective parenting as predictors of adolescent boys' antisocial behaviour and peer difficulties: Additive and interactional effects', *Journal of Research on Adolescence*, vol 14, p 99–125.

Bowlby, J. (1979) *The making and breaking of affectional bonds*, London: Tavistock.

Buchanan, C. and Heiges, K. (2001) 'When conflict continues after the marriage ends: Effects of post-divorce conflict on children', in J. Grych and F. Fincham (eds) *Interparental conflict and child development*, New York: Cambridge University Press, pp 337–62.

Cassidy, J. (1990) 'Theoretical and methodological considerations in the study of attachment and the self in young children', in M.T. Greenberg, D. Cicchetti and E.M. Cummings (eds) *Attachment in the preschool years: Theory, research and intervention*, Chicago, IL: University of Chicago Press, pp 87–119.

Cialdini, R. and Goldstein, N. (2004) 'Social influence: Compliance and conformity', *Annual Review of Psychology*, vol 55, pp 591–621.

Criss, M.M. and Shaw, D.S. (2005) 'Sibling relationships as contexts for delinquency training in low–income families', *Journal of Family Psychology*, vol 19, pp 592–600.

El-Sheikh, M. and Harger, J. (2001) 'Appraisals of marital conflict and children's adjustment, health, and physiological reactivity', *Developmental Psychology*, vol 37, no 6, pp 875–88.

Emery, R.E. and Coiro, M.J. (1995) 'Divorce: Consequences for children', *Pediatric Review*, vol 16, pp 306–10.

Freud, A. (1936) *The ego and the mechanisms of defense*, New York: International Universities Press.

Gelles, R.J. (1976) 'Abused wives: Why do they stay?', *Journal of Marriage & the Family*, vol 38, no 4, pp 659–68.

Haley, J. (1976) *Problem-solving therapy*, New York: Harper & Row.

HCPC (Health and Care Professions Council) (2008) *Confidentiality – Guidance for registrants*, London: HCPC.

Hetherington, E., Frankie, G. and Katz, D. (1967) 'Effects of parental dominance, warmth and conflict on imitation in children', *Journal of Personality and Social Psychology*, vol 6, no 2, pp 119–25.

Humphreys, C. (2006) 'Relevant evidence for practice', in C. Humphreys and N. Stanley (eds) *Domestic violence and child protection: Directions for good practice*, London: Jessica Kingsley Publishers, Chapter 1.

Lamborn, S.D., Mounts, N.S., Steinberg, L. and Dornbusch, S.M. (1991) 'Patterns of competence and adjustment among adolescents from authoritative, authoritarian, indulgent, and neglectful families', *Child Development*, vol 62, pp 1049–65.

Reder, P., Duncan, S. and Gray, M. (1993) *Beyond blame: Child abuse tragedies revisited*, London: Routledge, cited in P. Reder and S. Duncan (1999) *Lost innocents: A follow-up study of fatal child abuse*, London: Routledge.

Reder, P. and Duncan, S. (1999) *Lost innocents: A follow-up study of fatal child abuse*, London: Routledge.

Short, L.M., McMahon, P.M., Davis Chervin, D., Shelley, G.A., Lezin, N., Sloop, K.S., et al (2000) 'Survivors' identification of protective factors and early warning signs for intimate partner violence', *Violence Against Women*, vol 6, no 3, pp 272–85.

Sidebotham, P., Brandon, M., Bailey, S., Belderson, P., Dodsworth, J., Garstang, J., et al (2016) *Pathways to harm, pathways to protection: A triennial analysis of serious case reviews 2011 to 2014: Final report*, London: Department for Education (http://seriouscasereviews.rip.org.uk/wp-content/uploads/Triennial_Analysis_of_SCRs_2011-2014_Pathways_to_harm_and_protection_299616.pdf).

Steinberg, L. (2001) 'We know some things: Adolescent–parent relationships in retrospect and prospect', *Journal of Research on Adolescence*, vol 11, pp 1–20.

Strube, M.J. and Barbour, L.S. (1984) 'Factors related to the decision to leave an abusive relationship', *Journal of Marriage & the Family*, vol 46, pp 837–44.

Zubrzycki, J. (1999) 'The influence of the personal on the professional: A preliminary investigation of work and family issues for social workers', *Australian Social Work*, vol 52, no 4, pp 11–16.

9

Critical reflection: Using case studies to develop your own awareness in practice

In this book we have compiled a number of case studies that have been developed from our own practice experiences and presented in narrative form. Each case is different, but all have been written with the intention of showcasing the importance of critical reflection in the context of practice. Drawing from Schön's 'reflection in and on' action perspective, we have tried, in doing so, to raise awareness of theory, research, reflexivity and language. By combining the story of the case with critical reflection and then applying different theoretical frameworks to that experience, we have been able to find new ways of knowledge making. In focusing on the experience and the everyday practices of social work activity, we have also been able to reconsider and develop ideas that may be valuable for practitioners, and thus create a process of learning.

In each chapter, we have tried to challenge certain underlying assumptions, beliefs that may have been present in the discourse of our organisation, generated from wider society or inherent in our own personal and social views. By attempting to make explicit our assumptions and values we have, in turn, sought to explore where these have emerged from so that we could acknowledge how this information has affected our decision-making. This has not always been easy. Telling a story about practice is quite straightforward, but articulating why an interaction between two or more people developed in the way that it did, and reflecting on the role we played in that encounter, means having a coherent understanding of who we are, how our knowledge has been constructed and what it is we value. It means being closely connected to our social and cultural selves.

For us to have reached this understanding and connected with each case study, we have had to approach the story from the position that there is no one truth or one version to the story told. We have tried to convey this by exploring the perspectives of all the actors we were in interaction with. We recognise that everyone will have a different view of the same encounter and these views are influenced in different ways because we are all individuals – we have lived different lives and had different experiences. The important thing for us when writing each chapter was to try and understand why we thought in the way that we did – what was it that was influencing our thoughts, and how were these affected by the places we were situated in?

We do recognise that this has happened more often in some chapters than in others; while writing this book we have realised that it is difficult to concentrate on both the political and the social context at the same time. Therefore, some case studies spend more time discussing the political or organisational context because we felt it was important to recognise that the broader social context impacted on the individuals and the organisation central to that story. The macro story was, therefore, a central part of the micro story.

In all the case studies, however, the common theme of power has emerged. These narratives have often focused on how this element of practice can be difficult to understand or manage in certain situations. When the issue of power has arisen, we have therefore attempted to reflect on why power is a contentious subject so that we can try to understand how particular dynamics can alter the way a person feels in that given moment: powerful or powerless. This activity has been illuminated throughout and from what we can see, its importance appears to depend on the people present in that given interaction: their position and their motives.

Another common theme to emerge from all the case studies is emotion. We have, as a result, tried to pay attention to the emotive and affective content of each narrative. We have recognised that critical reflection often stems from those encounters that have left us with feelings of discomfort. This is because practice is a deeply emotional activity; to ignore feelings and emotions would be similar to denying the fact that practitioners are human. Current performance management cultures can often stifle the sentiments of social workers, and this is a concern. Critical reflection can be a difficult process to engage with if the emotional aspects of practice encounters are not considered effectively.

Reflection in social work is, therefore, an important area of practice, and has been highlighted as such in recent Knowledge Skills Statements issued by the Department of Education (2016). The Knowledge Skills Statements emphasise that if social workers are to develop their expertise, they need to be able to challenge any prevailing professional conclusions in the light of new evidence or practice reflection. A social worker needs to always be research aware and critically reflective if they are to prioritise children's needs, identify development, health and education, all the while ensuring active participation and positive engagement with their family.

The narratives in this book have attempted to identify those child protection cases that are significant in the current context of teaching, research and practice. By connecting theory and research to practice, we hope that readers will do their own theorising and at times reach a different conclusion to the ones that we did. We have drawn from different theories and models in each case study to try and highlight that social workers might want to do the same. Social work has the advantage of being situated in the middle of a number of different disciplines and drawing from their theory rich perspectives.

By using Schön's (1983) theory to 'frame reflection', we have framed each case study in a different way each time, using different theories to explore each dilemma. The first chapter, 'Applying a person-centred approach', draws on two different perspectives — person-centred and symbolic interactionism — before concluding with systems theory and demonstrating that another approach can be employed at a later stage, if required. This chapter demonstrates that different theoretical perspectives have both strengths and weaknesses, and that it is important for practitioners to ensure that they consider these elements when utilising them in practice. The benefit of drawing from a range of theoretical perspectives is that it enables practitioners to develop their knowledge and explore the way in which situations in their practice evolve in more detail.

Chapter 2, 'Managing different professional perspectives', draws on the sociological perspectives of dramaturgy, performativity and professionalisation. Erving Goffman (1959) is not usually used as a theoretical perspective in social work practice, but his work has been employed in this context to demonstrate how dramaturgical observations can be used to understand why practitioners might strive to accomplish credibility in the workplace. In doing so, the micro-organisational practices are examined as well as the way in which three individuals attempt to construct their professional self in front of each other. This case study highlights that the professional self is not an organic trait but rather, a dramatic character performance, one that arises from social interactions and staged scenes that take place inside and outside the office.

The theme of presenting an idealised self is explored further in Chapter 3, 'Challenging decisions', as the case study explores the way in which a social worker disagreed with a service unit manager's decision. This time, management theory is used to explore the notion of organisational conflict within a social work setting in an attempt to understand why decisions are made, withdrawn and then challenged. In turn, it demonstrates that what can easily be forgotten, when professionals become engaged in conflict, are the needs of the service user, which is an issue that must remain centre-stage and that is everyone's responsibility. By drawing from the Argyris and Schön's (1974) proposed model of single-loop and double-loop learning, the author demonstrates how a rational technical approach to understanding why different people respond to same situation in different ways can help all involved to critique their actions.

When this self-critique doesn't occur, organisational conflict can become toxic, turbulent and spread. This notion is explored in Chapter 4, 'Dealing with a colleague's suspension'. Moving away from the sociological to psychodynamic and psychosocial perspectives, the theories of affect, emotion and object relations are drawn on to explore how reactive actions can unsettle the dynamics of a team. All social workers are expected to use their emotional intelligence when in practice, but this chapter demonstrates that when an agency is trying to deal with a significant reduction in resources, an imminent Ofsted inspection and the fear a child will be harmed, dealing with specific performance problems can become unmanageable and lead to highly charged emotive and affective states taking priority.

Although the concept of relational conflict continues in Chapter 5, 'Once a risk always a risk – So what exactly are we assessing?', different theories are used to demonstrate how professional views can differ and what practitioners can do to assert their position. Drawing on literature that constructs knowledge relating to sexual abuse, risk and actuarial assessments, the author demonstrates how the practice of social work is an activity that is bound by and preoccupied with managing risk. In doing so, she demonstrates how this preoccupation with risk has often been driven by a rhetoric that risk can be controlled and that social workers are positioned as being responsible for determining what is safe and what is not.

The problem with working with the unknown, however, is that the concept of risk changes, depending on the position of the individual and their own values and views. This is discussed in more depth in Chapter 6, 'Dealing with attachment and trust issues', as the author explores the experience of unwittingly placing a child in an unsafe environment, in turn questioning how far professional relationships can be taken for granted. Drawing on the theory of attachment, the case study examines the importance of making connections and establishing positive relationships for children in care. It also recognises how gut instinct plays a part in social work practice, and how newly qualified social workers need supervision to communicate their feelings and actions.

Communication and how listening effectively can enhance practice and relationship building is also a key feature of Chapter 7, 'Working constructively with uncooperative clients'. Drawing on the theory of mind and space, the author demonstrates how empathy is required when building relationships, and how attention to the use of space and environment is the hallmark of good social work practice. Loosely drawing from Motivational Interviewing (MI) techniques, the author explores how the assessment process can be used to consider the needs of parent while simultaneously encouraging disclosure.

The book concludes with Chapter 8, 'Dealing with manipulative parents and unhealthy attachments', a private law proceedings case that the author personally struggled to make sense of while in practice. Drawing on the theory of the internal working model, the author uses Bowlby's work to explore a complex custody case that is exacerbated by acrimony and domestic violence. The author's open approach to discussing the issues faced show her struggling to deal with the hostile and emotive states of those involved, and how these, in turn, affected and challenged her own views, beliefs and identity.

The book concludes by highlighting to readers just how important it is, in this contemporary climate, for practitioners to develop their expertise in the field by openly identifying the difficult and uncomfortable situations they may face. It also identifies how these dilemmas may be overcome through reflecting critically on the views, actions and perspectives of all involved. All of the chapters show that establishing a safe space for critical reflection to take place is vital because this enables the process of questioning decisions and practice endeavours. This activity in turn provides timely opportunities to deepen and extend professional knowledge that will impact on the children and families that social workers work with. We hope that this book manages to go some way in inspiring debate and ongoing creativity for all the students, social workers and managers who read it.

References

Argyris, C. and Schön, D. (1974) *Theory in practice: Increasing professional effectiveness*, San Francisco, CA: Jossey-Bass.

Department of Education (2016) *Knowledge and skills statement for approved child and family practitioners* (www.gov.uk/government/uploads/system/uploads/attachment_data/file/524743/Knowledge_and_skills_statement_for_approved_child_and_family_practitioners.pdf).

Goffman, E. (1959) *The presentation of self in everyday life*, New York: Doubleday, Anchor Books.

Schön, D. (1983) *The reflective practitioner: How professionals think in action*, London: Temple Smith.

Index

Note: Page numbers in *italics* refer to terms in the glossary.